'*Investing Demystified* delivers, with great clarity and lucidity, the best possible advice you can get when it comes to personal investments and financial planning.'
Stéphane Guibaud, Professor of Finance, London School of Economics

'An important book that debunks common myths about investing. A must-read for ordinary investors.'
Anita Raghavan, *New York Times* and author of *The Billionaire's Apprentice*

'*Investing Demystified* is a must read for anyone concerned about investing or protecting their hard-earned money. Although a successful hedge fund manager, Lars won't try and tell you the next "great thing"; what he provides is a manual about how to think and act appropriately. Most professionals can't beat the market over time, let alone individuals. This book rams home that point and sets out a clear and simple guide to becoming a rational and ultimately more profitable investor.'
Ross Westgate, CNBC

'If you only read one book on how to manage your investments, read this one.'
Benjamin Pritchett-Brown, Investment & Pensions Europe

'Although the financial industry's reputation is at a low ebb, it's important to remember that, for the individual investor, there are more high-quality, low-cost savings vehicles out there than ever before. You just need to understand how to look for them and how to put them together. *Investing Demystified* offers invaluable help in doing this.'
Paul Amery, Index Universe

'In a world complicated by an over-zealous finance industry, it is refreshing to read *Investing Demystified*, a great and easy read that reveals the simple truth behind successful investments.'
Tets Ishikawa, author of *How I Caused the Credit Crunch*

'Doing something is better than doing nothing if you want to retire in comfort. But what can we do if we don't have an edge in the market? Lars Kroijer takes a refreshing look at how everyday people can improve their fortunes by taking some simple investing steps. But if you want to do better than that, then you will need to find yourself an edge.'
Dr David Kuo, The Motley Fool

'In a world of the next big investment fad, Lars Kroijer takes us back to the essence of smart investing: diversify, diversify, diversify. And don't overpay for that either.'
Coenraad Vrolijk, Managing Director of Bl...

Investing Demystified

Investing
Demystified

How to invest without speculation and sleepless nights

Lars Kroijer

Harlow, England • London • New York • Boston • San Francisco • Toronto • Sydney • Auckland • Singapore • Hong Kong
Tokyo • Seoul • Taipei • New Delhi • Cape Town • São Paulo • Mexico City • Madrid • Amsterdam • Munich • Paris • Milan

PEARSON EDUCATION LIMITED

Edinburgh Gate
Harlow CM20 2JE
United Kingdom
Tel: +44 (0)1279 623623
Web: www.pearson.com/uk

First edition published 2013 (print and electronic)

Pearson Education is not responsible for the content of third-party internet sites.

ISBN: 978-0-273-78134-9 (print)
 978-0-273-78153-0 (PDF)
 978-0-273-78152-3 (ePub)
 978-1-292-00762-1 (eText)

British Library Cataloguing-in-Publication Data
A catalogue record for the print edition is available from the British Library

Library of Congress Cataloging-in-Publication Data
Kroijer, Lars.
 Investing demystified : how to invest without speculation and sleepless nights / Lars Kroijer.
-- First edition.
    pages cm
 Includes Index.
 ISBN 978-0-273-78134-9 (pbk. : alk. paper)
 1. Investments. 2. Portfolio management. 3. Financial, Personal. I. Title.
 HG4521.K745 2013
 332.6--dc23
                                2013020569

10 9 8 7 6 5 4 3

17 16 15 14

Cover design by Kit Foster
Cover image: Shutterstock

Print edition typeset in 9/13 pt StoneSerITCStd by 3
Printed by Ashford Colour Press Ltd., Gosport

Contents

Acknowledgements

Since this is my first time writing about investments in a semi-technical way I have needed more help than the professors or personal finance professionals who often write about this topic. I am thrilled and honoured that such an accomplished and insightful group of people spent their time helping me. To start, I want to thank my wife, Puk Kroijer, for continuously supporting this project from the stage when it was still rumbling in my head. Soon after the rumblings were verbalised the publisher of my first book, Chris Cudmore, encouraged me to write a book and he and the team at Financial Times Publishing were again excellent at seeing the project through to conclusion.

A number of friends were also instrumental in the book's completion by giving comments on early drafts as I stumbled towards a coherent argument: Steven Felsher with his extremely thorough system of numbering each paragraph (there were 800+ in one draft), former office mate Edwin Datson, Mark Hunter, Stuart Hamilton, Chris Rossbach with his sharp pencil, Paul Amery from Index Universe, Coenraad Vrolijk from Blackrock, Morten Bech from the Bank of International Settlements, Stéphane Guibaud from London School of Economics, and my former professors Andrei Shleifer from Harvard University and Jay Light from Harvard Business School.

Finally, I would like to thank all those in and around the finance industry who consistently encouraged me to write about this subject and helped in various ways. While the book in general suggests investing in ways that lead to lower fees to the financial industry, the people I talked to had their customers' interests as their first objective. This kind of honest objective bodes well for the future of finance even while it is generally vilified in the popular press and is perhaps in for a rough ride in the years ahead.

Finally, this book is dedicated to Puk, Anna, Sofia and Sydney the dog; my four girls.

Lars Kroijer

About the author

Lars Kroijer graduated *Magna cum Laude* from Harvard University with a degree in economics and received a MBA from Harvard Business School.

Lars is the author of *Money Mavericks – Confessions of a Hedge Fund Manager* (second edition, 2012, FT Publishing). He currently serves on the Board of Directors of OVS Capital, Linden Grove Capital, Northlight Group, Steadview Capital and Maj sinAI (London, Mumbai/Hong Kong and Copenhagen-based hedge funds), and Shipserv Inc. (the leading online platform for shipping supplies with annual sales of about $4 billion). He has frequently appeared as a finance expert on a broad range of media, including the BBC, CNN, CNBC, Bloomberg, the *New York Times* and *Forbes* magazine.

Lars was the CIO of Holte Capital Ltd, a London-based, market-neutral, special situations hedge fund which he founded in 2002 before returning to external capital in the spring of 2008. Prior to establishing Holte Capital, he served in the London office of HBK Investments focusing on special situations investing and event-driven arbitrage. In addition, he previously worked at SC Fundamental, a value-focused hedge fund based in New York, and the investment banking division of Lazard Frères in New York. Whilst at graduate school, he held internships with the private equity firm Permira Advisors (then Schroder Ventures) and management consulting firm McKinsey & Co.

A Danish national, Lars Kroijer lives in London and is married with twin daughters.

Foreword

Today, most literature or other media on finance tell us how to make money. We are bombarded with stock tips about the next Apple or Google, read articles on how India or biotech investing are the next hot thing, or told how some star investment manager's outstanding performance is set to continue. The implicit message is that only the uninformed few fail to heed this advice and those that do end up poorer as a result. We wouldn't want that to be us!

This book starts with a very different premise. It starts with the idea that markets are actually quite efficient. Even if some people are able to outperform the markets, most people are not among them. In financial jargon, most people do not have an edge over the financial markets, which is to say that they can't perform better than the financial markets through active selection of investments different from those made by the market. Embracing and understanding this absence of an edge as an investor is a key premise of the investment methods suggested in this book, and something I will discuss at length.

Who is this book for?

It is for investors everywhere who have several things in common:

- They feel that they are not getting value for money from the finance industry and find it opaque, but realise how important investments are to their lives. They read about phenomenally wealthy finance types, but feel that in paying fees, for example, the results are poor. Thinking about the great phrase 'Where are the customer's yachts?', they don't even have a rowing boat.
- Ideally, they would like a simple portfolio of investments, but also want to feel that they can expect the best possible return for the risk they are willing to take.

■ They may well have investments with typical investment managers as (despite themselves) they fell for the snazzy ads that showed great historical performance, which perhaps wasn't matched post-investment.

■ They may have shares in blue chip companies like Google, Apple, Exxon or Vodafone, but at the same time recognise they are not expert stock pickers and consider that is something best left to the professionals.

■ They may also know a lot about finance and have a genuine interest in it, but with a busy day job are unable to devote a lot of time to their personal portfolio. They need a portfolio that helps them sleep better at night, knowing that their savings are well looked after without having to spend too much time on it.

■ They may have been directed by an adviser who they had retained to help simplify the jungle of investment products and were left unable to understand their portfolio mix. Perhaps without knowing if the adviser took a share of the high fees they were paying.

■ They probably also think about investing longer term. While this book certainly has many immediate action items it is the opposite of the 'Spot the next hot stock' or 'Make $10,000 a day without getting out of bed' genre.

■ They want a book on how to do a little bit better every year financially, with a big cumulative impact over time. If a hedge fund manager is a turbo-charged Ferrari, this book is akin to the grey Volkswagen that is a far better bet to get you safely to your destination in one piece.

So this book is about taking something as opaque and impenetrable as the financial market sector and demystifying it; thus *Investing Demystified*. Once investors realise that they do not have the investing edge to outperform the markets, and know that this is perfectly acceptable, the rational next step is quite logical and simple. I call this next step being the rational investor and the portfolio for that investor the rational portfolio.

So what is a rational investor?

The rational investor

The rational investor does not seek to outperform the financial markets, pay few fees and get higher returns for any level of risk, while incorporating individual tax and non-investment asset factors. He or she is rational about the low probability of having an 'edge'[1] in the markets and because of this insight will have a much improved financial performance.

1 The markets talk about investors 'having edge' – rather than 'having an edge' – or 'edging the market' but in the interests of legibility and understanding we have kept jargon to a minimum.

While I'm not expecting readers to know about finance, some basic knowledge is helpful. Someone without any finance knowledge may find it harder to distinguish between an unglamorous book that promises improved risk-adjusted performance over the long term and other appealing-looking products from the well-marketed finance industry that tell us we can all be Warren Buffett – or at least that we should try. No wonder that most people would rather aim to be a billionaire superstar.

However, to keep it an easily readable finance book, we will be relatively light on theory and complex maths. They play a central role in supporting the arguments made in this book as I'm keen that you understand that what I suggest is a practical implementation of the best theory on getting the optimum portfolio. But in the interest of readability I have tried to keep theory and maths to a minimum, and put some of it in boxes that you may choose to skip; likewise there are a limited number of footnotes and references for those who want to explore further.

This book uses words like estimate, guess, approximately, around, roughly, fairly, reasonable quite a lot. This is because the discussion is often about what will happen in the future and claiming certainty would be misleading. Most points are fair estimates of what we can expect and hopefully a framework of how to think about the issues. Reality will almost certainly turn out differently from what we forecast here, and perhaps even make a mockery of our logic if we try to be too exact. I use £, $, €, etc. interchangeably in the examples and discussion. This is deliberate as most of the topics discussed do not depend on currencies. Investors obviously care a lot about their specific currency exposure, but the issues faced by a sterling investor are very similar to those faced by a euro-based one.

Who am I to write this book?

This book draws heavily on my experiences managing a hedge fund and practically implementing investments, but also relies on academic research in portfolio construction. A one-time hedge fund manager writing a book about investments without edge may seem like a priest writing the guide to atheism. In my view, however, it is not at all inconsistent. The fact that some investors have an edge on the market does not mean that most people have it. Far from it. 'Edge' is confined to a very small minority of investors who typically have access to the best analysis, information, data and other resources. Most other investors simply can't compete, and would be worse off trying.

Paradoxically, for those who know me as a hedge fund manager (I wrote a book called *Money Mavericks* about my experiences of starting and running a hedge fund), I was interested in optimal portfolio theory before I even really knew about hedge funds. For a while I planned to get a PhD in the field and perhaps teach. As it turned out, I graduated from university with a lot of debt and had a lucrative offer from Wall Street. From there, I got my MBA and ended up being interviewed at a hedge fund. Events happened, as they say. So I have a lot of experience with optimal portfolio and general financial theory, but also experience operating in the financial markets. Since I stopped running my hedge fund in early 2008 (fortuitous timing) I have mainly focused on investing my own money along the lines discussed in this book, and have extensive experience of trading the products discussed.

part

one

Introduction

Introduction to markets and portfolios

Our objective

This book will help you – the rational investor – create a portfolio that will have the best returns for any risk level. You will think about risk, taxation and incorporating other assets in your portfolio. This approach will result in more cash being available in the future through better investment returns than other investment methods. This book is about sleeping well at night, confident that you have the best possible investment portfolio for someone who can't consistently outperform the market – and this covers the vast majority of investors.

This is perhaps an unusual book about investments. I will not tell you how to analyse company accounts, spot economic trends, identify great products, recognise the next hot stock or anything like that. Instead, I will try to convince you that you are probably among the vast majority of investors who are better off not trying any of that complicated analysis and then I'll tell you what to do with your investments on the basis of that premise. In other words, this is a book for investors who have no 'edge' over the markets.

In reality, very few investors have the edge to outperform the financial markets, where many thousands of investors with access to the best and most timely information, analysis and financial models compete. Those investors speak to companies, research analysts, economists, traders, customers and so on. Then they read any report, web-chat, filing, news piece, etc. before they analyse the information using the most sophisticated systems and financial models. Only then do they buy or sell. Despite that level of insight, it is not clear that professional investment managers as a group outperform the markets. We as investors are probably unable to consistently pick the winning managers among them, just like we can't consistently pick winning individual investments. But in both cases we can be sure that fees and expenses make the task of outperformance much harder. We are left with a realisation that we are far better off taking a step back and not competing in the financial market circus.

The absence of an edge does not mean that you should avoid investing. Doing so would exclude you from potentially exciting long-term returns in the equity markets, or benefiting from the security of highly rated government bonds. By embracing the fact that you do not have an edge or advantage to consistently outperform markets I will help you understand how to benefit from a simple and cheap portfolio construction that, despite its simplicity, is very close to the best both from a practical and a portfolio theory perspective. I call it the rational portfolio and those that implement it are rational investors because once you realise that you do not have the edge to beat the markets, I hope you will agree that what I suggest is the rational way of investing.

While most people would obviously rather have the magical ability to pick the market's winning stock every year, and soon be richer than Bill Gates, reality is that a vanishingly small number of people can consistently beat the markets or know others who can do it for them, and most are far worse off for trying. It's a huge positive step forward if you can embrace the fact that you do not have the edge to beat the markets. It will make you a better investor and leave you wealthier in the long run while spending less time worrying about your investments.

The rational portfolio that I'm going to propose is much simpler, yet more theoretical and practically robust than what most investors have today. Even before considering its massive fee advantage over more conventional investment portfolios this portfolio offers investors a superior risk/return profile because of its greatly diversified and optimised investments. Other advantages include excellent liquidity, ease of tailoring risk to suit individual needs and tax efficiency. So you are getting something better at a far lower cost.

Lower costs are possible because the rational portfolio is implemented through cheap index tracking products (investment products that try to mirror the performance of an index). Particularly in the equity part of the portfolio you can save about 2% a year in fees and expenses compared to many typical investment products that actively seek to outperform the market. To put this in perspective, if you have an income of £50,000 a year and save 10% a year from the age of 30 to 67 (so £5,000 at age 30, and every year thereafter going up with inflation at 2%), and the market gives you a return of 7% a year before fees, then at 67 the difference in your portfolio from the yearly 2% saving on fees is staggering (see Figure 1.1).

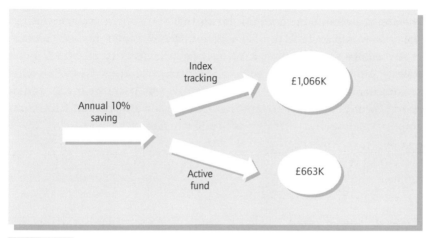

Figure 1.1   Fee-saving example

You are set to benefit from an increased wealth of £403,000 and retire as a millionaire! The money saved up every year amounted in total to about £281,000 at age 67, but the investment returns took your savings up to £1.06 million because you invested in the rational portfolio along the way.

You can re-run the example with other levels of savings or returns, or with just one investment. While you will be changing the numbers, the conclusion remains the same: unless you have an edge in the markets, the benefits from cheaply constructed rational portfolios are hugely significant over time. Remember this and act on it.

Where do we hope to end up?

There are three main themes to take away from this book.

1 We embrace that we do not have an edge

Investors who embrace that they do not have an edge are not necessarily unknowledgeable or naïve about the world of finance. In fact they might be the smartest person in the room. But they know something much more important: they do not think that they have the informational, analytical or other advantage to outperform the markets. Edge may exist in the finance world; we are simply acknowledging that we neither have it nor know someone who does.

Far too many people think that they have an edge, and far too few people have an incentive to tell them otherwise. Certainly not many you meet in the finance industry will do so. People working in banks, insurance firms, brokerage firms, media outlets, etc. get paid in many direct and indirect ways as a result of the fees paid to the finance industry. They have the backing of all sorts of marketing professionals who persuade investors that giving them money is the right thing to do, and the forceful backing of conventional wisdom that they are probably right. They are not.

Most of us are rational investors, and it's actually a pretty tall order to claim an investing edge. I hope that your reaction as we proceed will be, 'OK. Got it. I see why it's important. What's next?'

An immodest claim

A large majority of investors will make more money over the long term by investing as suggested in this book and by embracing the fact that they do not have an edge in the financial markets.

---

2 The components of the rational portfolio

The rational portfolio consists of the lowest possible risk investment combined with a portfolio of world equities, and potentially other government and corporate bonds. Adjusted for a few individual elements like risk and taxes, over the long term it will be very hard to outperform.

'If I don't have an edge, why invest at all?' That's a fair question that may be best answered by asking what the alternative is. Is it to put your cash under your mattress or buy jewellery that you can hide in the garden? What does 'not investing' actually mean? Leaving your money in the bank will yield little interest income and may mean taking credit risk with that bank. To put it simply, your money will not grow and its value will be eroded by inflation. In the example above, 'doing nothing' meant savings of £281,000 while the same savings invested with pretty reasonable assumptions in the rational portfolio meant savings of £1.06 million.

I hope to convince you that the rational portfolio suggested in this book is as close to theoretically and practically optimal as you will find and is how you will make more money from your investments over time. So the 'rational investing philosophy' is not the brainchild of yet another investment professional you may never have heard about (me), but instead is a practical and cost-efficient implementation of decades of work in portfolio theory by the sharpest minds in finance. While the benefits from the rational portfolio start accruing immediately, this is a long-term investment philosophy with a strategy and individual securities that you can hopefully keep for years or even decades.

Combining highly rated government bonds in the right currency, broad index-tracking products of world equities and possibly other government and corporate bonds in the right proportions through the best and cheapest products is core to rational investing (see Figure 1.2). I will quantify the risk/return profile of this portfolio and explain why low fees and expenses are core to long-term investment success. You may get bored with me talking about fees, but if you get expenses right you'll have come a long way.

The combination of the three asset classes that is best for you depends on your specific circumstances, particularly your attitude towards risk. I will give you the simple building blocks and help you to combine them. I will also discuss why some asset classes do not fit in the rational portfolio, including popular ones like property and commodities.

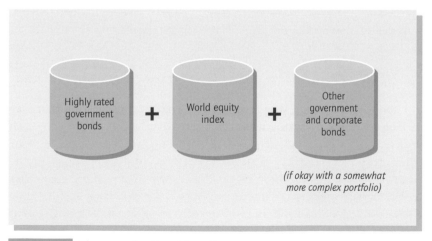

Figure 1.2   The core of rational investing

3 To get the full benefit of rational investing you should tailor your portfolio to your specific needs and circumstances

To start with you need to think about the risks of investing in the financial markets, and how that risk fits with your personal attitude towards risk. Add to this the fact that you should try to be as clever as possible about your tax situation, so that as tax regimes or your personal circumstances change you are in the best position to benefit. Getting all this right is no small task.

You need to consider your investment portfolio in the context of all your assets and liabilities, and how all of those interact. I will touch on what investing looks like in complete calamity situations, and also on the role that pensions and insurance play in the rational portfolio.

Finally you need to implement all this. I'm wary of suggesting specific products to buy as the development in index tracking moves so fast, but I will discuss a couple of offerings with the characteristics discussed above. These pass the 'what should I tell my broker' test; or, more likely these days, the 'what should I tell my internet browser' test.

The 60-second version

There are four things to take away from this book:

1 You almost certainly do not have an edge in the financial markets. That's OK. Most people don't, but you should plan and act accordingly.

2 There is an easy and cheaply constructed portfolio which is close to optimal. It combines the highest-rated government bonds with a world equity portfolio, adding other government and corporate bonds if you have the appetite for a bit more complexity. Get close to that in the right proportions, stick to it and you should do very well.

3 Your specific circumstances do matter a great deal. Think hard about your risk appetite and optimising your tax situation, but also pay attention to your non-investment assets and liabilities.

4 Be a huge stickler for costs, don't trade a lot and keep your investments for the very long run. Over time you will be far better off for having implemented the rational portfolio.

What is an edge over the markets and do you have it?

A key premise of this book is that we can't legally beat the markets consistently, or indeed know of an investor that can. It concedes having an edge over the markets. But what is meant by this?

Consider these two investment portfolios:

- **A**: the S&P 500 Index Tracker Portfolio
- **B**: A portfolio consisting of a number of stocks from the S&P 500; any number of stocks from that index that you think will outperform the index. It could be one stock or 499 stocks, or anything in between, or even the 500 stocks weighted differently from the index (which is based on market-value weighting).

If you can ensure the consistent outperformance of portfolio B over portfolio A, even after the higher fees and expenses associated with creating portfolio B, you have gained an edge by investing in the S&P 500. If you can't, you don't have an edge.

On first glance it may seem easy to have an edge over the S&P 500. All you have to do is pick a subset of 500 stocks that will do better than the rest, and surely there are a number of predictable duds in there. In fact, all you would have to do is to find one dud, omit that from the rest and you would already be ahead. How hard can that be? Similarly, all you would have to do is to pick one winner and you would also be ahead.

While the examples in this chapter are from the stock market, investors can have an edge in virtually any kind of investment. In fact there are so many different ways to have an edge that it may seem like an admission of ignorance to some to renounce all of them. Gut instinct may tell investors that not only do they want to have an edge, but the idea of not even trying to gain it is a cheap surrender. They want to take on the markets and outperform to make money, but perhaps also as a vindication that they 'get it', are street smart or somehow have a superior intellect.

The competition

When considering your edge who is it exactly that you have an edge over? The other market participants obviously, but instead of a faceless mass think about who they actually are, what knowledge they have and what analysis they undertake.

Imagine Susan, the portfolio manager of a technology-focused fund working for a highly rated mutual fund/unit trust (let's call it Ability) who like us is looking at Microsoft.

Susan and Ability have easy access to all the research that is written about Microsoft including the 80-page, in-depth reports from research analysts from all the major banks, including Morgan Stanley and Goldman Sachs, that have followed Microsoft and all its competitors since Bill Gates started the business. The analysts know all Microsoft's business lines, down to the programmers who write the code to the marketing groups that come up with the great ads. They may have worked at Microsoft or its competitors, and perhaps went to Harvard or Stanford with senior members of the management team. On top of that, the analysts speak frequently with their banks' trading groups who are among the market leaders in trading Microsoft shares and can see market moves faster and more accurately than almost any trader.

All research analysts will talk to Susan regularly and at great length because of the commissions Ability's trading generates. Microsoft is a big position for Ability and Susan reads all the reports thoroughly – it's important to know what the market thinks. Susan enjoys the technical product development aspects of Microsoft and she feels that she talks the same language as techies, partly because she knew some of them from when she studied computer science at MIT. But Susan's somewhat 'nerdy' demeanour is balanced out by her 'gut feel' colleagues, who see bigger picture trends in the technology sector and specifically how Microsoft is perceived in the market and its ability to respond to a changing business environment.

Susan and her colleagues frequently go to IT conferences and have meetings with senior people from Microsoft and peer companies, and are on a first-name basis with most of them. Microsoft also arranged for Ability personnel to visit its senior management at offices around the world, both in sales and development, and Susan also talks to some of Microsoft's leading clients.

Like the research analysts from the banks, Ability has an army of expert PhDs who study sales trends and spot new potential challenges (they were among the first to spot Facebook and Google). Further, Ability has economists who study the US and global financial system in detail as the world economy affects Microsoft's performance. Ability also has mathematicians with trading pattern recognition technology to help with the analysis.

Susan loves reading books about technology and every finance/investing book she can get her hands on, including all the Buffett and value investor books.

Susan and her team know everything there is to know about the stocks she follows (including a few things she probably shouldn't know, but she keeps that close to her chest), some of which are much smaller and less well researched than Microsoft. She is one of the best-rated fund managers in a couple of the comparison sites, but doesn't pay too much attention to that. After doing her job for over 20 years she knows how quickly things can change and instead focuses on remaining at the top of her game.

Do you think you have an edge over Susan and the thousands of people like her? If you do, you might be brilliant, arrogant, the next Warren Buffett or George Soros, lucky or all of the above. If you don't, you don't have an edge. Most people don't. Most people are better off admitting to themselves that once a company is listed on an exchange and has a market price, then we are better off assuming that this is a price that reflects the stock's true value, incorporating a future positive return for the stock, but also a risk that things don't go do plan. So it's not that all publicly listed companies are good – far from it – but rather that their stock prices incorporate an expectation of a fair future return to the shareholders given the risks.

When I ran my hedge fund I would always think about the fictitious Susan and Ability. I would think of someone super clever, well connected, product savvy yet street smart who had been around the block and knew the inside stories of success and failure. And then I would convince myself that we should not be involved in trades unless we clearly thought we had an edge over them. It is hard to convince yourself that this is possible, and unfortunately even harder sometimes for it to be actually true.

You just have to pick your moment

Warren Buffett is quoted as saying that 'just because markets are efficient most of the time does not mean that they are efficient all of the time'. To quote Buffett about investing is like quoting Tiger Woods about golf. He is a world-famous investor with a long history of being right, so we are all bound to feel a little deferential.

Buffett's words might be right of course. Markets might be perfectly efficient some or even most of the time and horribly inefficient at other times. But how should we mere mortals know which is when? Can you predict when these moments of inefficiency occur or recognise them when you see them? Clearly we can't all see the inefficiencies at the same time or the market impact of many investors trying to do the same thing would rectify any inefficiency in an instant. But can you, as an individual investor, spot a time of inefficiency?

I think that it's incredibly hard to have an edge in the market even occasionally. Be honest with yourself. If you have a long history of picking moments when you spotted a great opportunity, moved in to take advantage of it and then exited with a profit, then you may indeed occasionally have an edge. You should use this edge to get rich.

The costs add up

On average individual investors trying to beat the markets would not systematically pick underperforming stocks – on average they would pick stocks that perform like the overall market. They would have a sub-optimal portfolio that would not be as well diversified, but in my view the main underperformance comes from the costs incurred.

The most obvious cost when you trade a stock is the commission to trade. This has been lowered dramatically with online trading platforms but it is far from the only cost. A few others to consider are:

- bid/offer spread
- price impact
- transaction tax

- turnover
- information/research cost
- capital gains tax
- transfer charge
- custody charge
- advisory charge and
- your time.

Depending on your circumstances and portfolio size you may find that it costs more than 1% each time you trade the portfolio (the low, fixed, online charge per trade is only a small commission percentage if you trade large amounts). This is certainly less than it used to be decades ago, but for someone who is frequently trading their portfolio it will be a major obstacle to performance. In addition, capital gains tax amounts can add up for frequent traders and the 'hidden fees' like custody or direct or indirect costs associated with research and information-gathering come on top. The more this adds up to, the greater the edge someone will need just to keep up with the market.

I recently saw a particularly cringeworthy advertisement where a broker compared trading on its platform to being a fighter pilot, complete with Tom Cruise style Ray-Ban sunglasses and an adoring blonde. I remember thinking, 'I would love to sell something to whoever falls for that.' The platform makes more money the more frequently you trade, and the broker obviously thinks that you will trade more if you believe it'll make you be like Tom Cruise.

Some readers may dismiss this book as a load of rubbish. They may consider themselves to be sophisticated investors who can outperform the market. I hope this group at least has its opinions on edge challenged, and perhaps gets better at defining exactly what its edge is as a result of reading this book. But if you are going to actively manage your own portfolio I would encourage you to consider a few things:

- Be clear about why you have an edge to beat the market, and be sure you are not guilty of selective memory. Unlike predicting the winner of Saturday's football game, predicting that Google was going to double when it later did makes us appear wise and informed. Perhaps we are subconsciously more likely to remember that than when we proclaimed Enron a doubler. Because we add and take money out of our accounts continuously we are unlikely to keep close track of our exact performance and can continue the delusion indefinitely.

- Do not trade frequently. If you turn over your portfolio more than once a year you should have a really good reason to do so. The all-in costs of trading are high and greatly reduce long-term returns.

- Pick 12–15 stocks you feel great about that are not all in the same sector (preferably also not in the same geographical area) and plan to stick to those for a very long time. Warren Buffett says his favourite holding period is 'forever', suggesting that successful investors do not frequently trade in and out of investments.

- Do not start panicking if things go against you.

- You may decide you have an edge in one sector, geographical area or asset class. That's fine. Do exploit this edge, but invest like a rational investor in the rest of your portfolio.

- Continuously reconsider your edge. There is no shame and probably good money in acknowledging that you belong to the vast majority of people that don't have an edge. Investors who initially do well in the markets will often think it was skill rather than luck based on that first experience. Many reconsider later ...

How you cost your time spent managing your portfolio is individual to you (we each value our time differently) and while some consider it a fun hobby or game akin to betting, others consider it a chore they would rather avoid. Someone may spend 10 hours 'work time' a week on their portfolio which at an 'opportunity cost' of time of $50 an hour for 40 weeks is $20,000 a year on top of all the other costs discussed. This clearly makes no sense for a $100,000 portfolio and is too costly even for a $1 million portfolio. On top of everything else this investor would benefit from the reduced time involved in running a simple rational portfolio.

Should we give our money to Susan and Ability?

If you conclude that Susan is as plugged in and informed as anyone could be, why not just give her our money and let her make us rich?

Many investors do invest their money in the many tech-type products and Ability and its peers continuously develop mutual funds for everything you can imagine. There are funds for industrials, defensive stocks (and defence sector stocks for that matter), gold stocks, oil stocks, telecoms, financials, and technology. Many investors have become 'fund pickers' instead of 'stock pickers'. Even today, years after the benefits of index tracking have become clear to many investors there is perhaps $85 invested with managers that try to outperform the index (so-called 'active' managers) for every $15 invested in index trackers.

When investors pick from the smorgasbord of tempting-looking funds how do they know which ones are going to outperform in future?

Is it because investors have a feeling that IT stocks will outperform the wider markets?

If so, you are effectively claiming an edge by suggesting that you can pick sub-sets of the market that will outperform the wider markets? Consistently picking outperforming sectors would be an amazing skill.

Is it because of Susan's impressive CV (investors think that someone with her impressive background will find a way to outperform the market)?

If so, you are essentially saying that you know someone who has an edge (Susan), which is really another form of edge. This is the kind of edge many hedge fund investors claim. Funds will say, for example, 'through our painstaking research process we select the few outstanding managers who consistently outperform'. Maybe so, but that is also an edge.

Is it because investors feel Ability has come up with some magic formula that will ensure its continued outperformance in its funds generally?

There is little data to suggest that you can objectively pick which mutual funds are going to outperform in future.

Is it because your financial adviser considers it a sound choice?

First figure out if the adviser has a financial incentive, like a cut of the fees, in giving you the advice. The world is moving towards greater clarity about how advisers get paid, making it easier to understand if there is a financial incentive in recommending some products. Keep in mind that comparison sites also get a cut of the often hefty active manager fees. Now consider if your adviser really has the edge required to make this active choice. Unless he has a long history of getting these calls right I would question whether he has the special edge that eludes most (and would he really share this incredibly unique insight if he had it?).

They have done so well in the past

Countless studies confirm that past performance is a poor predictor of future performance. If life was only so easy – you just pick the winners and away you go ...

We are often driven by the urge to do something proactive to better our investment returns instead of passively standing by. And what better than investing with a strong performing manager from a reputable firm in a hot sector we have researched?

Mutual fund/unit trust charges vary greatly. Some charge up-front fees (though less frequently than in the past), but all charge an annual management fee and expenses (for things like audit, legal, etc.), in addition to the cost of making the investments. All-in costs span a wide range, but if you assume a total of 2.5% a year that is probably not too far out. So if someone manages $100 for you, the all-in costs of doing this will amount to approximately $2.5 a year come rain or shine.

If markets are steaming ahead and are up 20% or more every year, paying one-tenth to the well-known steward of your money may seem a fair deal. The trouble is that no markets are up 20% a year every year. We can perhaps expect equity markets to be on average up 4–5% a year above inflation. So you need to pick a mutual fund that will outperform the markets by 2%, before your costs, in order to be no worse off than if you had picked the index tracking exchange traded fund (ETF), assuming ETF fees and expenses of 0.5% a year. (ETFs, which are investment products that are traded like normal stock, will be discussed later.)

You need to pick the best mutual fund out of 10 for it to make sense!

To give an idea of how much the fees impact over time consider the example of investing $100 for 30 years. Suppose the markets return 7% a year (a 5% real return plus 2% inflation would be a reasonable expectation – see later) and the difference becomes all too obvious over time – see Figure 2.1. (There is a 2% fee disadvantage in this mutual fund case compared to the tracker fund.)

Ability and its many competitors go to great lengths to show their data in the brightest light, but a convincing number of studies show that the

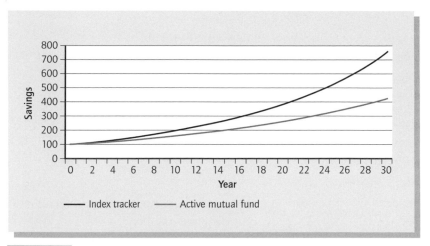

Figure 2.1   Index tracker versus mutual fund returns over 30 years

average professional investor does not beat the market over time, but in fact underperforms by approximately the fee amount.

There is of course the possibility that you are somehow able to pick only the best-performing funds. Suppose you had $100 to invest in either an index tracker, or a mutual fund that had a cost disadvantage of 2% a year compared to the tracker. Suppose also that the market made a return of 7% a year for the next 10 years. Finally assume that the standard deviation[1] of each mutual fund's performance relative to the average mutual fund performance was 5% (the mutual funds predominantly own the same stocks as the index and their performance will be fairly similar as a result). Figure 2.2 shows the returns of an index tracker compared to 250 mutual funds with those inputs.

Comparing an actively managed portfolio to an index tracker is unfortunately not as simple as subtracting 2% from the index tracker to get to the actively managed return. The returns will vary from year to year, and in some years the actively managed fund will outperform the index it is tracking. Some funds will even outperform the index over the 10-year period. If you can pick the outperforming fund consistently, you have an edge. If you can't, you should buy the index.

In approximately 90% of the cases in the 10-year example above, the index tracker would outperform the actively managed mutual fund, which is

---

1 A standard measure of risk that gives an idea of the range of returns you could expect and with what frequency.

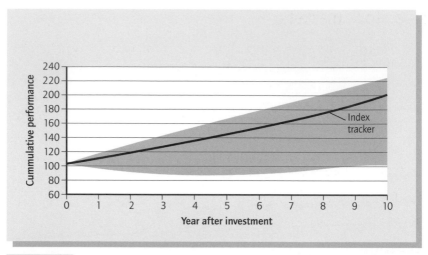

Figure 2.2 Ten-year performance of 250 active managers versus an index tracker

roughly in line with what historical studies suggest. So in order for it to make sense to pick a mutual fund over the index tracker you have to be able to pick the 10% best-performing mutual funds. That would be pretty impressive.

If you did not have an edge and blindly picked a mutual fund instead of the index tracker you would, on average, be about $30 worse off on your $100 investment after 10 years because of the higher costs. Had it been a $100,000 investment the difference would be enough to buy you a car.

You can bet your bottom dollar that the 10% of mutual funds that outperformed the index would trumpet their special skills in advertisements. Historical performance is however not only a poor predictor of future returns, but it can be very hard to distinguish between what has been chance (luck) and skill (edge). Just as one out of 1,024 coin flippers would come up heads 10 flips in a row, some managers would do better simply because of luck. In reality the odds are much worse in the financial markets as fees and costs eat into the returns. However, ask the manager who has outperformed five years in a row (every 50th coin flipper ...) and she will disagree with the argument that she was just lucky, even as some invariably are. Likewise some managers underperform the market several years in a row simply due to bad luck, but those disappear from the scene and thus introduce a selection bias as only the winners remain. This sometimes makes the industry appear more successful than it has been.

Outside stock markets

The discussion of edge is not exclusive to stock markets. You can have an investment edge in many areas other than the stock market and profit greatly from that edge, for example:

- Will Greece default on its loans?
- Will the price of oil increase further?
- Will the USD/GBP exchange rate reach 2 again?
- Will the property market increase/decrease?

The list goes on …

Being rational

For someone to accept that they don't have an edge is a key 'eureka' moment in their investing lives, and perhaps without knowing it at first, they will be much better off as a result. At this point you are at least hopefully considering a couple of things:

1 An edge is hard to achieve and it's important to be realistic about whether or not you have it.

2 Conceding that you don't have an edge is a sensible and very liberating conclusion for most investors. It makes life a lot easier (and wealthier) if you acknowledge that you can't better the aggregate knowledge of a market swamped with thousands of experts that study Microsoft and the wider markets.

3

What are the key components of the rational portfolio?

Once you have conceded that you don't have an edge on the market, unfortunately you are not done. In fact you have only arrived at the starting point of your rational journey!

Doing nothing with our assets is not a sensible solution: we need to put our money to use to get the best return for the risk we take, just like we would if we claimed we had an edge. Figure 3.1 shows a list of issues that a rational investor needs to think about. The remainder of this book covers these issues.

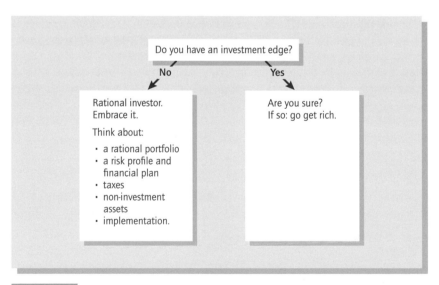

Figure 3.1   Issues that the rational investor must take into account

Asset split in a rational investment portfolio

In creating the rational portfolio we split our assets into the lowest-risk assets that preserve capital and risky assets that have to generate returns, and combine the two according to our risk preference. In the low-risk bucket we should have the highest-rated and liquid government bonds, ideally available in the base currency of our investments.

If we want to achieve anything other than the very unexciting return profile of low-risk government bonds we have to turn to riskier assets. We acquire these riskier assets not for the sake of adding risk, but because we hope to get great investment returns from them. The majority of rational investors are best off with a cheaply bought index tracker of world equities as their risky assets. It is a major evolution in the investing world that products tracking these indices are now readily available: just 15 years ago they were not.

Some books on investing involve intricate arguments about why certain geographical areas or sectors of the equity markets will outperform and provide a safe haven for the investor. On the contrary, the most diversified portfolio you can find offers the greatest protection against regional declines. Also, since we are simply saying 'buy the world', the product is very simple and should be super cheap. Over the long run that will matter greatly.

Someone willing to add a bit of complexity to the very simple portfolio of world equities and minimal-risk government bonds could add other government and corporate bonds (see Figure 3.2). While these additions make a lot of sense and I have them in my personal portfolio, unfortunately the product offerings in the space still leave something to be desired. Creating broad and cheap index-type exposure for bond portfolios is not as simple as for equities and there is a tendency for the products to be dominated by US and European securities in particular.

Elements of the rational portfolio are summarised as follows:

Asset class	Description
Minimal risk asset	UK, US, German, etc. or equivalent. Credit quality of maturity matching investor's time horizon.
Equities	World equity index or as broad as possible.
Other government bonds	Diversified return generating government bonds of varying maturities, countries and currencies; we have used those rated sub-AA as a good indicator.
Corporate bonds	Broad range of corporate bonds of varying maturity, credit risk, currency, issuer and geography.

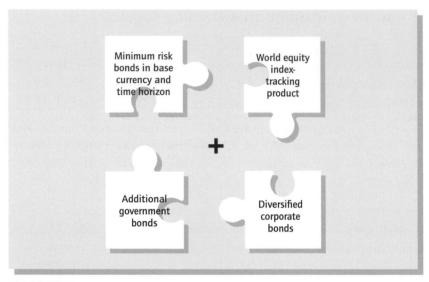

Figure 3.2   Elements of the rational portfolio

You may have noticed that there are some investments that are not part of this portfolio: property, private equity/venture capital, commodities, hedge funds, private investments (including angel capital, etc.) and so on. Buying these asset classes requires an edge. Whether you invest in regional property, a private equity fund or buy coal, you are claiming that you know something about future performance that the rest of the world does not. Also some of those investments are similar to the exposure you already have through your broad market exposures (at a small fraction of the cost) and are often very illiquid. The liquidity of the rational portfolio is one of its most under-appreciated features; having the ability to readily realise cash can be critical in some circumstances and something the rational portfolio provides.

Even during the darkest days of 2008–09, unless you had assets similar in size to a really rich oil sheik, you could unwind your portfolio at short notice if need be. If you badly need liquidity then having that option is priceless.

Understand the level of risk you are comfortable with

The products that rational investors use may be similar, but the proportions are not. If you have £105 and need £100 for heart surgery in a year, your risk profile is very different from someone with £100 at the age of

30 who needs £150 40 years hence. Our needs change over time as we age or our circumstances change. The risk you are willing to take at age 60 is typically very different from what you were willing to take at 40. Everyone is different and individual circumstances will determine what your mix of low-risk and riskier assets (like the equity markets) will be. The elements of the portfolio don't change, but the proportions of the risky assets do.

We need to gauge current market risk, but also think about less fun stuff like the risk of money in the bank, or the risk of markets heading down as badly as they have occasionally done in the past. With a large number of caveats, I want to use our understanding of the risks of the market to be better informed about risks in our investing.

In Table 3.1 I show how you should split your portfolio into its component parts, depending on your risk levels.

Table 3.1 The rational portfolio at different risk preferences

		No risk	Medium risk			High risk	
		Various portfolio compositions					
		A	B	C	D	E	F
Minimal risk asset		100%	67%	33%	0%	0%	0%
Risky assets:	World equity	0%	25%	50%	75%	85%	100%
	Government bonds	0%	3%	7%	10%	6%	0%
	Corporate bonds	0%	5%	10%	15%	9%	0%

So someone with £100 to invest and a medium 'C' risk profile could do as follows:

Allocation	Investment
£33	UK government bond tracker with maturity matching investor's time horizon
£50	World equity index tracker product
£7	Diversified return generating government bonds of varying maturities, countries and currencies, rated sub-AA
£10	Broad range of corporate bonds of varying maturity, credit risk, currency, issuer and geography.

I will discuss how I came up with the allocations above. Whilst the allocations are not an exact science and therefore do not have to be implemented in exactly the proportions illustrated, you would do very well if you implement your portfolio in a similar manner.

Of course our risk tolerances differ. Let's say that we have $100 now and need $110 in 10 years' time, and that we invest in the world equity markets where we expect real returns of about 5% a year. If we assume that performance every year will in fact be 5% we know that in 10 years our $100 will have become $162 and be far in excess of what we need. But that is not the whole story.

Since the equity markets are inherently risky, what can we say about the probability that we don't reach $110? Is it 1%, 2% or 20%? The answer depends on the risk of the equity markets. If we believe our expected return is $162 are we willing to move our allocations away from risky equities and into lower-risk bonds if it meant increasing our chances of reaching the $110, but with lower expected assets (because the bonds have lower expected returns)? Some people may, for example, be so risk averse that they would rather have expected assets of $120 with a 2% risk of not reaching $110, instead of expected assets of $162, but a 15% risk of not having $110 in assets. Which of the two types you are depends on your individual circumstance and attitude towards risk.

The numbers above may look complicated, but we can use them to think about the risk of our allocations in the context of our financial planning. Investment performance at times will differ significantly from average; how different will depend on the risk we take, and thinking ahead to how we react to bad outcomes will help us prepare for any eventuality.

Don't put all your non-investment eggs in one basket

As individual or institutional investors, the investment portfolio is only one out of several parts of our investing life. This is true when we consider risk, liquidity and taxes, but also when we consider the best investment portfolio.

Perhaps without thinking about it in those terms, many investors run the risk of putting all their eggs in the same basket. Someone may have a €1 million house with a €750,000 mortgage and a €100,000 investment portfolio. The investor has more than 90% of her gross assets tied up in the property market; if she were to invest in local property on top of this she would be buying more of an exposure that she already has plenty of. Similarly, if this was an Italian-based investor she already has plenty of exposure to the Italian economy. Putting her investments into Italian stocks would not diversify her exposure away from local exposure, as an investment into a broader index would.

There is a tendency for investors to be over-invested in their home markets; the British invest in the UK, Americans in the US, etc. Historically it was impractical and expensive to buy foreign securities, and perhaps the home bias has become an ingrained habit. Aim to diversify beyond the national borders. While many domestic firms may have international exposures as part of the business mix, as an investor you probably already have plenty of exposure to your home economy.

Incorporating non-investment assets in portfolio thinking is not a scientific optimisation, but rather a gut feeling. So when you consider your overall portfolio of assets and liabilities it is mainly the risk of interconnection between your assets you should worry about. Is there some event or risk that would affect all your assets in the same way? Could this event even lead to a crisis in your local bank and thus risk your deposits? Is there a way for you to diversify away from that risk in some of your non-investment assets, or are you at least making sure that your investment assets are diversified? Depending on your circumstances, factors such as your job prospects, the value of your education, a potential future inheritance, etc. may move more in tandem than you expect. A broadly diversified investment portfolio could one day be your safe haven in a nasty local storm.

Reducing tax has a large impact on long-term returns

The average individual or institutional investor should make good use of tax planning advice. The optimal portfolio and risk profile we have discussed above can be put together without too much outside help, but in the case of tax expert advice can make a huge difference.

Tax is a constant challenge. I will describe the tax benefits of the rational portfolio, but also discuss ways to save tax generally. Considering that taxes could take a huge chunk out of your returns, it's important to get it right.

Paying too much in fees destroys asset growth

One of the key drivers of long-term returns for the rational investor is low fees and expenses. The products involved in the creation of the optimal rational portfolio are fairly generic investment products and are cheap as a result. We are not paying anyone with the expectation that they do anything particularly clever – we are asking them to replicate an index (see Figure 3.3). Perhaps a monkey couldn't do it, but a computer certainly could.

The world of finance seems impossibly complex when it should be simple and transparent. Lower fees are a major benefit of simplifying a complex world, but importantly this has to be done while creating a stronger portfolio. We are not doing cheap for cheapness sake, but because it is a happy by-product of the simple portfolio construction that gives us the best risk/return profile. Throughout this book I will hammer home the point of low fees. If the only thing you take away from this book is getting charged a little bit less for a financial product the next time you invest, the book and time you spent reading it will have repaid itself many times over.

The benefit of paying lower fees may not look obvious at first. It typically does not reveal itself for a long time, until the compounding of better returns are really obvious, and even then there will always be some active manager or stock picker who claimed that you missed something obvious by not investing with him. Think of it as making a little bit of money

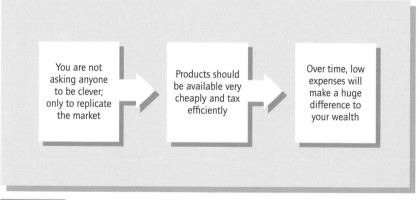

Figure 3.3 The simple solution

while you're sleeping; the lower fees and sensible investment strategy should make you sleep soundly at night. However, it's not one that leaves you sleepless with giddy excitement because of great outperformance compared to the general markets.

Implementation

The indices I suggest for your portfolio are extremely broad, transparent and liquid. As a result they should also be extremely cheap. The exact method of buying this index exposure depends on the specific tax situation, but since the underlying assets are so broadly traded, good products are generally available.

The past decade has seen a massive increase in the number of exchange traded funds (ETFs) and the amount of money invested in them. Similarly, index funds have had large asset inflows. Both developments are very positive for investors as it has increased choice when implementing the rational portfolio. With the greater number of product offerings, the fees charged have also declined. US-based Vanguard – one of the world's largest asset management firms – has been a major player in the drive for lower fees and even today has among the best product offerings at the lowest prices.

Because the development of index-tracking products continues to be so strong, future product development may well provide even better opportunities. At a fee of around 0.25% a year for world equity products there may not be much scope to significantly improve on the annual charges. But other features like tax structures or better indices to follow may improve the execution of the rational portfolio.

Generally, as a catch-all, I call any product that cheaply recreates an index-type exposure an index tracker. This could be an ETF or index fund, but also note that just because something is called an index does not make it a good choice for the rational investor. An index of companies with CEOs named Bob is an index, but that does not make it a relevant option in achieving our portfolio.

Speculate less, sleep better!

Becoming a rational investor can be a very significant moment in the investing life of some people, and those who have spent a large part of their investing lives frustrated with their inability to outperform the markets may find it a huge relief.

So what actually happens as a rational investor? The short answer is not a lot, and that is the point. But there are some on-going tasks that you could do or have someone help you with:

- You should see if there are better or cheaper products coming on the market to replicate the rational portfolio.
- You should consider if your risk characteristics have changed significantly, or if the world around you has changed so much that the portfolio mix no longer matches your risk profile.
- You should think about your tax situation and if there are better ways of optimising it.
- If your non-investment situation changes significantly you should consider how that affects your investment portfolio.

The points above may seem like a lot to do, but really are not. These are things you should consider irrespective of whether or not you are pursuing a rational portfolio, so there is no extra work involved.

The main non-financial benefit comes from the peace of mind a rational portfolio gives the investor. Someone who has accepted the fact that they do not have an edge should naturally be investing cost efficiently for the long term. They will not be spending a lot of time and financial resources contemplating the next hot stock tip from their golfing buddy or local tip sheet (even though the tipsters are very quick and vocal to boast about their winners). They will be doing other things with their lives and slowly get richer as a result.

For the brave: portfolio theory and the rational investor

Writing about portfolio theory is probably even less fun than reading about it, but this part is important so stay with me if you are interested in the theory behind this book. You should know that the investing style and portfolio construction in this book is not something I have come up with. It is a practical implementation of the generally acknowledged most advanced theory on the subject. Implementing advanced portfolio theory in the real world gives us the best possible portfolio and is actually very easy and logical for someone that does not have an edge on the markets.

The foundation of portfolio theory is that you have a riskless investment that you can optimally combine with a series of other investments. These combinations of investments create different portfolios with a range of individual risk profiles. Because of the optimal investment combination you get the best expected return for any level of risk.

Imagine the simple scenario where you can choose between investing only in two different things: the riskless investment and investment A. Since we know what return we will get from the riskless investment (otherwise it would not be riskless) we can plot the two options on a simple chart (see Figure 3.4).

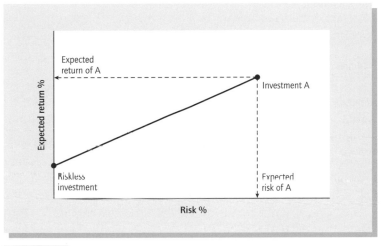

Figure 3.4   **A simple risk/return chart for two options**

The line between the riskless investment and A represent different proportions of the riskless investment and investment A; from 0–100% (all A) to 100–0% (all riskless).

In academic theory, the riskless investment was generally acknowledged to be short-term US government bonds. For practical purposes there was no risk that the US government would default overnight: thus 'riskless'. Those short-term US bonds still provided a return and that return was appropriately called the riskless return. The presence of this riskless return suggested that if you were not willing to take any risk with your investments whatsoever there would be the choice of investing in short-term US government bonds. Because this was the lowest risk security it was also accepted that it should be expected to carry the lowest expected return: there is no such thing as a free lunch.

Of course in today's world the term 'riskless investment' sounds almost like a contradiction in terms. At the time of writing the credit rating of the US, UK and French governments have been downgraded from the highest rating, the financial press is flooded with stories of government debt and deficits, and the number of issuers with the highest credit rating have dwindled since 2007. Granted that in the run up to 2007 investors acted as if everything was riskless, but that is another story.[1]

Investment A can be almost anything, but think of it as a share in Microsoft. Investment A carries a higher expected return than the riskless asset, but there is also some risk associated with that return. More risk for a higher expected return; again, no free lunch.

If you want no risk, you go all riskless, and if you want more risk, you buy investment A. If you want risk between the two, you combine them.

Adding assets

Now we introduce the possibility of another investment, B. Like A, B has its own expected risk/return profile. Importantly though, the movement in the price of A and B are not entirely independent of each other, measured by the correlation (relationship) between those stocks. Remember that word - correlation. It is one of the most important, yet overused, words in the world of finance.

Correlation gives an idea of how A and B move relative to each other. With a correlation of zero there is no relationship between the two, and a correlation of 1 suggests that they move in perfect tandem. If A goes up, so will B. At the danger of oversimplifying complex statistics, most stocks within a general stock market have correlations of roughly 0.5-0.9 with each other, although correlations can change a lot over time. This means that most stocks tend to move in the same direction. You would expect Microsoft and Apple to have a high correlation, while Microsoft and the price of wheat would be less correlated. The lower that two investments' correlation is, the more there are diversifying benefits of lower risk from investing in both of them instead of just one.

Adding the possibility of investing in investment B to Figure 3.4 gives the choices shown in Figure 3.5.

---

1   An important point on portfolio theory and the minimal risk asset that will be discussed later. In accepting that the minimal risk asset is not entirely without risk the line between it and investment A is theoretically not straight, but a curve. Depending on how the minimal risk asset and investment A move relative to each other you might actually end up in a situation where the lowest risk combination of the two is not the 100% minimal risk asset, but instead has some investment A in it. For the purpose of simplicity, I have ignored this possibility.

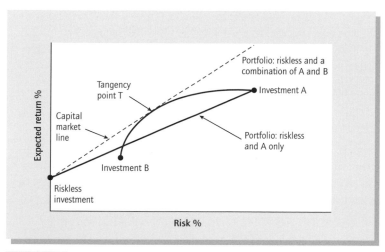

Figure 3.5   **Adding in a third option**

The line between A and B is not straight – this is because we assume A and B are not perfectly correlated and we benefit from the diversification of having two investments. Instead of a straight line, the curved line between A and B represents different proportions of A and B.

We can combine an investment in the riskless investment with any combination of A and B (any point on the curved line between A and B). As you see on Figure 3.5, if we draw a tangent line from the riskless investment point to the curved line then point T is where they meet. T is called the tangency point, and the line between the riskless investment and T is called the capital market line. Looking at the chart in this example, point T consists of roughly 40% of investment A and 60% of investment B (you can see point T is closer to B). You can also see from the chart that if you want the risk of point T or less, you get the highest expected return from combining point T and the riskless investment.

If we want more risk in our portfolio than point T (so on the dotted line to the right of point T) the best solution is to add leverage and invest the additional capital in the combination of 40% of A and 60% of B in this example. By adding leverage and buying more of the 40/60% T combination[2] we achieve

2 This leveraged portfolio assumes that we can borrow money at the riskless rate to invest in more of the T combination, which we can't. In reality, the cost of borrowing would be higher and the line would be flatter to the right of T than it would be to the left of T, to reflect this. If you were unwilling or unable to borrow money, the optimal portfolio at higher risk levels than T would consist increasingly of A and would be represented graphically on the curved line from T to A.

a higher return than if we had allocated more to investment A to get more risk in the portfolio. You can see that the tangent line that continues on from point T is above the curved line where the combination consists increasingly of only investment A.

The optimised market – minimise risk and maximise returns

All of this material may seem abstract and theoretical, but I hope to show how the implications for the rational investor are simple and straightforward as the combined forces of the market have already done the work for you.

Extending the theory discussed above to the whole market, there are endless combinations. Instead of just A and B we can combine thousands of investments as illustrated in Figure 3.6.

As shown in the chart, the new tangency portfolio T is no longer a combination of just two securities but a combination of the various combinations. By combining securities in different proportions we are able to create any risk/return portfolio in the shaded area. Since we want higher returns for a given level of risk we chose combinations of securities that get us to the bold curve. In portfolio theory this curve is called the *efficient frontier*. What the curve is telling us is that for each level of risk there is a combination of securities in the market that gives us the highest expected return. And by combining one of those points on the efficient frontier (point T) with the riskless asset we can create portfolios with the highest level of expected return for any level of risk.

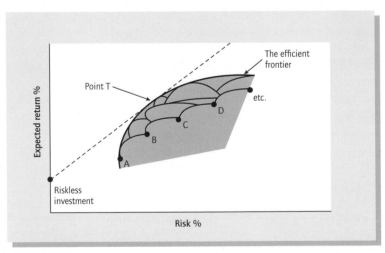

Figure 3.6 **Combining many investments**

I imagine some of my old economics professors would be aghast at the simplicity of the paragraphs above and the absence of long mathematical formulas. If you are interested in the maths and theory behind this summary of portfolio theory then *Modern Portfolio Theory and Investment Analysis* by Edwin Elton *et al.* (John Wiley & Sons, 2003) is a good textbook on the subject.

Bullshit in, bullshit out

One of the things I disliked about investment banking was building massive 50-page Excel models, outlining projections of companies and industries. We would often have little to go on in terms of projections other than short analyst reports which we would use to extrapolate all sorts of data to get 5–10 year projections with all the bells and whistles. We would call this 'bullshit in, bullshit out', suggesting that the financial models were only as good as the assumptions we put into them.

As with the large investment banking financial models, optimal portfolio theory is subject to getting our assumptions right. You probably noticed how casually the theory suggested that you input the expected risk and return for individual securities, and the correlation between them, and *voilà*, the efficient frontier and the tangency point are revealed. Or rather for about £50 you can buy software that will do that for you. But the world is obviously not that simple. Ask 10 market participants about the expected risk and return over the next year on Apple shares and its correlation with Microsoft, and you will get 10 different answers. Now ask the same people to do the same thing for all listed stocks and they will tell you that you are crazy – it's not realistic to have this kind of expectation for more than a small portfolio of shares, and besides, risk and return expectations, and correlations, change all the time. It simply can't be done.

The beautiful shortcut – follow the crowd

But here is the beautiful thing. If you generally believe in efficient markets, you don't need to worry about the portfolio theory above or collecting millions of correlations and thousands of risk-return profiles. The market's 'invisible hand' has already done all that for you. We don't think we are able to reallocate between securities in such a way that we have a higher risk/return profile than what the aggregate knowledge of the market provides. Buying the entire market is essentially like buying the tangency point T.

To some people it will seem like too bold an assumption that capital has seamlessly flowed between countries and industries in such a way that world markets are efficiently allocated. But if we asked: which country/industry/

▶

company is it that you want to reallocate money to/from contrary to the combined information and analytical power of millions of investors allocating trillions of dollars, and why? Accepting that investing internationally gives us greater choice and diversification than only investing in one country, we need to figure out some way to allocate between those choices. If we picked the countries/industries/companies on anything other than their relative market sizes we would essentially be claiming we knew something more than the markets.[3]

You can of course disagree with all of this and make claims like 'Microsoft will go up 20% next year regardless of the market and there is almost no risk that I am wrong'. Of course you might be right, but you are also clearly claiming an edge in knowing or seeing something that the rest of the market does not. Do that consistently and you'll be rich.

Going back to the example of having only the choice of the riskless investment and investment A, that is essentially where we end up. If we replace investment A with the world equity portfolio, and replace the riskless investment with the minimal risk asset, we have moved on from the world of portfolio theory to the real world with investments we can actually implement. We will see later that the minimal risk asset depends on the base currency of your investments.

Investment A in the chart, therefore, consists of many thousands of underlying equities from all over the world in the portfolio (see later). By combining the

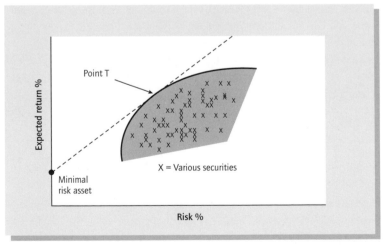

Figure 3.7 Combining the minimal risk asset and world equities

---

3 We are here assuming that capital can flow easily between countries and industries, which is increasingly a fair assumption.

minimal risk asset and A (world equities) in various proportions we choose various risk/return levels in the most efficient way, from minimal risk to the risk of the world equity markets, or greater than that if we borrow money. Point T is already the tangency point, or optimal portfolio, and we don't think we can reallocate money between the many securities in such a way that we end up with better risk/return characteristics (see Figure 3.7).

Later, when we add other government and corporate bonds, we will see that this is akin to when we added the possibility of investment B earlier. While adding a bit of complexity to the portfolio, the other government and corporate bonds enhance the risk/return profile of the whole portfolio.

The best theoretical and actual portfolio

The rational portfolio is a compromise: a compromise between what we would like to create in a theoretical world and what is available practically. In an ideal (theoretical) world we should own a small slice of all of the world's assets to maximise diversification and returns. This clearly is not possible in reality, but the rational portfolio is a very good simplification that we can actually implement. Because the asset classes of the rational portfolio have active and liquid markets for the pricing of thousands of individual securities, we don't need any specific insight to select securities in those markets. And because government bonds, equities and corporate bonds give a very good representation of the world's assets, a portfolio representing those asset classes is a very good simplification of what we should ideally be striving for in a portfolio. We can accept the premise that market forces have set a price on individual securities and the aggregate market at a level that is consistent with the risk/return characteristics of that asset class. Because equities are riskier, we get higher expected returns, etc. For other investments left out of the rational portfolio there is typically not a liquid and efficient market to set prices for the individual investments, so someone without an edge is unable to simply buy into the whole asset class and expect to get its overall risk/return.

So there is no theoretical inconsistency in being a rational investor – on the contrary. We don't think we know any better than the market about the risk/return profiles of individual securities or how they move relative to one another. By pricing securities, the market effectively incorporates the views of thousands of investors and presents us with the results of the market as it currently stands.

So what is 'the market'?

In equities, the market has often meant your local stock market. And if you invest in your local index in a cheap way you are doing better than by picking individual stocks or active mutual funds, but not as well as you could be. You could be picking a much broader geographical range of the world stock markets in proportion to their values.

So only publicly listed equities?

In order to keep things simple, we typically refer to the markets as the listed equity markets. If you invest in a combination of the minimal-risk asset and broad-listed equity markets in a cheap and tax efficient way, you are doing better than most. If you are willing to add a bit of complexity there's a lot of merit in adding other government and corporate bonds to your portfolio (see later).

Summary

- The 'invisible hand' of the markets has optimised the values of the investments available. We should celebrate this simplicity and buy the whole market. We don't think we can reallocate between securities to get a better risk/return profile.
- Combine the world equity markets with investing in the minimal risk asset to get to the kind of risk profile you want.
- The markets could mean for you only a broad range of equities, but adding other government and corporate bonds has a lot of merit.

The rational portfolio

4

The minimal risk asset – safe, low-risk returns

Buy government bonds in your base currency if credit quality is high

This chapter is about finding the lowest-risk investment as the base on which a riskier portfolio can potentially be built. Your choice depends on currency: for a sterling-denominated investor, short-term UK govenment bonds are a good choice. As discussed previously, there is probably no genuine riskless security in the world today, but the probability that the UK government will default is very low; thus minimal risk.

By comparison, a US-based investor buying short-term UK government bonds would have the same security of getting his principal back, but would incur currency risk as the GBP/USD exchange rate fluctuations add risk. So if, for example, the UK bond promised to pay the investor £101 a year hence for a £100 investment today, both investors are equally certain of receiving £101, but while the £101 would always be £101, the US dollar value of that amount could fluctuate quite a bit and is thus more risky. The US investor would therefore be better served by owning short-term US government bonds that are of similar credit quality to the UK government bonds where his returns would be independent of currency risk.

If your base investment currency is one where the government credit is of the highest quality, those government bonds will generally be a great choice for your minimal risk investment. While most investor's base currency is obvious (sterling for UK investors, dollars for US ones, etc.), and currency risk is a risk you would rather avoid, your base currency can also be a mix of currencies. It is essentially the currency that you think you will one day need the money in. So while I may live in the UK and probably have the majority of my future expenses here, I also spend a lot of time (and money) in Denmark, the eurozone and the US. Also, I may have future expenses for my children's education outside the UK, or my wife and I might live or retire abroad one day. By having my base currency as a mix of several currencies, albeit dominated by sterling, I will better match my future cash needs and leave myself less at risk of being caught out by a falling currency with potential expenses in other currencies.

Today there are three major credit agencies that rank the creditworthiness of bonds, namely Moody's, Standard & Poor's and Fitch. Here is how those agencies rate long-term bonds.

Long-term bond ratings	Moody's	S&P	Fitch
Prime	Aaa	AAA	AAA
Investment grade	Aa1 to Baa3	AA+ to BBB−	AA+ to BBB−
Non-investment grade	Ba1 to Ca	BB+ to C	BB+ to CCC
Default	C and lower	D	DDD to D

The credit agencies were widely discredited after 2008 when they wrongly gave high ratings to all sorts of sub-prime garbage, but in general they give you a good indication of the credit quality of a country's bonds.

Credit ratings change frequently. As you consider adding your minimal risk asset, you can see the latest credit ratings on Wikipedia by searching for 'List of countries by credit rating'. If the government credit of your base currency is listed here as AAA you have an easy choice for your minimal risk asset. With the adverse environment of government debt and deficits in recent years, the list of AAA-rated countries from all agencies has shortened. That said, if your home base currency offers AA or higher-rated bonds then it would be sufficient to accept those as your minimal risk asset. If we only accepted bonds with the highest rating, at the time of writing that would exclude bonds from major economies like the US, Japan and France, which is neither practical nor desirable for many investors (the UK was also recently downgraded from the top rating by Moody's and Fitch). While there is obviously a reason for these countries losing the highest rating it is worth noting that the financial markets trade the bonds at real yields that are among the most creditworthy in the world in any currency.

If your base currency is one without a highly rated bond available, you face a tougher choice. For all their undoubted economic successes over the past decades countries like Brazil, Mexico and India do not have highly rated government bonds (all approximately BBB-rated at the time of writing). As a Brazilian you could buy Brazilian short-term government bonds which would not be minimal risk or highly rated government bonds in one or a couple of foreign currencies, although this would involve a currency risk. Depending on the credit rating of your base currency government you may choose to take the credit risk of the domestic government bonds instead of taking the currency risk of highly rated foreign bonds, or perhaps even keep money in cash deposits in the local bank if that is considered a superior credit option to domestic government bonds (see the box on pages 49–53).

Older people in certain parts of the world, including Brazil, undoubtedly remember times of domestic economic turmoil and the thought of buying local government bonds as their minimal risk asset will seem like heresy. And they are right. These investors do not have essentially risk-free bonds in their local currency, however far the government has come. Perhaps one day the credits of these governments and many like them will grow in esteem to the point that they become the lowest-risk bonds in the world, but not today. In the past, many investors with a less-creditworthy domestic government essentially made their base investment currency the US dollar and would buy US government bonds for their base currency.

While the lower credit ratings of some government bonds mean that the bonds yield more, this is not a good reason to have them as your minimal risk or safe asset. As discussed in the next chapter, if you want to add returns to your portfolio you can do so by adding broad exposures of equities that have the added benefit of both being geographically diversified and adding expected returns.

Perhaps diversify even the very low risk that your domestic government fails

Investing in sub-AA credit ratings is a question of degrees. Some investors would be happy to invest in their BBB-rated local currency government bonds whereas others would rather invest abroad with currency risk than have an AA domestic-rated government bond. The choice partly depends on your situation and sensitivity to currency risk versus domestic credit risk. For those inclined to accept sub-AA domestic government bonds as their minimal risk asset I would encourage you to think about what else would happen in your portfolio if your domestic government defaulted. In most cases, a domestic government default would have a catastrophic effect on your portfolio and general life.

If you had diversified some of the domestic risk away by having your minimal risk asset as highly rated foreign bonds, such as German/UK/US government bonds, then you would at least have some respite when the domestic calamity hit. Also, some investors consider that having all your minimal risk assets invested in the bonds of just one government, however creditworthy, is a bad idea. Those investors argue that while the government bonds of Britain or Germany are highly rated today there is always some risk that they could fail, perhaps even spectacularly and quickly.[1] Because of this eventuality investors should diversify their minimal risk asset into a couple of different, highly rated government bonds, even if this means taking a currency risk for those bonds that are not in your base currency. My view is that if you are invested in government bonds that are among the most highly rated in the world the probability of a sudden default is so low that for practical purposes it is a risk you could feel safe taking.

Here are some recommendations for minimal risk assets depending on your base currency:

If your base currency is:	Primary suggested minimal risk asset:	Alternative minimal risk asset:
US dollar	US government bonds	Mix of world-leading government bonds (take a currency risk)
Euro	German or AAA/AA eurozone government bonds	Mix of world-leading government bonds (take a currency risk)
Sterling	UK government bonds	Mix of world-leading government bonds (take a currency risk)

1 For those who don't think government bonds can default I would encourage you to read *This Time is Different: Eight Centuries of Financial Folly* by Carmen Reinhart and Kenneth Rogoff (Princeton University Press, 2011). The authors make a mockery of the belief that governments rarely default and that we are somehow now protected from the catastrophic financial events of the past.

Other currency with AAA/AA government credit	Domestic government bonds	Mix of world-leading government bonds (take a currency risk)
Other currency with sub-AA domestic government credit	One or a mix of world-leading government bonds (take a currency risk)	Domestic government bonds (take a credit risk) or bank deposits if a strong credit bank

So your minimal or 'safe' asset is not necessarily your domestic government bond. Consider a Spanish investor who is after the lowest risk asset, and does not want to take a currency risk. This investor should not be buying Spanish government bonds that are quite lowly rated, but instead should buy German government bonds that are also euro denominated. If this investor did not want the minimal risk to be the bonds of just one government he could diversify by either adding other euro-denominated government bonds or accept the currency risk with highly rated non-euro government bonds.

In most countries there are domestic bonds related to the sovereign issuer, such as government-guaranteed regional, city or municipal bonds. Those and similar bonds could be reasonable alternatives as minimal risk assets, particularly if there are tax advantages to investing in them. However, make sure that the guarantee is bulletproof even in distress. If you get a superior yield from these alternative bonds compared to the standard government bonds, you are probably taking additional credit risk. Also be careful in thinking that adding these kinds of bonds provide you with additional safety; they are typically a poor diversifier of risk as they tie back to the same creditworthiness as the domestic government bonds.

Matching time horizon

In the discussion above, short-term bonds are the minimal risk asset. This is because longer-term bonds have greater interest risk (the fluctuation in the value of the bond as a result of fluctuations in the interest rate). Consider the example of a one-month zero-coupon bond and a 10-year zero-coupon bond that trade at 100 (zero-coupon bonds don't pay interest, only the principal back at maturity). Now suppose annual interest rates go from zero to 1% suddenly. What happens to the value of the bonds?

	T = 0		T = 1
Interest rate	0%		1%
One-month bond	100	→	99.9
10-year bond	100	→	90.5

The one-month bond declines a little in value to reflect an interest rate of 1%, while the 10-year bond declines to a value of around 90.5 to reflect the higher interest rate. Clearly something that can go from 100 to 90.5 fairly quickly (rate changes are rarely that dramatic) is riskier, even if your chance of eventually being paid in full has not changed.

However, in reality the time horizon for most investors exceeds the maturity of the short-term bond. Someone who is interested in maintaining a position in the minimal risk asset for five years will be taking an interest rate risk over that five-year time horizon whether buying new three-month bonds every three months, or buying a five-year bond and keeping it to maturity.

But if the time horizon is such that you think five-year bonds make sense, you shouldn't necessarily just buy the five-year bond and hold it to maturity. A year hence, your bond would only have four years to maturity and therefore no longer match your time horizon.

The best way to address this issue is not for you to constantly buy and sell bonds to get the right maturity profile (here you would sell the now four-year bond and buy another five-year bond), but to buy the bonds through a product like an exchange-traded fund or investment fund that trades the bonds for you. (These 'access products' will be discussed in detail later.) Such funds will offer products like 'Germany 5–7 years (to maturity) government bonds', 'UK 10–12 year government bonds', etc. Buying one or a couple of these products to match your desired minimal risk asset and maturity profile is a cheap and low-hassle way to ensure you have the right minimal risk asset in your profile.

So investors with a longer time horizon should therefore buy longer-maturing minimal-risk bonds. As a reward for taking the interest rate risk associated with the longer-term bonds they typically yield more than the short-term bonds, as illustrated in Figure 4.1.[2]

So if you need a product that will not lose money over the next year, pick short-term bonds to match that profile. However, if you – like most people – are after a product that will provide a secure investment further into the future, pick longer-term bonds and accept the attendant interest-rate risk.

---

2 There are cases where the yield curve is reversed and shorter-term bonds yield more than longer-term ones, but these cases are less frequent.

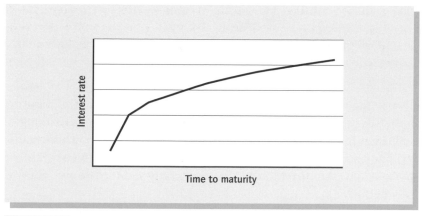

Figure 4.1   The typical bond yield curve

You should therefore consider the time horizon of your portfolio and select the maturity of your minimal risk bonds accordingly. If you are matching needs far in the future (like your retirement spending) there is certainly merit in adding long-term bonds or even inflation-protected bonds (see below) to your portfolio. Long-term bonds compensate investors for interest-rate risks by offering higher yields and you have the further benefit of matching the timing of your assets and needs.

Another good alternative is to mix the maturities of your minimal risk assets. You may have some assets that you won't need for decades, and others you think will be needed in 5–7 years. In that case, there is nothing wrong with picking a couple of different products with different maturities to match that profile.

Inflation-protected bonds

Normally when people quote a bond yield they refer to the nominal yield. The nominal yield consists of the real yield plus inflation. (So if a bond offers a 2% yield then that simply means that you get £2 for a £100 bond; if you assume inflation at 1%, then the real yield would be 1%.) So as an investor, in most bonds you have an inflation risk on top of the interest rate risk. To address this inflation concern several governments have started issuing inflation-protected bonds where the buyer is promised a real return. The inflation-indexed bonds work by linking the principal to an inflation index like the consumer price index (in the US) or the retail price index (in the UK). As those indices go up with inflation, so does the amount you are owed by the government.

The market has grown explosively since the British government started issuing these bonds in 1981, but are still not nearly as widespread as the regular bonds: there are currently about $1.5 trillion outstanding compared to world government bonds of over $40 trillion. These bonds are an interesting development and provide investors with a way to avoid the inflation risk inherent in the bond markets, and I would recommend UK and US investors in particular to consider them.

The threat of inflation is a real concern for a lot of savers and these new bonds offer a good way to address that concern. While you still take an interest-rate risk and should match maturities to your maturity profile, at least your inflation risk is mitigated.

In recent inflation-linked bond issues several issuers were able to issue bonds that had a negative real interest. Think about that. You lend someone money, potentially even for a very long time, and they promise to pay you back less than what you lent them in terms of what that money can buy. It may seem crazy, but that is the reality of the world we live in right now. This does not mean that these are not good bonds to own, just an illustration that interest rates are low now and the cost of owning a bond that will be extremely likely to repay you is high.

What will the minimal risk bond earn you?

Most people with even a peripheral interest in finance realise that at the time of writing, in spring 2013, interest rates are currently at or near a historical low. So investors should not expect to make a lot of money investing in the minimal risk asset in any currency. In fact, with nominal interest rates near zero, inflation means that investors in short-term government bonds will experience negative real returns. So while your £100 invested in a government bond may, with almost certainty, become £105 in five years' time, the purchasing power of that £105 will be less than that of the £100 today. This is, of course, still better than if you had held the £100 in cash for five years – in that case the purchasing power would be even lower.

Without putting too fine a point on it, that obviously isn't great, but there is not a lot you can do about it. If you are after securities with minimal risk then the yields are just very low right now. Instruments that offer higher returns come with more risk of not getting paid and anyone who tells you otherwise is not telling you the whole story.

Figures 4.2 and 4.3 show what UK and US government bonds (so in £ and $) will currently earn you, by maturity, both in real and nominal terms.

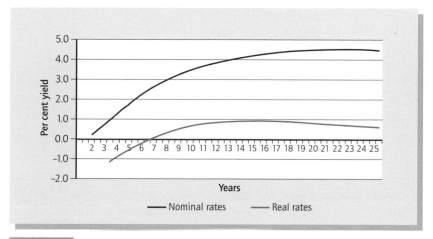

Figure 4.2   **Current UK government bond yields**

Based on data from www.bankofengland.co.uk

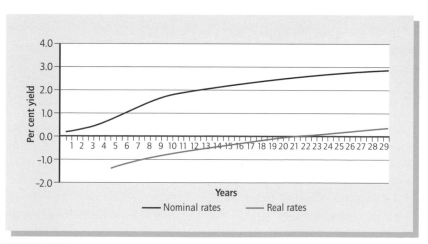

Figure 4.3   **Current US government bond yields**

Based on data from www.treasury.gov

While the outlook for generating very low-risk real returns is thus fairly limited (at the time of writing), these are continuously moving markets and it is worth staying on top of them as rates change. What you can see from Figure 4.2, for example, is that if you wanted to buy UK government bonds now, you could expect to earn a just under 1% real return a year for a 20-year bond. Likewise, for a five-year bond you should expect a negative return of about 0.5% a year.

What you can also see from Figures 4.2 and 4.3 is the current market expectation of future inflation (the difference between the lines). So, for example, the markets are assuming that there will be approximately 4% annual inflation in the UK for the next 25 years, but only around 2% for the next five years, suggesting higher inflation in the longer term. Inflation is bad for many things, one of which is tax. (While the benefits you get from your investments are based on real returns and the future purchasing power of your money, you pay taxes on the nominal return.)

Suppose you invest £100 for a nominal return of 2% the following year, then you could be liable for tax on your £2 gain, even if 2% annual inflation had eroded the real gain (so the purchasing power a year hence would still be £100 in today's money even if the nominal amount had become £102). Compare that to a zero inflation rate environment with a 0% nominal/real return and your £100 would still be £100, both in real terms and nominally, at the end of the year. There would be no gains to pay taxes on.

If the charts above give you the sense that the returns you get in any one year from owning UK or US government bonds is stable, reconsider. Figure 4.4 shows the annual return from holding short-term (sub one year) and long-term (more than 10 years) US bonds since around the Depression. What you can see is that the annual returns move around a fair deal for both, but far more for the long-term bonds. This is because those bonds will move in value far more as the interest rate or inflation fluctuates.

It can be hard to do an objective, like-for-like comparison of historical and current returns as the market view of the creditworthiness of government credit has not been constant, but Figure 4.4 suggests that the returns from longer-maturity bonds are not without risk. If your investment horizon for the minimal risk asset was approximately 10 years and you had gained access to the government bonds through an ETF or index fund, your annual fluctuations would have looked roughly like Figure 4.4. It will probably be a surprise that something that is considered as safe as US government bonds can fluctuate as much as the chart suggests.

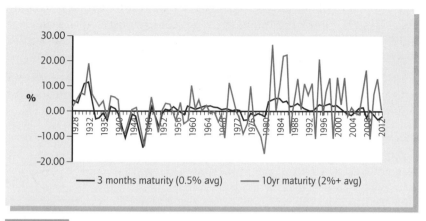

Figure 4.4 Inflation-adjusted US government bond returns since 1928

Based on Bureau of Labor Statistics and Federal Reserve St. Louis

There are a few points to note from the charts above:

- Real return expectations from the minimal risk asset are currently near an historic low.

- Returns from these minimal risk assets have fluctuated quite a bit, because of changes in inflation and real interest rates, and can reasonably be expected to do so in the future.

- You can generally expect higher returns from investing in longer-dated bonds. If that matches your investment horizon then hold your minimum risk bond portfolio through a suggested access product like an ETF or index fund. But note that particularly for longer-dated bonds the yearly fluctuations in value can be significant.

In the interest of keeping things simple in the following examples, I have assumed a real return of 0.5% a year from the minimal risk asset. As you can see in Figure 4.4 while that is too high for current short-term bonds, it is more reasonable for longer-term bonds and in line with historical returns from short-term bonds.

Do not believe your cash is safe in the bank!

Although interest rates are quite low, many investors still hold large deposits in cash at their financial institutions without considering the credit risk. I would caution against blindly doing this.

▶

About 120 countries in the world have a system whereby the state guarantees deposits with financial institutions up to a certain amount in cases of default. While this varies by country it means that the first £85,000 (in the UK) or €100,000 (in many EU countries) of deposits with a bank is guaranteed by the government. The guarantees are in place to lend confidence to the financial system and avoid runs on the banks. Without a bank guarantee we would be general creditors to the bank and have to gauge bank credit risk, something most depositors are not equipped to do. (Of course, if you have your money with a bank deemed 'too big to fail' the bank won't fail without the government also failing.)

If you hold cash deposits with one or more financial institutions in excess of the deposit insurance then you are a general creditor of that institution in the event that it fails. This means that if you have £200,000 in deposits with a bank and the credit insurance is only for £85,000, the last £115,000 is not covered.

A good friend of mine sold his successful IT business a while ago for a very large cash amount. He was never really that interested in finance, and just left the money in an account with his financial institution while he took some time off. This was a large, double-digit, million-dollar amount and the financial institution was the insurance company AIG. He got concerned when one morning he read in the *Financial Times* about all the issues with AIG and how it could potentially go bust. When my friend contacted AIG there was initially some confusion about the kind of account he held and for a while my friend thought his money with AIG was going to be lost in the general abyss of a spectacular financial collapse. In the end, he along with all the other creditors of AIG kept his money, but the experience certainly put the statement that an investment is 'as good as money in the bank' in perspective.

On a much smaller scale, I had some cash in a lesser-known bank in excess of the government credit guarantee. I had agreed to put most of the money on time deposits where I would get a slightly higher interest rate of 2.5%. Coincidentally I discovered that the bank bonds were trading in the market at a yield of approximately 5% a year. In simple terms, the market was telling me that I was taking a credit risk on the non-government guaranteed portion of my deposit that the market estimated at 5% a year, but getting paid 2.5% for it. Not a great idea!

Who backs the deposit insurance?

The deposit insurance scheme is only as good as the institution that has granted this guarantee. If you were holding cash with a Greek bank and relied on the deposit insurance protection from the Greek government you would clearly not be as secure as with the same guarantee from the German government.

In the recent bailout of Cyprus, the restructuring that was initially suggested involved depositors both above and below the guaranteed amount taking a cut in their deposits (in the end, only larger depositors had part of their holdings confiscated), suggesting that bank depositors in that country were indirectly exposed to the creditworthiness of that government in addition to that of the bank holding their money.

Local banks fare horribly if the government defaults; the banks are tied strongly to the local economy, which is suffering. On top of facing a poor economic climate, the banks will have lost a lot on their holding of government bonds. The correlation between the troubles of your government and your bank is thus very high, and the protection you were hoping for may be absent as a result. This is bad news, particularly as your bank and government default may well happen at the same time as other things in your life are being negatively affected by the same economic factors; you may have lost your job, your house may decline in value, and so on. It is exactly in that circumstance that you want the diversification of investments and assets that the rational portfolio provides.

A way to address the potential lack of security of your cash in the bank is to buy securities like AAA/AA government bonds or other investment securities that closely resemble cash (such as money market funds, etc.). Importantly, securities like these still belong to you even in the case of a bank default, and while the process of moving that security to another financial institution could be cumbersome, you are no longer a creditor to a failed bank, which gives you far greater security in a calamity.

While investments like stocks and bonds held in custody at a bank still belong to you if the bank goes bust, you should be careful about holding too many assets at risky banks. Once an institution defaults, the process of finding out who exactly owns what can take time. There have even been cases where the segregation between client assets and bank assets have been less firm than it legally should be, rendering it even harder to regain the investments that are legitimately yours, in the face of bank creditors claiming that the same assets belong to them.

Also, in a future bailout like the ones we have seen in Southern Europe it may be that not only your cash is confiscated, but that institutions find a way to take some of your securities as well. It's all a mess worth avoiding, so unless there is a compelling reason not to do so I would encourage you to place your cash and investment assets with very credible banks.

Particularly pre–2008, some less-known banks offered very generous interest rates on deposits compared to the more conservative traditional banks (these turned out to not be so conservative either, but that's another story). In the UK, the Icelandic banks in particular were guilty of this, but there were many others. (The rate differential provided the potential for profits from the perspective of the depositor at the expense of the soundness of the banking system.) If the depositor guarantee was indeed iron clad (i.e. the government would not try to get out of the depositor guarantee under any circumstances) then depositors were incentivised to withdraw cash deposits from the more conservative high street banks and deposit the money with the bank that offered higher deposit interest rates. If the gun-slinging bank went bust (like some did later) the government would ensure the depositor would not suffer. If the gun-slinging bank stayed in business, the depositor would benefit from higher rates.

A couple of years ago I was approached by someone who was planning to start a bank. His pitch did not involve great new markets or interesting products, but rather what he called an 'arbitrage' on the credit insurance of the government. His arbitrage involved offering customers extremely high deposit rates, but only up to the amount of the government deposit insurance, and thus attract sizeable deposits. He would use the deposits to offer loans to renewable energy investments that also had government guaranteed rates of return, while capturing a spread for the bank (and himself presumably) in the middle. He claimed that his scheme was entirely legal and within banking regulations (I suggested he double checked this). I don't know if this man was able to start his bank, but it gives a good picture of the kind of thinking that can drive some of the more gun-slinging banks out there. Also, it shows how important it is for governments to get bank regulation right in the face of the many people who constantly try to game the system. It is not an easy task.

I feel like a pessimist in writing about the dangers of cash deposits. It is certainly the case that in more than 99% of cases the thought behind the term 'safe as money in the bank' or 'cash is king' means exactly that; that it is entirely safe. My logic is based more on how things fit together and trying to avoid several bad things happening at the same time. If you consider the unlikely scenario of the bank where you hold most deposits going out of business, that scenario probably involves a lot of things that are also not good for your investing life. Regardless of what your risk profile is as an investor, you should be sure that you get properly compensated for the risks you are taking, and that you think about what happens in a calamity. The risk to your cash deposits in the case of a bank default is no different.

Summary

- Cash deposits are not entirely without risk. Don't hold cash in excess of that which is guaranteed by the government at one bank, and do worry about which government has issued the deposit insurance on your cash.

> ■ By holding investment securities like government bonds (or products like ETFs for government) instead of cash with a financial institution, you are often in a far better situation to recover these securities in the event of a bank failure.

Buying the minimal risk asset

Because of costs in trading bonds most investors in short-term bonds have to accept that the bonds in their portfolios will not be super short term,[3] and that you will be taking a little bit of interest rate risk as a result. The most liquid short-term bond implementation products like ETFs or index funds that represent the underlying bonds have average maturities of 1–3 years. The slight interest rate risk that comes from holding bonds with 1–3 year maturities is a reasonable compromise between the theoretical minimal risk product and one we can actually buy in the real world. For most investors with longer-term investment horizons other implementation products typically have different ranges of maturities like 5–7 years, 7–10 years, etc. to suit your preferences.

How much of the minimal risk asset you should have in your portfolio and what maturities it should have depends on your circumstances and attitudes towards risk. If you are extremely risk averse you could have your entire portfolio in short-term minimal risk assets, but you could not expect much in terms of returns with that. I will revert to what sample portfolios look like when you start introducing more risk, but the availability of the minimal risk asset is of critical importance to all investment decisions:

■ You can use the minimal risk asset as part of your portfolio to adjust the risk profile. In the simple scenario where you can only choose between the minimal risk asset and a broad equity portfolio, you could weigh the balance of those two according to the desired risk. The minimal risk bonds would have very little risk, whereas the equities would have the market risk. How much risk you want in your portfolio

---

3 Imagine the scenario where you want to hold one-month government bonds. Tomorrow the bonds are no longer one-month to maturity, but 29 days. Is this ok? How about 2 days hence? How much you are willing for the maturity to deviate from exactly 30 days is up to you, but in reality there is a trading and administrative cost associated with trading bonds. It would simply not be feasible to stay at exactly 30 days to maturity at all times.

would be an allocation choice between the two (we will later add other government and corporate bonds).[4]

■ For some investors, the minimal risk asset *is* their optimal portfolio. If you are unwilling to take any risk whatsoever with your investments and willing to accept that this means low expected returns, this is it.

Summary

■ If your base currency has government bonds of the highest credit quality (£, $, €, etc.) then those should be your choice as the minimal risk asset.

■ If your base currency does not offer minimal risk alternatives you have the choice of lower-rated domestic bonds where you take a credit risk, or higher-rated foreign ones where you take a currency risk. Keep in mind that a domestic default will probably happen at the same time as other problems in your portfolio, and the domestic currency would probably devalue, rendering the foreign currency denominated bonds worth more in local currency terms.

■ If you want no risk at all you should buy short-term bonds. If you have a longer investment horizon, then match the investment horizon with the maturity of your minimal risk bond portfolio. You will have to accept interest rate risk even if you avoid inflation risk by buying inflation-adjusted bonds.

---

4 Certain corporate bonds trade with lower risk premiums than many governments. The view is that these corporates are lower credit risk than many governments – not hard to believe – and although they do not have the ability to print money, nor do governments in the eurozone. The reason I believe that you should not consider these bonds as the minimal risk asset is more practical. Compared to government bonds, the amount of corporate bonds outstanding for any one company is minuscule and you would probably not be able to trade them as cheaply and liquidly as government bonds.

World equities – increased risk and return

Buy equities from around the world

In order to move the portfolio towards the promise of higher returns you need to increase your risk/return profile by buying publicly listed equities (referred here simply as equities). I am not recommending you buying equities because I have some insight that equities are set to have an outstanding performance relative to other assets. It is because I consider equities to be the highest expected return asset class (at the highest risk) and the most easily bought, in a diversified fashion, of the three groupings of investments that I think someone without an edge should invest in. The three are: the minimal risk asset, equities and other government and corporate bonds. Later we look at why other asset classes are excluded from the portfolio. But here the question is: which equities?

Figure 5.1 is a chart of the Dow Jones, the world's oldest stock market index that was created to track the US stock market since its inception in 1896. From a start of around 40 in 1896 that index is trading at around 13,000 today.

As I will discuss further in the next chapter, far from all equity markets have been as successful as the Dow and we can't extrapolate the Dow performance to the wider world. When estimating the returns we can expect from investing in equities it is important to incorporate the returns of all equity markets.

From the perspective of the rational investor, each dollar invested in the markets around the world is presumed equally smart. This means that we should own the shares in the market according to their fraction of the market's overall value. So if we assume that the market refers only to the

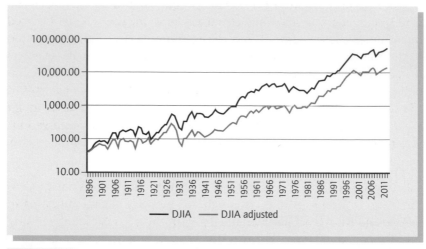

Figure 5.1 Dow Jones index since 1896 ('normal' and adjusted for inflation and dividend reinvested)

US stock market and that Apple shares represented 3% of the overall value, then 3% of our equity holdings should be Apple shares. If we do anything other than this, we are somehow saying that we are more clever, more informed – that we have an edge on the market.

But why stop at the US market? If there is $15 trillion invested in the US stock market and $2 trillion in the UK market there is no reason to think that the UK market is any less informed or efficient than the US one. And likewise with any other market in the world that investors have access to. We should invest with them all, in the proportions of their share of the world equity markets within the bounds of practicality.

Many investors overweigh 'home' equities. The UK represents less than 3% of the world equity markets, but the proportion of UK equities in a UK portfolio is often 35–40%. Investors feel they know and understand their home market. Perhaps they think they are able to spot opportunities before the wider market, although in fairness the concentration is often because of investment restrictions or because investors are matching liabilities connected to the local market. Various studies suggest that this 'home field advantage' is perceived rather than real, but we continue to have our portfolios dominated by our home market.

If you over- or underweight one country compared to its fraction of the world equity markets you would effectively be saying that a dollar invested in an underweight country is less clever/informed than a dollar invested in the country that you allocate more to. You would essentially claim to see an advantage from allocating differently from how the multi-trillion dollar international financial markets have allocated which you are not in a position to do unless you have an edge. So besides it being much simpler and cheaper, since investors have already moved capital between various international markets efficiently, the international equity portfolio is the best one.

Take my situation as an example. As a Danish citizen who has lived in the US and UK for over 20 years I might instinctively be over-allocating to Europe and the US because I'm familiar with those markets. But in doing that I would implicitly be claiming that Europe and the US would have a better risk/return profile than the rest of the world. This might or might not turn out that way, but the point is that we don't know ahead of time. Or you could find yourself making statements like, 'I believe the BRIC (Brazil, Russia, India and China) countries are set to dominate growth over the next decades and are cheap.' Perhaps you'd be right, but you would also be saying that you know something that the rest of the world has not yet discovered. This does not make sense unless you have an edge.

The advantage of diversification

The world equity portfolio is the most diversified equity portfolio we can find. To give an idea of the benefits of diversification in the home market consider Figure 5.2, which suggests the benefits decline as we add securities in the home market. This makes sense. Stocks trading in the same market will tend to correlate greatly (they are exposed to the same economy, legal system, etc.), and after picking a relatively small number of them you have diversified away a great deal of the market risk of any individual stock. So you could actually gain a lot of the advantages from the US index funds by picking 15–20 large capitalisation stocks and sticking with them, assuming they did not all act like one. (If you only added stocks from one sector that all moved in the same way the diversification benefits would be far lower.) It is not the rational US portfolio that you have achieved (you claimed an edge by selecting a sub-set of 15–20 stocks and deselecting the rest of the market), but from a diversification perspective you have accomplished a lot.

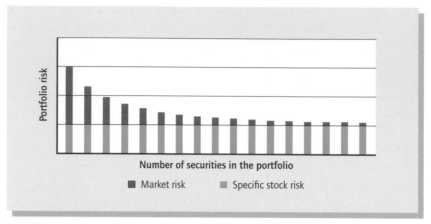

Figure 5.2 Portfolio risk and diversification

By expanding the portfolio beyond the home market we achieve much greater diversification in our investments. This is because we spread our investments over a larger number of stocks but, more importantly, because those stocks are based in different geographical areas and local economies. Decades ago we didn't really have the opportunity to invest easily across the world, and while it's still not seamless for investors in many places, investing abroad in a geographically diversified way is a lot easier than it used to be.

So, in summary, the key benefits of a broad market-weighted portfolio are as follows:

- The portfolio is as diversified as possible and each dollar invested in the market is presumed equally clever, consistent with what a rational investor believes. (I bet a lot of Japanese investors wished they had diversified geographically after their domestic market declined 75% from its peak over the past 20 years.)

- Since we are simply buying 'the market' as broadly as we can it's a very simple portfolio to construct and thus very cheap. We don't have to pay anyone to be smart about beating the market. Over time the cost benefit can make a huge difference. Don't ignore that.

- This kind of broad-based portfolio is now available to most investors whereas only a couple of decades ago it was not. Most people then thought 'the market' meant only their domestic market, or at best a regional market. Take advantage of this development to buy broader-based products.

If for whatever reason you are unable to buy a broad geographic portfolio like the one described above, then buy as broad a geographic portfolio as you can and get as large a fraction of the market as you can. So if you can only buy US stocks, buy the whole market – like a Wilshire 5000 tracker instead of an S&P 500 tracker – if the costs are the same. If you can only buy European stocks, buy that whole market, etc.

Do alternative weightings do better?

Many works on investing suggest that value investments (shares with low price/book or price/earnings ratios) and smaller companies both outperform the general market over time. Various indices and products have been created to cater to this argument.

In short, I don't think rational investors should buy alternative weighted investments as proxies for their market exposure. By actively de-selecting a portion of the market (the higher growth or larger companies) investors are claiming that others who have invested in those companies are somehow less informed than themselves, which is a grand statement and inconsistent with rational investing. It is probably fair to assume that all those investors in the growth or larger companies are highly experienced and informed, have read all the relevant books on investing and are well aware of all the aspects of historical outperformance of various sectors of the markets. They are not stupid; in fact they are as much a part of the market as the value or smaller company investors are. Do you really think that the trillions of dollars that follow companies like Google and Apple are somehow from ill-informed investors and that you know more about the markets than they do to the extent that you can de-select those stocks?

Anyone who suggests an alternative weighting to that of the overall market looks more like an active investor than a passive one. Likewise, the implicit cost of the part of the portfolio that diverges from the general index can easily approach the fee levels of an actively managed fund. Suppose an alternative weighted index has an overlap of 66% with the wider market, but costs 0.3% more a year to implement. In that case you are paying 1% a year on the part of your investment that is different from the general market, or fees akin to those demanded by some active managers.

I also think that many of these alternative weighted indices are created to match what has had the best historical performance and thus be easier to sell. If stocks with high price/earnings (P/E) and growth rates had been the best performers over the past decades many alternative weighted indices would consist of that market segment, complete with charts outlining the great reasons why that trend could be expected to continue. We would be guilty of fitting the product to past returns and essentially saying that we had the insight that the future would be like the past.

On top of the active de-selection of some parts of the market that it implies, my main issue with small company investing has to do with implementation. Actively implementing a portfolio of smaller companies is very expensive as the execution trade is subject to large bid/offer spreads and price movements if you trade in any size. But even if you could pass the hurdle of costs, you are still left with the same question: do you really know enough about the markets to claim an edge to the extent that you over-weigh these stocks at the expense of other stocks in the market? What is it you know that the wider market doesn't?

Whether you are picking a North American Biotech index, the Belgian index, an index of commodities stocks, etc. you are essentially claiming an edge and advantage in the market as if you were picking Microsoft shares to outperform.

To ensure that this book is not without a 'get rich quick' scheme here is one. Buy whatever index you think is sure to outperform and sell short the broader index against it with as much money as you can borrow. Now wait for the world to prove you right, ensure you riches and the financial media to turn up and write articles about your investing brilliance.

In summary: stick with the broadest and cheapest market.

What are world equities?

Today, the total value of the equity markets in the world is $40–50 trillion. As you would expect, this value has grown dramatically over the past decades, rendering what seemed like massive drawdowns in 2008–09 appear as minor blips on what looks like a certain upward trajectory.

The increase in the size of the world market capitalisation is not only because share prices went up. Many new shares were listed on the stock exchanges and particularly outside the US and Europe new markets took off in spectacular fashion. There was also an increase in population, an increase in GDP and savings, privatisations of state-owned enterprises, and more countries moving from planned to market economies, all which contributed to the large rise.[1]

1 Some emerging market companies listed their shares on Western exchanges to increase credibility and foreign companies thus make up a meaningful part of some exchanges.

The US is, by some distance, the largest equity market in the world. The market value of the shares listed in the US is approximately $15 trillion, with Apple and Exxon as the two most valuable companies at the time of writing. Although the US stocks represent the largest country fraction of world equities this share is smaller than it was even a decade ago as rising emerging markets have come to represent an ever-greater share of world equities.

Market capitalisation data changes continuously, so in looking at the split of current market values for the various countries in the world (see Figure 5.3) bear in mind this could have changed since publication.

While different world indices include country exposures in slightly different ways Figure 5.3 shows roughly the exposure you would have if you buy a product that tracks world equities. Since some 'world' indices do not include all the countries with functioning equity markets, the weightings of those that are included are slightly higher. The list of markets and weightings should be available on the website of any product provider you are considering.

It is worth noting that various countries have greater or smaller stock markets relative to their national economies (see Figure 5.4). The US currently represents approximately 35% of world equity markets, but its share of the world GDP is only just over 20% (and declining). Some countries have a longer history of stock listings and perhaps a more

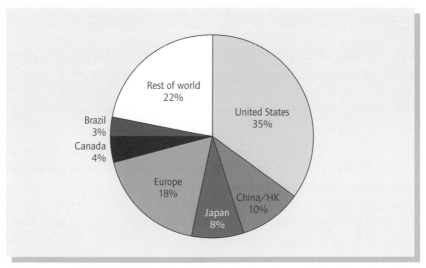

Figure 5.3 World equity market value

Based on data from www.worldbank.org

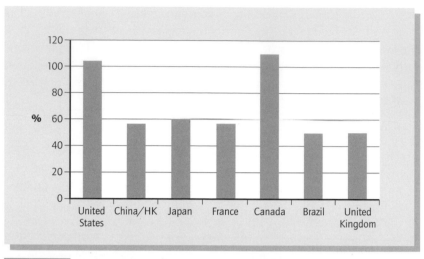

Figure 5.4   **Equity market value versus country GDP**

Based on data from www.worldbank.org and www.imf.org

favourable legal system for publicly quoted stocks. Likewise, because most companies today have significant operations abroad we should not expect the stock market valuation to be a precise reflection of the domestic economy. But whatever the reasons, as a world equity investor you should not expect your geographic exposure to exactly match that of economic output.

While I think it would be ideal if all countries had roughly similar GDP/market value ratios, as then the portfolio would be even better diversified, I think it is more important to be weighted in line with market values in a world index. If there are risk/return benefits from reallocating capital between markets we can trust the efficient markets to do so, and as a result trust our market value-based portfolio to be efficient.

When you buy a world equity product you will naturally incur foreign exchange exposure as the majority of the underlying securities will be listed in a currency other than your own. For example, when you as a UK-based investor buy the sterling-denominated world equity index tracker you will indirectly be buying shares in the Brazilian oil company Petrobras. Petrobras is quoted in the Brazilian currency (the real (R)) so in order to buy the Petrobras shares, the product provider has to take the sterling amount and exchange it for reals, and then buy the stock (see

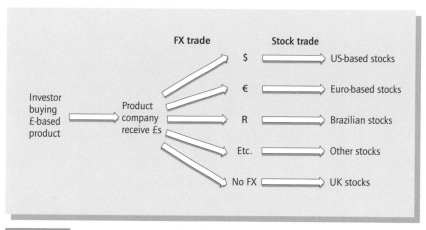

Figure 5.5   An example of stock and currency exposure

Figure 5.5). Likewise with all the other currencies and securities represented in the index.[2]

In the example shown in Figure 5.5 you are now exposed both to the fluctuation in the share price of Petrobras and also movements in the GBP/Real exchange rate (see Figure 5.6 for an example).

In this example, I assumed that the Petrobras share price went from R20 to R25 while the £/R rate went from 3.2 to 3.1. The aggregate impact of this on the portfolio was that the £100 investment went up in value to £129 because of the mix of share price appreciation and the £/R currency movement.

The many different stocks and currency exposures in the world equity portfolio add further to the diversification benefits of the broad-based portfolio exposure. If your base/home currency devalued or performed poorly, the diversification of your currency exposure would serve to protect your downside.

Some investment advisers argue that you should invest in assets in the same currency that you will eventually need the money in. So a UK

2 The trading set-up may sound cumbersome and expensive, but major product providers naturally have off-setting flows that reduce trading, but are also set up to trade FX (foreign exchange) and stocks very cheaply, or have derivative exposures or sampling that can also reduce costs and keep things simple.

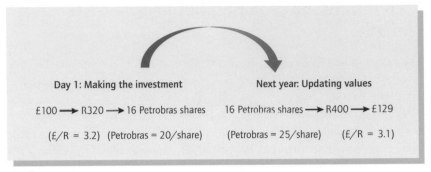

Figure 5.6 Combined impact of share price and currency movement

investor should buy UK stocks, a Danish investor should buy Danish stocks, someone who eventually needs money in different currencies should buy a mix (if you have different costs in different currencies), etc. There is some merit in currency matching specific and perhaps shorter-term liabilities, but the matching is better done by purchasing government bonds in your home currency (the minimal risk asset). If you worry that major currencies fluctuate too much for you, I question whether you should be taking equity market risk in the first place.

The broader investment and currency exposure is favourable not only from a diversifying perspective, but also as protection against bad things happening in your home country. Historically, whenever a currency has been an outlier it has performed poorly because of problems in that country (there are exceptions to this rule of thumb), and it is exactly in those cases that the protection of a diversified geographic exposure is of the greatest benefit to you.[3]

---

3 Currency-hedged investment products do exist but in my view the ongoing hedging expense adds significant costs without clear benefits, and on occasion further fails to provide an accurate hedge. Besides, many companies have hedging programmes themselves, meaning that a market may already be partially protected against currency moves, or have natural hedges via ownership of assets or operations that trade in foreign currencies (like Petrobras owning oil that trades in US dollars).

Expected returns: no promises, but expect 4–5% after inflation

The return expectation from equity markets is driven by our view of the 'equity risk premium'. The equity risk premium is a measure of how much extra the market expects to get paid for the additional risk associated with investing in equity markets over the minimal risk asset. This does not mean that stock markets will be particularly poor or attractive right now; it means that investors historically have demanded a premium for investing in risky equities, as opposed to less-riskier assets. We also assume that investors expect to be paid a similar premium for investing in equities over safe government bonds in future as they have historically.

The size of the equity risk premium is subject to much debate, but numbers in the order of 4–5% are often quoted. If you study the returns of the world equity markets over the past 100 years (see Table 5.1) the annual compounding rate of return for this period is close to this range. Of course it is impossible to know if the markets over that period have been particularly attractive or poor for equityholders compared to what the future has in store.

The equity risk premium is not a law of nature, but simply an expectation of future returns, in this case based on what those markets achieved in the past, including the significant drawdowns that occurred. Economists and finance experts disagree strongly on what you should expect from equity returns in future and some consider this kind of 'projecting by looking in the rear-view mirror' wrong. In my view, the long history and volatility of equity market returns gives a good idea of the kind of returns we can expect in future. Equity market investors have in the past demanded a

Table 5.1 Returns 1900–2011 (%)

	Nominal[1]	Real[1]	Risk[2]
World equities	8.50	5.40	*17.50*
Short-term US government bonds	3.90	0.90	
Equity risk premium		**4.50**	

[1]Nominal: before inflation. Real: after inflation.
[2]See Chapter 6 for a discussion of issues relating to risk measures.

Source: Credit Suisse Global Returns Handbook 2012

4–5% return premium for the risks that equity markets entail, and I think there is a good probability that investors in future are going to demand a similar kind of return premium for a similar kind of risk in the equity markets.

A criticism of using historical returns to predict future returns is that this predicts higher returns at market peaks and lower returns at market lows.[4] Historical returns looked a lot better on 1 July 2008 than on 1 July 2009 (after the crash), and perhaps because you were attracted by the high historical returns in mid–2008 this was exactly the time that you invested in equities. Combining high historical returns with low expected risk at the time made equity markets look very attractive at precisely the wrong moment.

I understand why some criticise the expected return, but think that the length of data mitigates this. With hundreds of years of data across many countries (some have used only US data in the past, but that introduces selection bias by excluding markets that have performed poorly), incorporating great spectacular declines, great rises, and everything in between, I think historical data is the best guide to the kind of risk and return we can expect from equity markets in future.

Practically speaking, investors have been unable to buy the whole world of equities for many years. One of the leading index providers, MSCI, only started tracking a 'world index' in late 1960s, but finding liquid products that actually followed this or similar indices did not start in earnest until decades after that. Figure 5.7 shows historical returns for the MSCI World Index since inception. In this case, I think the time horizon is too short (40+ years) to use the data to make predictions about future world equity returns, when we have longer historical data sets (albeit not as an index done at the time).

---

4 You can also estimate the equity risk premium by looking at the dividend yield of the stock markets, or the average price/earnings ratio. Combining either of these measures with longer-term earnings growth estimates could also yield an estimate of projected stock market returns. The problem as I see it with either of these measures is that both use quite short-term financial data and combine that with a highly unpredictable long-term growth rate to extrapolate something as uncertain as future stock market returns. Alternatively, some suggest using surveys asking investors what their projections for the market returns are. While interesting (different countries often have very different results) these surveys have been criticised for being heavily sentiment driven and more about a desired return than one actually expected.

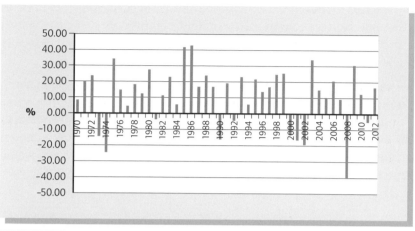

Figure 5.7 MSCI World index since inception (dividends reinvested)

Lars's predictions

So, in simple terms, on average I expect to make a 4–5% return a year above the minimal risk rate[5] in a broad-based world equity portfolio. This is not to suggest that I expect this return to materialise every year, but rather that if I had to make a guess on the compounding annual rate in future it would be 4–5% (see Table 5.2). Note that while the equity premium here

Table 5.2 Expected future returns (including returns from dividends) (%)

	Real[1]	Risk[2]
World equities	4.5–5.5	*20.00*
Minimal risk asset	0.50	
Equity risk premium	**4–5**	

[1]After inflation.
[2]See Chapter 6 for a discussion of issues with risk measures.

5 While the historical risk premium was calculated as a premium to short-term debt, the minimal risk asset return expectation of 0.5% is not as short-term (highly rated real short-term debt returns at the time of writing have negative yields). However, historically the short-term real return has been closer to 0.5% and this is what the equity risk premium is based on. Also, the current yield curve suggests that the negative real interest rate will not last forever.

is compared to short-term US bonds I would expect the same premium to other minimal risk currency government bonds because the real return expectation of short-term US government bonds is roughly similar to that of other AAA/AA countries like the UK, Germany, Japan, etc.

For those who consider these expected returns disappointing, I'm sorry. Writing higher numbers in a book or spreadsheet won't make it true. Some would even suggest that expecting equity markets to be as favourable in the future as in the past is wishful thinking. Besides, a 4–5% annual return premium to the minimal risk asset will quickly add up to a lot; you would expect to double your money in real terms roughly every 15 years!

> The power of compounding never ceases to amaze me. If I dropped my daily Starbucks visit and put the £4 daily savings into the equity markets at a 5% annual return I would have almost five times the current average national income in the UK in savings on the day I turned 70 (I am 40 now).

Many of you may be uncomfortable with having important stock market expectations simply being based on something as unscientific as historical returns or my 'guesstimate' of that data. Perhaps so, but until someone comes up with a reliably better method of predicting stock market returns it's the best we have and a very decent guide. Also, we know that the equity premium should be something – if there were no expected rewards from investing in the riskier equities we would simply keep our money in low-risk bonds.

Another problem with simplistically predicting a stable risk premium is that we don't change it in line with the world around us. It probably sits wrong with most investors that the expected returns in future should be the same in the relatively stable period preceding the 2008 crash as it was during the peak of panic and despair in October 2008. Did someone who contemplated investing in the market in the calm of 2006 really expect to be rewarded with the same return as someone who stepped into the mayhem of October 2008?

Someone willing to step into the market at a moment of high panic would expect to be compensated for taking that extra risk, suggesting that the risk premium is not a constant number, but in some way dependent on the risk of the market. At a time of higher expected long-term risk, equity investors will be expecting higher long-term returns. The equity premium outlined above is an expected average based on an average level of risk.

In summary

In the interest of making something as complicated as the world financial markets into something almost provocatively simple, Figure 5.8 outlines where we are in terms of returns after inflation.

As an investor who seeks returns in excess of the minimal risk return you can add a broad portfolio of world equities. You can reasonably expect to make a return of 4–5% a year above the rate of minimal risk government bonds, which we expect to be about 0.5% a year, although expect that return to vary significantly for a standard deviation (see Chapter 6) of about 20% a year.

If the world equity markets are too risky for you, combine an investment in that with an investment in the minimal risk bonds to find your preferred level of risk. In brief:

Minimal risk	Low risk	Medium risk	High risk
100% minimal risk	75% minimal risk	50% minimal risk	0% minimal risk
0% equities	25% equities	50% equities	100% equities

Or you can do any combination of the above that suits your individual circumstances.

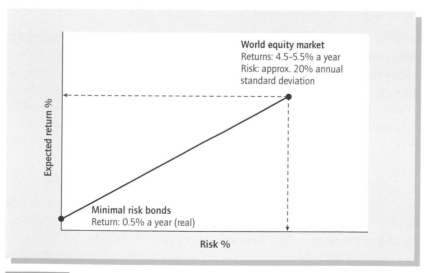

Figure 5.8   Where are we now?

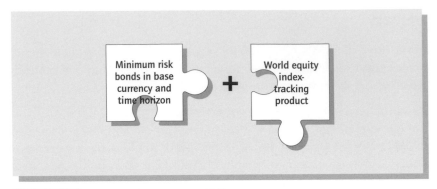

Figure 5.9   The simple rational portfolio

Buy the broad equity exposure cheaply through index-tracking products. This is important. Later (in Chapter 14) I will discuss exactly which products you can buy to achieve the exposures above, subject to your tax circumstances.

If you do as recommended in this chapter you will, over the long term, do better than the vast majority of investors who pay large fees needlessly and consequently get poorer investment returns. And keep in mind that this portfolio can be created by combining just two index-tracking securities; one tracking your minimal risk asset and one tracking the world equity markets. An excellent portfolio with just two securities (see Figure 5.9): who said investing is difficult?

If this seems too simple, remember that the world equity exposure represents an underlying exposure to a large number of often well-known companies in many currencies all over the world. Your two securities thus get you a mix of amazing diversification along with a minimal risk security that gives you the greatest amount of security possible. How much you want of each depends on the risk/return profile you want.

The risk of equity markets

Understanding the risk you take to get returns

It seems that every pre-bubble period is characterised by an abundance of changing paradigm stories or that 'this time it's different', only for history to repeat itself and markets falling. What follows are the inevitable stories about people who saw it coming and those who predict further gloom.

While nobody really knows what will happen to the stock markets, we can make some observations about the risks we take in investing in them. Figure 6.1 shows world and US equity market risk over the past 25 years, illustrated as the trailing 12-month standard deviation (SD) of the returns (explained below).

What you immediately notice is that the risk moves around a lot – it won't surprise you that the markets moved around a lot during the 2008–09

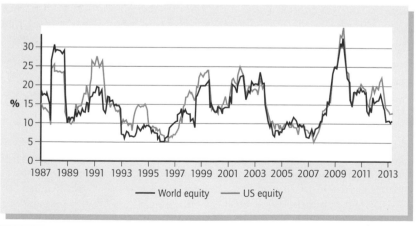

Figure 6.1   Risk of equity markets (trailing 12 months standard deviation)

financial crisis (notice the spike in 2009 where the standard deviation was over 40% for world equities), while market returns were far less volatile in 2007, right before the crisis. What you also notice is how closely tied the world and US risks appear. This is not a surprise as the US market is the largest component of the world market, but also because the world is far more interconnected than it used to be. But what we can also see from Figure 6.1 is that expecting a standard deviation of the equity markets of 20% on the basis of how it has been in the past is not a terrible guess.[1]

The standard deviation is important as it is meant to give you an idea of how much returns may vary. It assumes that returns are distributed around an expected average return of all the many potential outcomes, and the standard deviation tells you how different from the average return many outcomes will be. A higher standard deviation means that more outcomes are very different from the average outcome, while a low standard deviation suggests that most outcomes are clustered around the average outcome. While we don't know what the future outcome will actually be (unless you have a crystal ball), the standard deviation helps us understand how great a variation there may be in actual future outcomes.

The standard deviation

Table 6.1 gives you an idea of how frequently you may lose a lot of money, depending on the risk you think equities will have. The higher

---

1 For those willing to engage in some complex maths there is a better way to predict the future volatility of stock markets. When looking at the price of an option on a stock market index the only variable that is not readily observable is the expected volatility (the other inputs are: the strike price of the option, the current price of the index, time to maturity and the interest rate). Using the Black-Scholes option pricing formula we can obtain the implied volatility. Looking at the implied volatility for options with various maturities we can see how volatile traders expect the market to be in future. In the past, the implied volatility of index options have been better predictors of future market volatility than using the historical volatility of the stock market. For the S&P 500 index you can look at the VIX index, which gives the implied volatility for that market for the coming month, but expect the implied volatility to be very different depending on the market, maturity and strike price you are looking at.

Table 6.1 Losses according to standard deviation (SD)

Exp return:	5.0%	Number of SDs and losses to equities				
	SD	1.00	1.28	1.64	2.00	3.00
	Probability	15.9%	10.0%	5.0%	2.3%	0.1%
	Frequency/yrs	6	10	20	44	741
Risk	15.0%	−10%	−14%	−20%	−25%	−40%
levels	20.0%	−15%	−21%	−28%	−35%	−55%
(SD)	25.0%	−20%	−27%	−36%	−45%	−70%
	30.0%	−25%	−33%	−44%	−55%	−85%
	35.0%	−30%	−40%	−52%	−65%	−100%

the standard deviation the more frequently you will lose a lot of money.[2] A 20% annual standard deviation for equity returns may be a reasonable guess in future, but as you can see from Figure 6.1, the standard deviation does vary a lot over time. Table 6.1 shows how much you would lose at standard deviations of between 1 and 3 (so increasingly unlikely and big losses), if the standard deviation of the markets was 15–35% and you assumed that the markets on average return 5%.

So while it is obvious that greater risk generally means more fluctuating outcomes, the standard deviation helps us quantify it. Instead of putting a finger in the air and making vague statements like 'losing 20% in a year is pretty unlikely', the standard deviation can help us be more specific if we have a view on how risky the market is. And greater specificity helps us understand the potential frequency of different losses when investing in the market.

As an example, if you believe that the standard deviation of your returns is 20% and the expected return is 5%, then you know that there is roughly a 15.9% probability (or risk) (one standard deviation) that a £100 investment will turn into £85 one year later. (The mean expected return was £105, but with a standard deviation of 20% a one-standard deviation loss would be a £20 loss for a £85 result.) If we assumed a 25% standard deviation there would be a 15.9% probability that our £100 had become £80. You can also

---

2 You can look up the probabilities associated with various standard deviations and get a fuller explanation of standard deviation in general, on Wikipedia. This also shows the recognisable 'bell-shaped curve' of the normal distribution.

see that a 2 standard deviation outcome is something that only happens 2.3% of the time (so about every 44 years), but if the standard deviation we expect in future is 25% and we are unfortunate enough to have a 2 standard deviation loss in one year, we would lose 45% (5% expected return minus 2 × 25%).

So what does this mean for you?

Going back to Figure 6.1 you can get a decent picture of what risk you take by investing in the two markets. (Simplistically, I suggest using a 20% standard deviation.) You can then take this risk and use the standard deviation table (see Table 6.1) to estimate how frequently you may expect to incur various levels of losses in the equity portion of the portfolio. While using the standard deviation is not an exact science in this context (we don't know nearly enough about future risk to say that there is precisely a 15.9% or 2.3% chance of the loss), at a basic level the standard deviation can help us understand the probability of various things happening to our equity portfolio, and thus help us plan our finances.

This may seem like finance mumbo jumbo, but you should try to understand it because it gives you an idea of how much money you can make or lose from investing in equity markets.

The standard deviation is useful, but hard to predict and has some flaws

The large fluctuations in the risk of the equity markets shown in Figure 6.1 suggest that we should generally be cautious about claiming too much precision in estimating the risk of an investment portfolio.

Consider the increase in the market risk during the 2008–09 financial crisis. If you had allocated assets to equities because you thought they had a risk profile similar to the historical one, you would find yourself at the height of the crisis with an equity portfolio far riskier than that. Equities are more volatile in times of crisis, but this is also typically where you have already lost a lot of money investing in them. If you shied away from equities at the peak of the crisis because they were now riskier than before, you would be selling equities and probably lock in a big loss, perhaps at the bottom of the market. In order to avoid this, you must make a conservative enough allocation to equities so that you can afford both the occasional losses but also the increased risk that inevitably comes with that decline.

While the standard deviation is a useful concept it is certainly not a perfect measure of risk. One of its drawbacks is that it does not properly account for skew or 'fat tails'. What this means is that outcomes that are considered highly unlikely if you look only at the standard deviation, in reality happen a lot more. This is very important as otherwise we would massively under-estimate how frequently we can expect to incur very large losses from our equity portfolio. At the time of writing, the standard deviation of the S&P 500 is around 15%; if we assume an expected return of 5% a year we can see from above that a 40% loss would be a 3 standard deviation event (a 45% move from the 5% expected outcome). We can also see that if we blindly used the standard deviation we would expect this to happen every 741 years, when we know that in reality it happens every couple of decades.

Understanding that highly unlikely events happen more than suggested by the standard deviation is important when we consider the risk of our portfolio. Large losses can and probably will happen, and almost certainly happen more than the simple standard deviation will have us think. How much more is hard to predict, but be ready for the possibility, and avoid just blindly using the standard deviation to understand your risk, even if some textbooks and finance practitioners seem to think that this method is the answer. It's not.

If you are confused about all this, don't despair. You are not alone, and until a couple of decades ago this stuff was rarely mentioned even in academia. Just remember that the standard deviation gives you a reasonable idea of how much money you can make or lose and is therefore useful for planning the portfolio, but also remember that unlikely bad events with large losses happen far more than the standard deviation suggests, and be ready for surprises.

You can lose a lot!

Most often when we talk about standard deviations we worry less about the small swings in values; we worry more about losing a lot of money quickly.

With an increase from around 40 at its inception in 1896 to trading at around 13,000 at the time of writing, the Dow is a manifestation of the equity market's staggering success story and a neat illustration of the riches that are to be gained from investing in stock markets. That said, the progress of the Dow has not been without its losses, most notably around the Great Depression. Figure 6.2 shows the worst losses the Dow has incurred since its inception.

It is obvious that investing in the stock markets can lose you a lot of money.

Figure 6.2 is a great way to put things in perspective. A super-simple and non-mathematical way to use the chart would be to say, 'If there is a crisis that is as bad as the 1930s depression, at least we know that then the stock market declined by over 80%.' Or, 'If the 2008 financial crisis was to be repeated we know that in that case the markets declined by 50%.'

While future events that lead to losses in the market may not look like past ones, this kind of simple comparison is a useful way to frame risk.

Recovering from the magnitude of losses like those in Figure 6.2 can take a long time, even if you were able to endure the painful losses and hold on to your equity position. Keep in mind that had you invested $100 in the Dow before the 1930 declines started you would have been left with only about $15 at the bottom, challenging even the most patient investor.

Figure 6.3 shows how long it took in years for the Dow to recover from the declines shown in Figure 6.2.

The point is that even once you have hit the bottom it may take a long time to be dug out of that hole, and in many cases longer than most investors' time horizons.

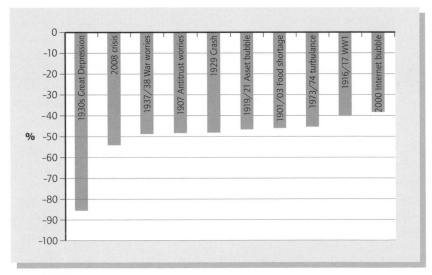

Figure 6.2 Biggest losses in the Dow Jones since 1900

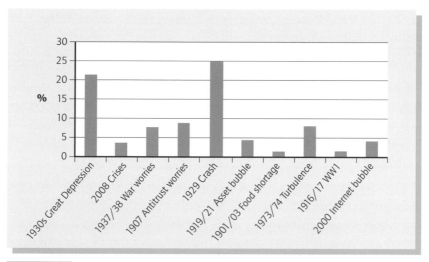

Figure 6.3 Time (in years) for the Dow Jones to recover from losses

Don't assume that markets always bounce back

Of course the charts above are based entirely on the US stock market and specifically the Dow, a small subset of that market. People often use the US stock market for data analysis as it is not only the place with the most comprehensive data sets but it has, at least historically, dominated financial academic circles. Until only a couple of decades ago it was not as simple to get international data seamlessly and even if you did get the data it was not easy to analyse.

One of the problems with using US-based data is the large selection bias that is introduced. The twentieth century was the American century and the stock market reflected this success. But just because we use data from a very successful century in a very successful geographical area does not mean that things will be like that in future.

Imagine if you were an investor in the Russian stock markets or government bonds just before the 1917 revolution. You would have lost everything without hope or recourse. Likewise, there have been many instances of large-scale and irrevocable losses for investors. When studying the charts above there may be a dangerous tendency to believe that 'it may take a while, but equity markets will always come back'. They may not.

The disadvantage with the view that markets will always bounce back is that some investors will want to 'average in' to falling markets, i.e. buy on weaknesses, dips, etc. After all, if markets always bounce back, the reasoning goes, you will eventually be fine. That thinking is akin to a gambler going to a casino, betting on red and keeping on doubling down whenever he loses. That strategy works really well until the one time when it really, really doesn't work and you run out of money.

Some may view the rebound from the 2008 financial crisis as evidence that markets do always bounce back, and that historical instances of complete and 'un-rebounded' losses are exactly that: history. To those I would say, look at Japan.

In Figure 6.4 the main Nikkei index is trading at an approximate 65% discount to its peak in the early to mid–1990s. When I was studying economics at university in the early 1990s, I remember how often we considered the Japanese miracle. We were told how special characteristics like lifetime employment and superior production techniques had led to Japan's spectacular rise and the implication was clear: Japan would continue to prosper. But already as I headed to business school in 1996–98 there were few mentions of the Japanese economic miracle, other than the odd case on auto production techniques.

Even if the Nikkei does recovery fully it is entirely possible that this will be so far into the future as to be irrelevant for many current readers' financial lives. From the vantage point of 1990 many would have predicted the chart shown in Figure 6.4 to apply to leading European or US markets, not

Figure 6.4 The Nikki index since its peak

Japan. So don't exclude the possibility that this can happen in your local equity markets or even the wider world equity markets.

We don't know what is to come, but it's dangerous to extrapolate too much from historical data alone. We don't know what we don't know, and it is hard to incorporate this factor. Over the next year, decade or century we could be blessed with peace and prosperity, or some completely unpredictable calamity. Looking at how the US stock market reacted to the dire events in the twentieth century may give us an indication of how the world stock markets will react in future, but it's also quite possible that future losses will look very different.

Diversification and the false sense of security

Although correlations between various national stock markets have generally increased over the past decades, the benefits from diversification are still clear. Local companies, in general, are more dependent on the global markets than they were decades ago, but there are still unique characteristics to national economies. The latter operate in different legal and political climates and while they may be dependent on local factors such as access to commodities, skilled labour, tourism, etc. they are also influenced by natural disasters (as in Japan) or political upheaval (as in the Middle East). Diversifying away from such exposures in one region or country makes a lot of sense.

The main problem with higher correlation in down markets is that we are not always afforded the protection of diversification when we really need it. We are probably less concerned that the volatility of our monthly returns is slightly higher because correlations are higher than expected if this happens in a market where we are up 10% a year (see Figure 6.5). But if we are down 40% because of high correlations between our different investments then we care a lot. If we believe that the correlation between investments is more or less a constant number we would have understated our portfolio risk in bad markets and be more exposed to losses than we thought. Increased correlation was a factor that affected a lot of investors in the 2008 crash, when not only did various international stock markets correlate, but also several supposedly uncorrelated asset classes did so as well. (Certain government bonds were a notable exception, being the safety asset in the turbulence.)

A major selling point of the US sub-prime investment proposals was that there had never been a case where all housing markets in the US had

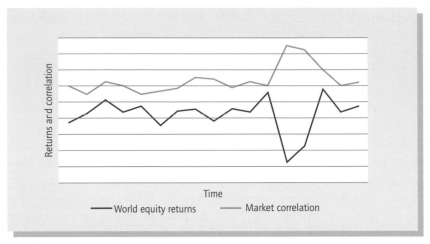

Figure 6.5   World equity returns and correlation between markets
(illustration only)

declined at the same time. This diversification was supposed to provide
great investment security and was a major driver of the high ratings
and attractiveness. In simple terms, investors did not believe that the
housing markets in Miami, Las Vegas and Dallas would all collapse at
the same time and were therefore willing to provide more debt at a low
cost. During the crash, correlations between the various housing markets
shot up to the point at which they acted like one market instead of
providing diversification against a location specific decline. The resulting
eggs of embarrassment on the face of the financial community and huge
monetary losses became all too obvious.

Some people look back at historical market declines that used to be more
geographically contained and wish they had had the chance then to
diversify internationally. Now they can diversify, but correlations are up.
You can't have it all. Over time, as cross-border capital flows to foreign
equity markets increase and the world generally becomes more interconnected because of trade or information flows, correlations will probably
increase even further. Higher correlation means that we would be fooling
ourselves if we think diversification alone protected us against bad things
and we accepted higher risk in our portfolio as a result.

Risk rethought

To some, standard deviations or skew might sound like an archaic finance-related term that will get us all in trouble. What I'm suggesting is not to use this as an exact science, but rather as a tool that gives a general idea of what the perceived risk of investing in equities will be in the future. The next step is to figure out how to use that in understanding the risk of our portfolio.

Other than basing things on a gut feel or what we glean from newspapers, we can get a more accurate sense of where things stand. A future market standard deviation of 20% is clearly not the same as one of 40%: the market is expecting far less risk. Similarly, you can't just assume that future returns are distributed like the neat bell curve of the standard deviation – they are not. Understanding that there is skew helps to explain this; it makes more sense that really bad events can and probably will happen on occasion despite the standard deviation suggesting that it is as unlikely as being hit by a meteor.

This chapter has been less about giving answers than about informing the gut feel that investors probably already have about the equity markets. In the long run we can expect good returns from equities, but this is not without risks, and those risks can be unpredictable and severe. We'd better plan for that.

Adding other government and corporate bonds

The main focus of this book has been on creating a simple, yet powerful and robust portfolio for the rational investor. The message is hopefully clear: find your minimal risk asset and combine it with the broadest possible, yet cheaply acquired equity index, preferably one representing world equities. Do so in proportions that suit your desired risk profile and in a tax efficient way (see Chapter 11). If you do this and read no further, in my view you are already doing better than the vast majority of investors, private or institutional.

This chapter slightly muddies the waters for those investors who are willing to accept a bit more complexity, namely the addition of other government and corporate bonds. The addition of these asset classes further adds diversification to your portfolio and therefore enhances the risk/return profile.

Figure 7.1 shows a portfolio including government and corporate bonds, instead of just the minimal risk asset and equities, which gives us higher expected returns. We can expect a better risk/return profile by adding these other government and corporate bonds to the minimal risk asset and world equity portfolio because the correlation between these additional bonds and the equity portfolio is not perfect (they don't move in step and there are therefore diversification benefits from having some of both).

If the correlation between other government and corporate bonds and equities is 1 (i.e. they are perfectly correlated) there would be a straight line between the other bonds and equity points in Figure 7.1. Instead, by combining the other bonds with equities your portfolio will take on the risk/return profile like that of the curved line in Figure 7.1 (100% equities

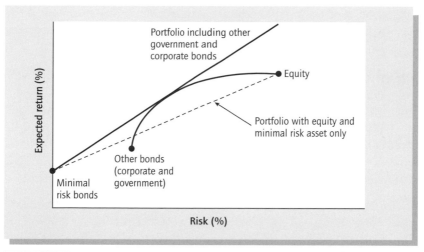

Figure 7.1   **A portfolio that included government and corporate bonds**

is the 'Equity' point and 100% other bonds is the 'Other bonds' point).[1]
We are essentially benefiting from the diversification benefits that the
other government and corporate bonds add to the portfolio.

So what is the difference between the minimal risk bonds and the other
government bonds we are now looking to add? Think of your minimal risk
bonds as the core of your portfolio. This is not where you are looking to make
money, but where you are looking to take a minimal risk. I am then adding
all other government bonds, other than the minimal risk bonds that are
already in your portfolio. So if your minimal risk bonds are UK government
bonds, then the other government bonds you should consider adding are all
but UK government bonds. It only makes sense to add government bonds
that add expected returns to the portfolio (see later). If you added German
government bonds to the UK ones you had as the minimal risk asset then
the low yield of the German bonds would not add returns to your portfolio.
And since you had the capital-preserving minimal risk asset already in the
form of UK government bonds the German ones would not add much to
your portfolio (unless you wanted a couple of different bonds as the minimal
risk asset and included the German bonds for this purpose).

It may come as a surprise to some that the bond markets in the world
actually exceed the equity markets by a healthy margin of about $30–40

---

1 As discussed elsewhere these graphs are mainly for illustration, particularly as the
risk and correlations change continuously.

trillion, or more than double the US annual GDP (US government debt/ GDP is approximately 100% at present).[2]

Adding government bonds

There are good reasons to add government bonds to your rational portfolio in addition to those you already hold as your minimal risk asset. Despite the world's increasing international interdependence government bond portfolios are geographically diversified. Figure 7.2 shows government debt by geographical sector.

It is probably not surprising to many that the US debt is right at the top, considering the size of its economy, but that Japan is there alongside it may surprise some. With its very large debt/GDP ratio of over 200% Japan has managed to remain very indebted, but without incurring high, real interest rates as a result.[3]

As with equities, when adding other government bonds we would normally try to invest as broadly and cheaply as possible, and allocate in accordance to the relative values that the market has already ascribed to the various securities. However, you should amend this and not buy other government bonds in the proportions of the bonds outstanding that are shown in Figure 7.2.[4]

Earlier, we discussed how a highly rated government bond in the right currency provided the best investment for risk-averse investors, albeit at very low interest rates (at the time of writing). As an example, if I'm a UK-based investor looking for the lowest-risk investment for the next five

---

2 Note that a lot of debt (about $28 billion) is issued outside the country of the issuer. This may be a French company issuing debt in the US in dollars. This is important in that you may buy a bond in the US, but have the underlying exposure as that of a French company.

3 At the time of writing, shorting Japanese government debt is a popular hedge fund trade as the managers deem the debt levels unsustainable, but according to a Japanese hedge fund manager friend of mine the arguments used are hardly new and in his view this is not a 'slam dunk' trade. Time will tell.

4 As a first gut feel of why this 'buy the world' strategy may not work for everyone, consider that over half your government bond portfolio would be Japanese and US government bonds. This not only adds quite a bit of concentration risk to two issuers, but also adds currency risk and minimal real expected returns due to the low/negative real yields on those bonds.

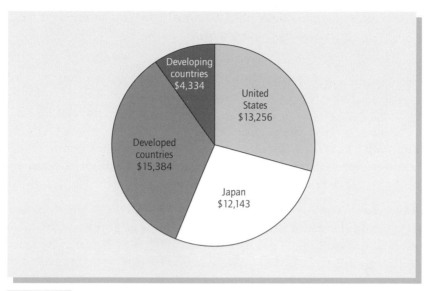

Figure 7.2   Government debt in $ billions

Based on data from Bank for International Settlements, end quarter 2 2012, www.bis.org

years in sterling, I should buy five-year UK government bonds, perhaps in the form of inflation-protected bonds.

As we are now considering adding other government and corporate bonds to the rational portfolio of minimal risk bonds and equities, we should not just blindly add all the world's government bonds (see Figure 7.3). We already have exposure to UK government bonds and therefore do not need to include more of these in the portfolio,[5] we would just be doubling up on an exposure already taken to be the minimal risk investment.

How much the exclusion of the minimal risk asset from the world government bond portfolio changes the profile of the remaining portfolio depends on your base currency. If your base currency is $ or yen, then you

5 One minor caveat to this argument; if the mix of maturities you added to get to your minimal risk asset is very different from the overall mix of maturities issued by that government then it makes sense to amend the minimal risk allocations. So if you only had very short-term bonds in your minimal risk allocation, yet are willing to add more risk in the form of equities and other bonds, it makes sense for this allocation to include some longer-term bond exposure from that same government.

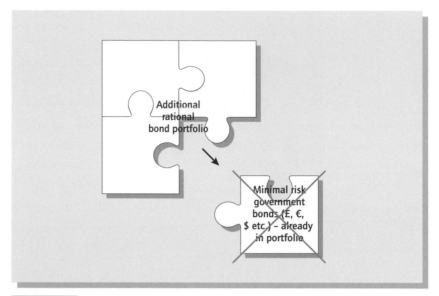

Figure 7.3   Don't blindly add in more minimal risk government bonds

would have reduced the universe of government bonds by a quarter. On the other hand, if your base currency is my native Danish kroner (with AAA-rated government bonds), then the impact on the world government bond portfolio would be negligible.

Only add government bonds if they increase expected returns

We discussed earlier how when adjusting for inflation investors in several highly rated government bonds should actually expect to earn a negative return, at least for short-term bonds. At the time of writing, the major countries with AAA or AA rating that offer a safe haven in their domestic currency but with little or no real return include Australia, Switzerland, Japan, Germany, the UK and the US, among others.

Consider the example of a sterling-based investor with UK government bonds as her minimal risk portfolio, contemplating adding other government bonds to her rational portfolio. From the UK bonds she gets almost no real returns, but also takes almost no risk. If she were to add bonds from the AAA- or AA-listed countries above she would also get no return, but would be taking currency risk. So she would get no greater returns from the foreign bonds, but take more risk.[6]

The rational investor thus has little to gain from adding AAA or AA government bonds to her portfolio other than as a minimal risk asset. If she was after a lower-risk portfolio she could add more of the minimal risk bonds (UK government bonds in this example). If she was willing to accept more risk in the portfolio she could get additional expected returns by either adding equities or government bonds that had a higher real return expectation than that offered by her minimal risk asset.

One caveat to excluding the other AAA/AA government bonds from the rational portfolio (see Figure 7.4): if you think there is credit risk in your minimal risk asset, then it may make sense to spread your investments among other AAA/AA credits. For example, if you are a UK investor and don't consider the UK government's credit entirely safe, then you could split your minimal risk investment into a couple of different AAA/AA bonds to diversify the credit. By diversifying you decrease the concentration risk of having your minimal risk asset from just one issuer (the UK government in this case), although it means taking currency risk with the other government bond holdings.[7]

The above is a departure from portfolio theory. According to portfolio theory you should add all the world's investable assets in proportion to their values, and combine those investments with the risk-free asset to get to your desired risk level. Here I'm suggesting that you should only add assets that have a positive real expected return higher than your minimal risk government bonds, as you are otherwise adding currency risk without adding real expected returns.

---

6 There is of course the possibility that the other currencies appreciate against sterling. So if you held US bonds and the dollar went up in value relative to the pound, those bonds would be worth more in sterling terms. That being the case, although this risk can also lead to you making money it is not a risk you get compensated for taking in the form of higher expected returns.

7 By adding other safe bonds to your minimal risk bonds you are also diversifying your interest rate risk away from that of just one currency (you have exposure to a couple of different yield curves), but for the purposes of keeping the portfolio simple I don't think this diversification is worth the added complexity and currency risk of those bonds.

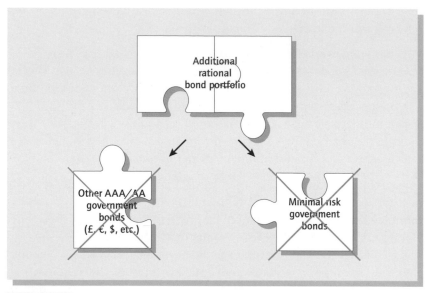

Figure 7.4   Typically, do not add other AAA/AA credits

The government bonds we should add to the rational portfolio

If the above seems like excluding a lot of government bonds, remember that you have only removed those already in the portfolio (the minimal risk asset) and other government bonds without meaningful additional expected real return (but with currency risk).

After omitting the minimal risk asset and other AAA/AA government bonds because of their low yield, the bonds you should consider adding to your portfolio are real return-generating government bonds (the rest) and corporate bonds (see Figure 7.5). And here we are still talking many trillions of dollars of potential investments.

Which government bonds you are left to invest in depends on how highly rated are the bonds that you want to eliminate. If you were only to eliminate bonds that were AAA rated and wanted to invest in the remaining then those would be distributed as shown in Figure 7.6.

What you will notice is that this list is dominated by the US and Japan, 'only' AA rated by S&P at the time of writing, and thus not deemed entirely without risk. But if you, like most investors, take the view that

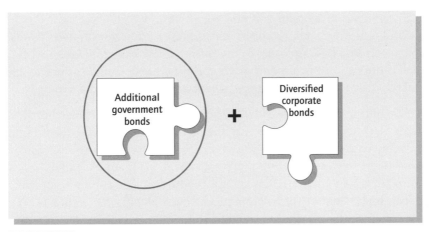

Figure 7.5   Add real return-generating government bonds to the portfolio

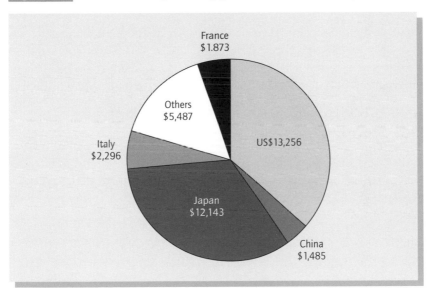

Figure 7.6   Below AAA government debt in $ billions

Based on data from Bank for International Settlements, end quarter 2 2012, www.bis.org

these AA-rated bonds still did not offer enough expected real return to be worth adding to the portfolio (besides being the minimal risk for investors in those currencies), and that you only wanted to add government bonds rated below AA (to get additional yield), then the remaining world government bonds would be distributed as shown in Figure 7.7.

The way to read Figure 7.7 would be as follows:

I am an investor who, in addition to my minimal risk asset and equity portfolio, wants to add a diversified group of other government bonds. Since I already have exposure to my minimal risk government bonds and don't think government bonds from countries rated AAA/AA offer enough yield to be interesting, which government bonds should I be adding?

While in principle you should buy the bonds rated below AA according to their market values, in reality it is not practical for some investors to find investment products that represent so many different countries. Instead you might buy an emerging market government bond exchange traded fund (ETF) and combine that with a product covering sub-AA eurozone government bonds. The combination you end up with would not be exactly in the proportions of the sub-AA-rated bonds in Figure 7.7, but get you a long way towards adding a diversified group of real return generating government bonds to your rational portfolio.

Bond yields move a lot. Even at the height of the 2008 financial crisis the yield on 10-year Greek government debt was 5–6% compared to the current unsustainable levels. This was considered a safe investment although events since suggest that it wasn't and provide a good example

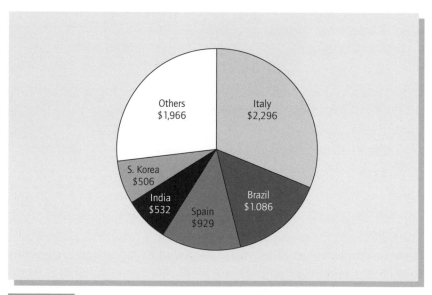

Figure 7.7 Below AA government debt in $ billions

Based on data from Bank for International Settlements, end quarter 2 2012, www.bis.org

of how the credit quality of an individual government can decline at an alarming pace if the markets lose confidence in repayment. Despite the fact that the government bonds in the sub-AA chart (see Figure 7.7) are geographically diversified investments, you should expect some correlation between them. Not only do some of the European countries operate in the same currency and open market (the EU), but all countries are subject to changes in the world economy, besides their unique domestic changes, and are similarly vulnerable to changes in market sentiment.

Table 7.1 shows the yields on various selected 10-year government bonds that fit into the real return-generating government category at the time of writing. While the table below is for 10-year bonds only (you should try to get a mix of maturities) it gives you an idea of the interest you can expect from these lower-rated bonds.

Table 7.1 Ten-year yields: selected sub-AA governments

Country	Percentage	Country	Percentage
Kenya	12.4%	Turkey	6.5%
Pakistan	12.1%	South Africa	6.2%
Greece	11.4%	Indonesia	5.5%
Nigeria	11.1%	Spain	4.7%
Brazil	9.7%	Mexico	4.7%
India	7.8%	Italy	4.4%
Russia	7.0%	China	3.4%

Based on data from www.tradingeconomics.com

These yields are in local currency-denominated bonds. Since the expected inflation on the Brazilian real is greater than that of the euro the inflation-adjusted return is not as high as suggested above. In other words, Brazil is not as poor a credit risk as suggested by the table.

In addition, it is unfair to say, for example, that you would expect to make a nominal 11.4% return from Greek bonds. The high return implies an increased probability that Greece will default or that you will somehow not be paid in full.

There are some further points when considering adding other government bonds to the portfolio:

■ As you add additional government bonds from these lower-rated countries do so in a range of maturities. On top of diversifying geographically this will avoid concentration of the interest rate risk. Practically, adding these bonds is best done via buying a range of ETFs or low-cost investment funds that buy the underlying bonds for a low fee. For example, you could buy an emerging markets bond ETF that will give you an underlying exposure to the wide range of lower-rated government bonds in different maturities that you are looking for. Likewise, with some of the sub-AA-rated developed country government bonds. By holding the bonds via ETFs or investment funds you don't have to worry about buying new bonds as old ones mature. The provider will do this for you and ensure that your maturity profile remains fairly stable, which is what you want.

- Be careful that you don't add concentration risk when you are meant to be diversifying. In Table 7.1 (that excludes the AAA bonds only) if your minimal risk asset had been US bonds and thus excluded, Japanese bonds would have been over 50% of the remaining amount. These charts and tables should serve to remind you to broadly diversify your government bond holdings to those that add real returns – not increase concentration risk to one issuer (e.g. Japan).

- Buying the government bonds listed above in proportion to their shares of all sub-AA-rated government bonds would be an expensive administrative headache, and there are no access products like ETFs or index funds that do exactly that for you. But if you don't get the proportions exactly right that is fine too. Perhaps buy some low-cost emerging market government bond funds and add to those some exposure to below-AA developed market government bond funds. If you do this roughly in proportion so that each country's or region's share is roughly similar to that of its share in Table 7.1 then that is a good approximation.

- Keep an eye out for changes in the make-up of real return-generating government bonds. Some of the bonds rated lower than AA may have increased in credit quality to the point where they don't really add real returns in excess of your minimal risk asset, or perhaps more likely some of the governments rated AA or above may have declined in credit quality to the point where they are worth adding as a real return generator. I look forward to re-reading this book in 10 years' time and with the benefit of hindsight seeing which governments moved up or down in credit quality. Look to make these changes as you rebalance your portfolio occasionally. Since your real-return generating government bond portfolio is well diversified, changes to it will hopefully not be too dramatic, but likewise keep in mind that unlike the minimal risk asset, world equities and corporate bonds, this is the one segment of the rational portfolio where a broad-index-type access product like an ETF or index tracker will be unlikely to suit your needs. You probably have to put a few products together yourself to create a portfolio of sub-AA-rated government bonds, the make-up of which will change over time.

Adding corporate bonds

In addition to adding sub-AA government bonds you should consider adding a board portfolio of corporate bonds to your portfolio (see Figure 7.8).

Traditionally, whenever investment books like this one have proposed investment in corporate bonds (as most do) they were referring to US-based bonds. This was because their audience was often made up of US or dollar-based investors, and besides, foreign bonds were expensive and impractical to buy. While the ease of investing in non-US bonds is rapidly improving, the US dominance is still prevalent, at least relative to the US share of world GDP, at around 20%. We saw earlier that the world equity portfolio's largest constituent by a wide margin is also the US, and if you only add US corporate bonds you will not get the diversification benefits of international exposure. But this is not just true of US investors. Any investor that adds corporate bonds only in their home geography may have diversified asset classes, but at the same time have

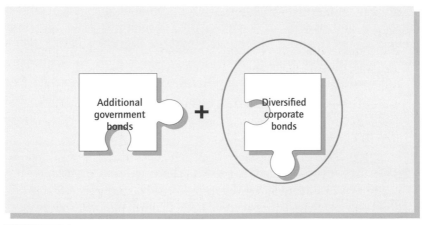

Figure 7.8   Add diversified corporate bonds to the portfolio

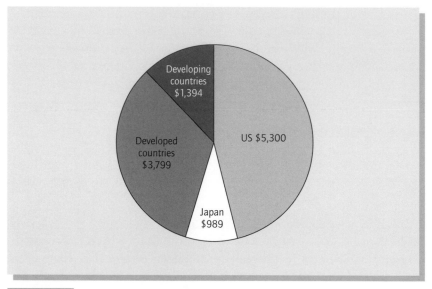

Figure 7.9 World corporate debt in $ billions

Based on data from Bank for International Settlements, end 2011, www.bis.org

increased geographic concentration. Adding a broad portfolio of international corporate bonds can rectify this concentration issue.

Looking to the future, the non-US portion of world corporate debt is likely to increase further and thus augment the importance of getting both the asset class diversification of adding bonds and also the geographic diversification of adding international ones to your rational portfolio.[8]

When you add corporate bonds to your rational portfolio, consider Figure 7.9 and make sure you diversify internationally. At this time, around 55% of the world's corporate bonds are non-US, and like the US ones represent thousands of individual bonds of different maturities, industries, geographic areas and credit qualities. Ignoring the great diversification benefits from adding index-tracking ETFs or funds made up of these many thousand foreign bonds to your rational portfolio would be an omission.

8 We have left out the large and broad market of financial institution debt. This includes interbank debt, but also various obligations issued by financial institutions. This is less of a transparent market for the rational investor and someone with the broad exposures discussed in this book already have a lot of the same exposures via the existing bond and equity positions in their portfolio.

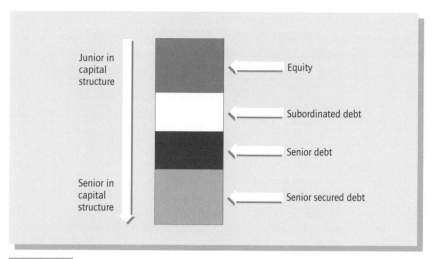

Junior in
capital
structure

Senior in
capital
structure

Equity

Subordinated debt

Senior debt

Senior secured debt

Figure 7.10 Placement in the capital structure

It makes sense that while there are very high-yielding bonds, in general
return expectations from bonds are lower than equities. As a bond holder
you are a lender – to either a corporation or government – whereas as
an equity holder you are an owner. The seniority of the capital structure
reflects this. In receiving the distribution of the cash flows of a company
the debt holders are entitled to their interest payments before dividends
are paid to equity holders. Likewise, in default, debt holders have the first
claim on the assets of a company. A lower expected return is the price of
this superior place in the capital structure (see Figure 7.10).

Just as all the various layers of seniority in the capital structure are represented in the world corporate bond portfolio, the bonds vary significantly
in maturity. And as with the case of government bonds the longer-maturity
corporate bonds of similar credit quality typically yield more than their
shorter-term peers.[9]

If history is any guide ...

Compared to equity returns, figuring out historical returns for broad bond
indices is not straightforward. Until fairly recently there was a dearth

---

9 Occasionally the yield curve is inverted (long-term yields are lower than short-term
  ones). This is when the market is expecting the interest rate to drop in the future.

of investable index products available to investors who wanted bond exposure, other than perhaps that of the major country government bonds or US corporate bonds. Things are slowly getting better and the next decade will see further expansion in the amount of fixed-income products available for the retail investor.

The historical indices that do go back some time have a heavy US bias and until recently broad-based indices were hard to come by, much less ones you could actually create as a product. Table 7.2 shows the performance data for some broad bond indices.

Although the time period shown in Table 7.2 is far too short to make meaningful conclusions, 2008 stands out as an interesting data point. Both the US aggregate and global government bond indices had positive returns in a terrible equity market.

The outperformance of highly rated bonds in a tough market environment points to the potential advantage of adding fixed income to the rational portfolio. As equity markets collapsed, investors sought security in highly rated bonds. There was a belief that whatever happened, the bonds would be repaid at maturity, while nobody knew what would happen to equities.

The large decline in the Barclays US High Yield index in 2008 was no surprise. Companies with high-yield bonds outstanding were dependent on a benign economic environment to repay their debts. With a collapsing

Table 7.2 Various bond indices performance 2002–12 (%)

	2002	2003	2004	2005	2006	2007	2008	2009	2010	2011	2012
Barclays US Aggregate Bond Index (a)	10.3	4.1	4.3	2.4	4.3	7.0	5.2	5.9	6.5	7.8	4.2
Citigroup World Government Bond Index (b)	19.5	14.9	10.3	−6.9	6.1	10.9	10.9	2.6	5.2	6.4	1.7
Barclays US High Yield Corporate Bonds (c)	−1.4	29.0	11.1	2.7	11.9	1.9	−26.2	58.2	15.1	5.0	15.8

(a): Broad mix of US bonds, government and other.
(b): Government bonds of over 20 countries, weighted by market capitalisation and including a range of maturities.
(c): Sub-investment grade ratings only.

market and grim forecasts as a result of the crash, those future repayments were put in doubt and investors sold high-yield bonds as a result.

Generally, I would caution investors about reading too much from this short data period. There is no saying that future crises or correlations will be like those of the past. In fact, as a writer based in Europe I find it entirely conceivable that a future crisis could easily involve government credit issues with their bonds declining in value instead of being a safe asset. If so, you could easily see both equities and government and corporate bonds collapsing at the same time.

So while there is no certainty as to what might happen in a future crisis, adding other government and corporate bonds to the portfolio makes good sense. We are adding bonds from a very broad range of countries, maturities, currencies and risk levels, and with both government and corporate issuers. This kind of asset class diversification to the world equity portfolio as a return generator is likely to serve the portfolio well, with lower-risk and more-diversified returns.

Getting practical

As we look to add bonds to the portfolio, here are a few pointers:

- Buy a broad-based bond exposure, both in terms of geography and type of bond.
- Buy index-tracking products where available. You generally don't want to pay the higher fees of active management, but in the case of adding bonds cheaply actively managed funds may be a good choice when index trackers are unavailable.
- Look for new product development. Particularly in the bond space this will be important. My prediction is that the broadly available bond offering will be much expanded in the years ahead and you will probably be able to benefit from this.

Later, when discussing implementation (see Chapter 14) I'll describe a couple of good alternatives to gain broad and cheap bond exposure as part of your rational portfolio.

Typical criticisms of adding bonds to a portfolio

Compared to equities there are fewer good bond indices and they are not as well known

True. Many investors don't even know they exist. But what we care about is the availability of products that represent a broad range of bonds, both geographically and by type. Although this sector is still not up to the level of equities it is improving.

You will tend to overweight the debt of indebted countries and companies (they have more debt outstanding as a fraction of company value or GDP)

True. But the prices should reflect the higher indebtedness. In the future there could be government bond indices driven by the GDP of a country, but those that exist are still not that widespread.

In certain countries the trading of bonds is very expensive, rendering them a bad risk/return prospect

The key thing to figure out is if you are at a cost disadvantage compared to other market participants. If you are, it may make sense to stay away. If costs are just high for everyone, the higher costs should be reflected in the price and not affect the bond's risk/return profile.

The income from bond coupon payments renders them tax inefficient

Important point. If you are unable to find tax-efficient products (ETFs, etc.) you may consider tax-advantageous bonds in your geographic area, such as municipal bonds in the US. A tax disadvantage can easily eliminate any investment advantage.

Bond products only represent a portion of the total bonds outstanding

It would be impractical and/or impossible to buy a small portion of all outstanding bonds in the world. Indices try to ensure that they can be practically implemented and thus avoid small and illiquid bonds; as with equity markets (to a lesser degree) this is a simplification we have to live with.

Bonds are mainly dollar denominated. This is an issue for non-US investors

Yes, a large portion is in dollars. This is because of the US's dominance of government and corporate bonds, but also because many that issue bonds in currencies other than their home currency do so in dollars. You can partly alleviate this problem if your minimal risk asset is not US government bonds and thus exclude them from your other government bond allocation. Also, don't ignore the large and increasing number of international corporate bonds.

> **It is expensive to trade bonds**
>
> Unless you are a big institution you should buy products like ETFs, bond index funds or even cheap managed bond funds that acquire the bonds for you. With the exception of buying government bonds directly from the treasury, you can typically only buy bonds in larger ticket sizes and by buying aggregating products like ETFs or index funds scale and cost advantages are gained that are hard for the individual investor to match. (This is also discussed later in Chapter 14.)

Corporate bond returns also depend on credit quality

Earlier we discussed how the equity risk premium to the minimal risk bonds is about 4–5% a year. What about risky governments and corporate bonds?

Corporate bonds rank above equities in the capital structure of firms and therefore have superior rights to cash flows or capital. It therefore seems reasonable that corporate bonds should have a lower return expectation than equities. How much lower obviously depends on the mix of corporate bonds in the index. At the time of writing, the yield to redemption for the Finra/Bloomberg US investment grade and high-yield indices were as follows (www.bloomberg.com/markets/rates-bonds/corporate-bonds):

Current yield
US investment grade 3.13%
US high yield 5.65%

For government bonds, we saw earlier what the yield on a 10-year bond was for various 'risky' countries. But as was the case with those government bonds we can't simply deduce from the data above that high-yield bonds always will do better than investment grade ones. The high-yield bonds are likely to have a much higher default rate (just like higher-yielding government bonds will default more often), and the return net of those defaults will be lower than in the unlikely case where all the high-yielding bonds are repaid in full.

Return expectations of the rational portfolio

Below are some estimates for returns of the various asset classes we have discussed so far in this book. Based on a mix of academic research, historical returns, a study of the financial markets and my own judgement

I have outlined what I would consider reasonable expected returns for each asset class, above the rate of inflation as follows:

Annual real return expectations

Minimal risk asset	0.50%	(UK, US, German government debt or similar)
'Risky' government bonds	2.00%	(sub-AA-rated countries)
Corporate bonds	3.00%	(mix of maturities, countries and credit quality)
World equities	5.00%	(4.5% equity risk premium)

In later sections, we look at individual attitudes towards risk. The minimal risk asset is obviously deemed to have little risk (thus the name), and we have discussed previously how a reasonable estimate of risk for equity markets is a 20% annual standard deviation. While we can reasonably estimate the risk of the government and corporate portfolio relative to the minimal risk asset and equities (with government bonds closer to minimal risk, and corporate bonds closer to equities), how the various allocations act relative to each other is harder to predict.

Although you have added diversification to your portfolio by adding risky government and corporate bonds, adding bonds is not always guaranteed beneficial. The correlation between those assets and the rest of your portfolio is likely to be higher during duress than in a steady state, even as some higher-rated bonds may increase in value as a safe haven during a storm.

Adjusting the rational portfolio

Before we introduced risky bonds into the portfolio things were easy. If you wanted no risk, you could pick the minimal risk asset; if you wanted a lot of risk, you could pick a broad-based equity portfolio. If you wanted a risk profile in between the two, you allocated between the two. And do this in a cheap and tax-efficient way. Simple.

Adding other bonds to the portfolio gives additional diversification benefits to the portfolio, but does so at the expense of more complexity. When deciding on what portion of your portfolio you should allocate to bonds, start by going back to your premise as a rational investor. We assumed each dollar invested in the world markets is equally well informed, and as a result we should try to replicate the exposures of all markets.

The split of the approximately $100 trillion market that is world equities, and world government and corporate bonds, is roughly as shown in Figure

7.11. But after adjusting the portfolio to exclude the minimal risk bonds and other highly rated and low-yielding bonds, the split is quite different. Figure 7.12 is the same pie chart but excluding AAA/AA-rated government bonds.

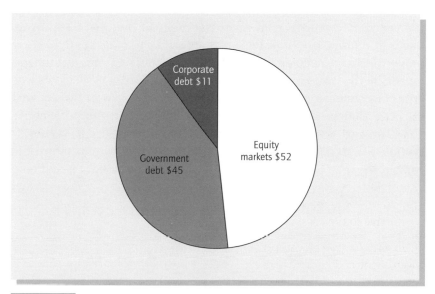

Figure 7.11 World debt and equity split (in $ trillion)

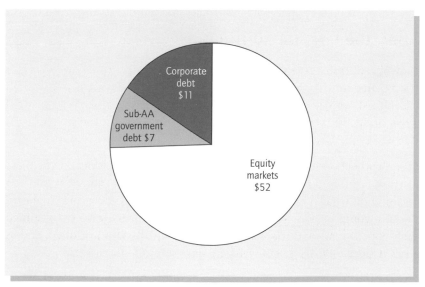

Figure 7.12 Adjusted world debt and equity split (in $ trillion)

Using this mix of assets as a rough guide to our portfolio allocation we could allocate our risky investments as follows:

World equity markets   75%
Sub-AA government debt   10%
Corporate debt   15%

If you combine your investment in the minimal risk asset with investments in equities, risky government bonds and corporate bonds in those proportions you are doing well. You will have allocated your investments roughly in the same proportions as the aggregate market participants who have been choosing between a wide array of investable assets in search of the best risk/return. If you now do so in a cost- and tax-efficient manner, while thinking about your risk levels, you will have created a very strong portfolio. Graphically this updated portfolio is illustrated as point T in Figure 7.13.

If your risk preference is lower than point T, you combine the 'T' portfolio (as in Figure 7.13) with the minimal risk asset to get the desired portfolio risk.

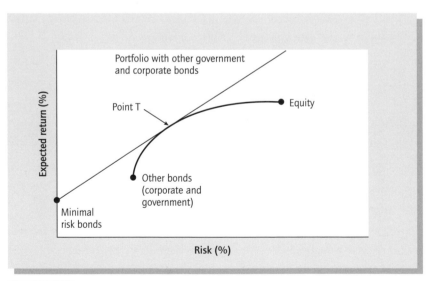

Figure 7.13 The updated portfolio

Using equity risk insights in the context of a full rational portfolio

My reason for focusing on equities is that we have good data to gain some meaningful insights about the risk of investing in equity markets, whereas it's harder to be exact about the overall portfolio risk. This is because while we can try to quantify the risk of government and corporate bonds, it is harder to predict how those move relative to each other and to equities (correlation) with any accuracy, and therefore what the aggregate portfolio risk is.

Extrapolating an understanding of equity market risk to the overall portfolio you need to bear the following in mind:

- Try to understand the risks you are taking with an investment in the world equity markets.

- Realise that your minimal risk asset is not entirely without risk, but has a far lower risk than the equity markets. Longer-maturity bonds will fluctuate more in value than shorter-term ones.

- Other government and corporate bonds will typically have a risk level between equities and the minimal risk bonds. The riskier the bonds, the more they will be like equities and perhaps move in price more like equities if markets drop, but it is hard to be exact about that. As a very rough rule of thumb, assume that the other government and corporate bonds have slightly less than half the risk of equities, but will move more like equities in terrible markets than when markets are stable.

The rational portfolio allocations

So, now we have a rational portfolio as shown in Figure 7.14. Incorporating the points above about the relative proportions of risky government and corporate bonds relative to equities, the rational portfolio could look like that in Table 7.3.

The allocations shown in the table are the best because they are based on the proportions of values that the market already ascribes to them, with the caveat that I have excluded non-return generating, highly rated government bonds. So apart from those highly rated bonds, the ratio of equities, government and corporate bonds is in line with the market value proportions in the world today. And if we allocate along the same lines as the efficient markets we will achieve maximum diversification and the best risk/return profile.

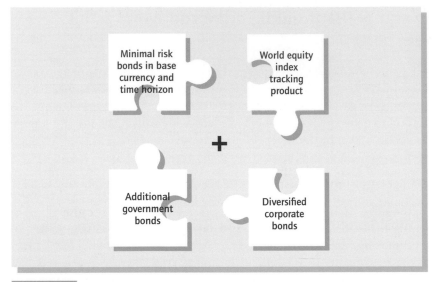

Figure 7.14 The rational portfolio

Table 7.3 The rational portfolio at different risk preferences (percentages)

		No risk	Medium risk			High risk	
		Various portfolio compositions					
		A	B	C	D	E	F
Minimal risk asset		100	67	33	0	0	0
	World equity	0	25	50	75	85	100
Risky assets:	Government bonds	0	3	7	10	6	0
	Corporate bonds	0	5	10	15	9	0

We need to take a combination of equities and other government and corporate bonds and combine that with our 'safety asset', the minimal risk asset. How much risk we want is then determined by how much of the minimal risk asset, and how much of the combination of the other asset classes, we want. Construct your portfolio in this way and you will have an outstanding portfolio for the long run.

In implementing the portfolios outlined above look for products that, as closely as possible, represent the various asset classes:

Asset class	Description
Minimal risk asset	UK, US, German, etc. or equivalent credit quality of maturity matching investor's time horizon.
Equities	World equity index or as broad as possible.
Other government bonds	Diversified, real return-generating government bonds of varying maturities, countries and currencies; we have used those rated sub-AA as a good indicator.
Corporate bonds	Broad range of corporate bonds of varying maturities, credit risk, currency, issuer and geographic area.

If the strategy for investing above seems simple, it is because it is. As a rational investor who is willing to add a bit of complexity to the all minimal risk/equity mix from earlier, we are simply adding real return-generating bonds in the proportions that they exist in the world. We think that the normal functioning of the market has caused the prices of the many debt and equity securities to be such that they reflect the risk/return characteristic of that security.

Of course not every investment in the world is perfectly efficiently priced. If this was the case, and everybody believed it, then there would be no trading. Everyone would accept that the prices reflected all information and the security's risk/return contribution. But that is not the point. The point is that we do not think that *we* are in a position to know better than the prices set by the market and as a result should not try to reallocate our portfolio to get better returns.

Special case: if you want a lot of risk

Theory and practice collide in the case where an investor's risk preference is higher than point T in Figure 7.13. Theory suggests that the investor should borrow money and use that borrowed money to buy more of the 'T' portfolio.[10] In reality many investors either don't ever want to

---

10 The straight line between minimal risk, point T, and up to the right assumes that the investor can borrow at the same rate as the minimal risk bond. In reality the borrowing rate for the investor would be higher and the curve to the right of point T would be flatter to reflect the lower expected return (higher borrowing costs) as risk increases.

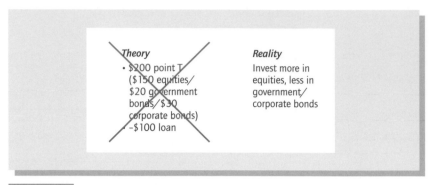

Figure 7.15 Higher risk-preference investors

borrow to invest or simply can't find the money to do so. Particularly post-2008, when geared investors got burned badly as loans got called at the worst possible time, investing with borrowed money is often not a real or desired alternative.

For investors with a higher risk preference than point T, I would suggest buying more of the world equity portfolio and fewer bonds (instead of borrowing money to buy more of the mix of equities and bonds) – see Figure 7.15.

If you want even more risk than being 100% invested in world equities there are leveraged ETFs. Simplistically, the way they work is that the provider takes your £50 and uses that as collateral to borrow another £50, and then invests the £100 (in the case of a 50% leverage product). You will then have the exposure to the market of £100 despite only having invested £50. This obviously works well if markets are going up, but will quickly hurt badly in declining markets.

Incorporating other assets

This book is about making portfolio management straightforward and efficient. The overall message is simple:

- Recognise that you are a rational investor.
- Create a very simple investment portfolio consisting of minimal risk assets and the broadest possible equity index, perhaps adding other government and corporate bonds.
- Think about your risk profile and how it may change over time and as the world around you changes. Adjust your portfolio accordingly.
- Implement the portfolio in a way that is tax efficient. The suggested portfolio will already be extremely liquid, which is great. Get help on taxes if you need it.
- Make sure you purchase the portfolio in the most cost-efficient way. This is worth a bit of time up front.
- Don't get impatient. The rational portfolio will be much better for you over time, but you will probably not see the cost and portfolio construction benefits immediately.
- In my view, at this point you are doing better than 95% of the investing community. The remaining 5% have an edge and you can't compete with that. Nor should you try.

Your investment portfolio is obviously not the whole story; you have other assets and potentially liabilities. For an individual this could be a house, private investments, stake in a family business, a plot of land, and perhaps even less tangible elements like a future inheritance, your education or skillset. For an institution the asset base could be future business prospects, your people, etc. Likewise your liabilities could be manifold, other than just the mortgage on your house.

What else do you have?

Many investors think of their investment portfolio as separate from the rest of their lives. While that is probably convenient, an investment portfolio should be seen in the context of, or at least be influenced by, the other assets or liabilities a person or institution has.

Most investors tend to take quite concentrated risks, often without giving it too much thought. As an example, if you work in the property sector in the UK, own a house in London and stand to inherit a share of the family property business one day, you already have significant exposure to the UK economy and particularly the property sector. You may have a diversified rational portfolio with your investments, but you are still taking a large concentration risk in your overall economic life. If the UK property market went down the drain you would be in a rough spot, despite having done the right things in your investment portfolio. It could well be that the diversification benefits you gained from having a broadly diversified portfolio were dwarfed by the fact that the rest of your assets were so concentrated. You might be losing your job and any potential future job prospects, your house may decline in value and your inheritance be worth less, all for the same reason.

As unpleasant as the plight of the UK investor would be in the above scenario, compare it to the situation of an investment portfolio composed exclusively of UK property stocks. In that case all the assets would be falling at the same time and there would be no respite anywhere. The investor would have failed to take advantage of the opportunity to diversify and paid the price for it.

Similarly, consider if you owned a lot of shares in the company you work for. While companies are interested in aligning the interest of share-holders and employees, you would be taking a great concentration risk if something went wrong in the company. Not only would your investment in company shares probably be a far greater portion of your portfolio than if you did not work there, but you would have your job prospects and investment assets tied up in the same company. This is great if you were one of the first to join Microsoft, but horrible if your employer was Enron. Of course in many cases company shares or options are a part of compensation packages and obviously better to have than forego, but I would caution you against blindly adding to the concentration.

While it is of course possible that the UK property market or the company you worked for collapse for the same reason as the wider world economy, and therefore stock and bond markets also collapse, by having an international investment portfolio at least you guard against localised risks. Someone from Greece today, Argentina around the turn of the century, Thailand/Indonesia/South Korea during the Asian crisis in the late 1990s or any of the other countries that have defaulted over the past decades would perhaps better appreciate the advantages of avoiding local concentration risk. This was doubly true if they had mistakenly deemed local government bonds free of risk and to their horror found that they were not. The graveyard of financial history is filled with investors who claimed things to be different this time around or thought their country or area of expertise was immune to various risks.

> Taking the argument a step further you could actively de-select your market in your investment portfolio. Instead of buying the world equities market, you could buy the world, ex-UK. The trouble with this of course is that most countries with the notable exception of the US only represent a small fraction of the overall world equity markets, and the advantages of this kind of diversification are therefore negligible. As the US markets represent over a third of the wider world equity market, de-selecting the US from the world equity portfolio may make sense for US investors who are worried about significant existing US exposure in their overall assets. Non-US investors will benefit less from this de-selection and at any additional costs it would probably not be worth the additional diversification benefits.

Other assets

Individual investors often tend to think too narrowly about incorporating all their assets when thinking about their personal portfolio. Your personal assets include everything, including intangible assets, and even potential liabilities. Here are a few ideas, some of which may seem far-fetched:

> **Tangible assets:**
> - Investment portfolio
> - Future pension (who guarantees it?)
> - Security and generosity of government safety net
> - Insurance policies

▶

- Property holdings (do you own a house?)
- Private investments
- Company shares or options
- Future inheritance (morbid perhaps, but do you have a sense of timing and how it is invested?)
- Car and other possessions

Intangible assets:

- Education and qualifications
- Languages you speak
- Current job and prospects (if you work in finance you already have a lot of direct and indirect exposure to the financial markets, and may want to temper adding to it through your investment portfolio)
- Previous job experience (will affect future earnings potential)
- Partner's education and job
- Geographic flexibility

Liabilities:

- Flexibility of liabilities – will you certainly incur them?
- Future school fees or health bills
- Mortgage
- Credit cards, car, etc. loans (if you have any liquid assets you should never have loans like this – they are far too expensive)
- Tax (including tax you would incur to realise assets)
- Are any liabilities not fixed, but move up and down with the economy? How do they correlate with your assets (it's better if they decrease as asset values decrease)?

Think of everything and think out of the box to compile your lists.

Of course it would be great if the performance of your various assets in no way correlated, but unfortunately that is not very realistic. Most things link to the economy somehow.

If we were presented with perfect data sets regarding the values, risks and correlations of an investor's other assets we would be able to do some sort of scientific optimisation of asset allocation. That, however, is almost impossible. The idea of taking assets, including intangible ones, and optimising allocations based on them probably sounds like nonsense to most people. But while we don't have the data or desire to do these calculations in a scientific way it's still worth nurturing your gut instinct about how this all fits together.

A simple way to start thinking about the non-investment assets is asking yourself if there is something you really don't want to happen, and go from there. Would you be in trouble if the local property market collapsed, or if you lost your job? Would you be able to adapt if the skillset you had educated yourself to was no longer required? Would the causes of these events trigger problems elsewhere in your overall asset base? Could you adapt?

Imagine the scenario where a major local business ceased trading. The thought processes of someone locally who was affected may look as follows:

Asset	Impact	Comment
House	↓↓	Down with damaged local economy
Job	↓↓↓	Probably lose job
Job prospects	↓↓	Don't have other skills needed locally
Private investments	↓	Loan to friend who depended on that local business
Investment portfolio	↔	Diversified
Company pension plan	↓	Plan should be funded, but no longer backed up by company guarantee

In the context of an investment portfolio we want to minimise the probability that these things happen at the same time as a large decline in your investments. It could be that the industry you worked and were trained in all of a sudden shifted to China or India with job losses and bleak prospects for you as a result. This would be bad news for you. But in a case like that you can take solace from the fact that while this hurts you locally your rational portfolio is broadly diversified and perhaps not declining at the same time as everything else in your life is going wrong.

There is no generalised way to reduce the concentration risk outlined above. If you find yourself with too great a concentration risk try to find ways to divest some of the assets that add to this risk and re-invest those in a more diversified portfolio like the rational one. Unfortunately many people only worry about these issues after misfortune has hit.

Not just geography

I had a friend who was a successful internet entrepreneur. He had made some money from selling his internet business and was now launching the next one.

Because of the risk he perceived in his own business he did not invest too much of his money into the new venture. He thought the risk of it going badly was too high for him to risk his life savings. As a result, he invested his savings in various internet firms he respected and thought he understood quite well. It seemed to make sense; he was investing in what he knew.

Of course what happened was the massive internet crash that took everything down with it. His second venture failed – it ran out of cash as nobody wanted to invest more in the internet sector. Unfortunately this happened for the same reason and at the same time that my friend's internet stocks plummeted in value.

Many people would probably consider my friend's actions quite reasonable. He was aware of his concentration risk in his second company and diversified away from it, even including investing in other countries with his cash. But in the end the diversification was a false one – he was not diversified because the value of all his assets linked back to the same assumption, namely the internet continuing its meteoric rise.

Currency matching

Before the 2008–09 crash foreign-denominated mortgages were all the rage in certain parts of Europe. In theory it was simple. You could buy a property in Poland in zloty and finance that purchase with a Swiss franc-denominated mortgage. Instead of paying high single-digit interest rates on a Polish mortgage you would pay next to no interest on your Swiss franc-denominated mortgage because of the lower Swiss franc interest rate. Similarly some friends financed the purchase of their expensive London apartment with a mortgage based in Japanese yen and paid little in interest on their mortgage.

In both these cases there was a currency asset/liability mismatch. It may seem tempting to make only small interest payments in a foreign currency, but these set-ups involve foreign currency risk.

The financial markets are obviously aware of the interest rate differential and the forward rate (the rate at which you can trade the currency in the future) should reflect the interest rate differential. So if zloty/Swiss franc is at 3.50 and the nominal interest rate differential is 5%, all else being equal, the one-year forward currency rate is 3.50 × 1.05. If the spot rate moves less than 5% in the following 12 months the mortgage holder will be in profit; the interest differential plus change in principal outstanding would be lower than the payment on a domestic mortgage.

It is perhaps quite instructive that post the 2008–09 crash these mortgages are increasingly rare. The mortgage borrowers essentially took a large currency bet that currency markets were inefficient, which they were probably ill equipped to take. When the crisis hit and investors escaped to 'safe' currencies like the Swiss franc, the currency rallied from about 2 to 3 zloty per Swiss franc, and the zloty equivalent amount of mortgage outstanding went up. This happened exactly at the same time as house prices declined in Poland. Someone with a 1 million zloty house and 80% mortgage before the crisis, might have found themselves with a 750,000 zloty house and a 1.2 million zloty equivalent mortgage (0.8million × 3/2). Many investors went bust as a result.

The point is you have to weigh up a potential currency asset/liability mismatch against the benefits of diversification that investing abroad and in other currencies brings. If you have significant and specific liabilities in one currency it makes sense to have at least matching assets in that same currency in minimal risk-type investments (or like keeping the mortgage in the same currency that your house will one day be sold in) before diversifying investments into other currencies.

The institutional investor

Thinking about all your assets and liabilities in a portfolio context is not exclusive to the individual investor. Imagine you run a Florida-based insurance company. Your speciality is insuring beachfront properties in the Miami area against hurricanes. Business is good – so much so that you are in no rush to pass on any of the risks to the reinsurance companies. Like any insurance company you are building a reserve account from the premiums you collect in case a hurricane hits the coast and you have to pay out on lots of insurance policies.

Next you are presented with an excellent investment opportunity for your reserves; a property investment company that primarily invests in the same region of Florida. The project promises great returns, and you feel doubly good since you are already somewhat of an expert on the area. As a result you put a large part of your reserves into the project. After all, what's not to like? Actually, there is a lot not to like …

The insurance company has taken a massive correlation risk between its assets and liabilities, and exposed itself to the perfect storm (no pun intended). Should a hurricane hit the coast the insurance company would see the size of its liabilities (the insurance policies) increase dramatically at the same time and for the same reason that the value of its assets (the property development) go down in value. On top of this there would probably be fewer buyers of property assets even at a lower price, as liquidity tends to dry up in distressed situations and the company would have a hard time realising the cash value when it was most needed. Bad, bad news.

The example above is fictitious; in reality no reasonable insurance company would put itself in such a situation, or the overseeing regulator would stop them (like they did with mortgage banks before 2008!). But the lesson remains: the combination of your assets and liabilities, and the risk you are willing to take, matter a great deal in your investment portfolio.

Other assets rethought

The material in this part of the book on incorporating all assets and liabilities in an 'all-in' approach to portfolio management may be seen as an extra or 'nice to know' area of portfolio management, but in my view every investor should consider it seriously. It's an area that is developing as financial firms get better at understanding and incorporating additional information they have about you, hopefully with the result that they can more easily offer cheap products that are tailored specifically to your needs. While it is not central to the theme of the book I would strongly encourage you to think about your broader assets and how things fit together. If your broadly diversified investment portfolio only represents about 10% of your overall asset base and the remaining 90% is highly correlated and dependent on the same factors, the diversification of your investment portfolio may actually give you a false sense of security.

What is omitted from your rational portfolio and why

Avoid investments that require an edge or those you already have exposure to

It wouldn't surprise me if the portfolio I have suggested has many sceptics. It probably looks too simple to make much sense, and leaves out several successful asset classes that have dominated not only the financial press, but also our popular culture. I live in London, a city which has seen an incredible rise in property prices over the past decades. Because of this most investors take for granted that any reasonable portfolio consists at least partly of domestic property. London is one of the places in the world that came through the crash relatively unscathed so the fans of property maintain their continuing belief.

In this chapter, I discuss other popular asset classes and their absence from the simple rational portfolio. We will see that appreciating that we are without an edge is even more important as we move away from the public equity and bond markets and into sectors that are typically closer to the local economies that we individually know and feel a part of. It may seem strange to have a whole chapter on things to leave out of your portfolio, but it is important to remember why: the portfolio in this book is for people who have no edge to outperform, and should be a simple and cheap portfolio as a result. The rational portfolio is certainly simple and cheap, and requires no edge in the three asset classes it suggests: the minimal risk asset, world equities and other government and corporate bonds. The asset classes discussed in this chapter will undoubtedly make many investors phenomenally rich in the future, but those will either be investors who have a great edge, charge others a lot of fees or are lucky. Since you don't want to count on luck, can't charge other people large fees and have no edge – and probably have a lot of exposures anyway – you should stay away. The eliminated asset classes are still important because you need to be sure that you know they have been considered and that there are good reasons for leaving them out.

A few recurring issues with these other asset classes make them unsuitable for the rational portfolio:

■ You don't have an edge or special insight/knowledge to pick the outperforming sub-set of the asset class.

■ The whole asset class does not necessarily have return expectations in excess of the minimal risk asset in future.

■ You already have exposure to the asset class via companies represented both in your broad equity and potentially corporate bond exposures. Do you really need to increase them further?

■ The other asset classes can be very illiquid – do you get compensated with higher returns for this disadvantage?

■ Other asset class exposures can be very expensive in fees and expenses. Unless you have a great edge in picking the right products this can destroy any return advantage.

■ There is a good case for adding quoted property investments to the rational portfolio although only in limited size relative to the overall equity investment. But because it is small and you may already have this exposure indirectly elsewhere in your rational portfolio, and for the sake of simplicity, property investments have been excluded from the simple rational portfolio.

So, the excluded asset classes discussed in this chapter are:

■ property
  ■ direct investments, private property funds
  ■ residential property
  ■ quoted property holdings
■ private equity, venture capital and hedge funds
■ commodities
■ private investments
■ collectibles.

Mortgage-backed, mortgage-related and asset-backed securities, other types of quasi-government debt and other debt instruments issued by financial institutions are also excluded. This is because some of them fall into the property category, and others are alternatives to the minimal risk investment, particularly in cases where the investments are quasi government and there are tax advantages. Also, a lot of the exposures those kinds of debts give you are captured indirectly elsewhere in the portfolio, but they are without easy products to gain access to – so in the interest of simplicity and ease of implementation these additional investment possibilities do not add enough additional value to be included. Financial institutions' debt is a gigantic market (bigger than the corporate debt market), but less of a relevant product for the rational investor as a lot of it relates to the wholesale funding market for financial institutions and there are no easily accessible products available to most retail investors.

Property – don't do it unless you have an edge

Rational investors would not expect to do any better than the general property market, less any cost disadvantage they may have, so the best expected return from property would be that of the whole sector in the relevant area. Someone investing in private/direct property projects or private funds that invest in property often invests in the same geographical area as their other assets and as we have seen this exposes them to a great concentration of risk in their overall portfolio as a result. There is a good chance that whatever may cause the local/regional property market to decline could affect other local assets, in addition to the value of investors' private homes. Unless you get compensated for this concentration risk by getting higher expected investment returns, the concentration is a risk worth avoiding and as you are without an edge you would not predict this outperformance.

Likewise, consider the illiquid nature of private property investments. While even very large investors can liquidate world equity market investments in a short period of time, trying to sell a direct property investment or a stake in a private investment when you need the money is rarely a recipe for success. And while there have clearly been successful property booms, if you are selling at a tough time for property assets generally then others probably need to sell property at the same time. With liquidity drying up for those investors who are forced to sell their investments, this situation is terrible.

One of the reasons so many investors are fascinated by property investments has to do with physical proximity. People who are interested in investing often can't help themselves spotting a great investment opportunity and where better to see it than right in front of you. You might see a decrepit building in a great location and wonder why nobody is fixing it up, and think that you might just be the best-positioned investor to do it. Or hear through a friend that planning permission is going through for an upscale development that would lift the value of an adjacent building, and so forth. Like a lot of people in London, I have been guilty of feeling like a property expert and thought I was an astute property investor until I realised that I had just been lucky and bought into a rising market.

I don't doubt that many property investors are people with local connections or insight to do this well. Perhaps they have an edge, but unless you are one of those plugged in people, you probably do not have an edge in the property markets. And like the argument of picking active equity managers, picking property investment funds suggests an indirect edge if you claim to be able to pick a manager who has an edge.

So how do you know if you are one of these investors with an edge in property markets? As in the public equity markets it is not always easy to know if you have an edge. Those who perform poorly have a great excuse and those that perform well in the property market are unlikely to think it is luck and will always have other great reasons: they saw something others didn't, knew something, understood something and heard something. Something. Just be honest with yourself as you consider your edge. It can be expensive to think you have it if you don't.

Has residential property really been that great?

The best estimate of residential property performance is the Case-Shiller House Price index which represents the price changes in US residential homes. Professor Robert Shiller describes the housing index along with other interesting ideas in his excellent book *Irrational Exuberance* (Princeton University Press, 2005). To my knowledge there isn't a property index that covers all forms of residential property investment across many countries that goes back many decades for us to analyse.

Using the Case-Shiller index as a proxy for residential property investments since 1890 we can compare the returns of the housing market to an investment over the same time period in short-term US government bonds (see Figure 9.1).

The first thing to note is that over the past century we would have done far better investing in US government bonds than in residential property. It is

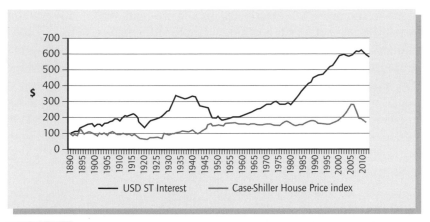

Figure 9.1 Inflation adjusted Case-Shiller House Price index versus short-term US government debt

of course easy to criticise analysis like this for not correctly incorporating rental income (or the ownership benefit of not paying rent), maintenance and improvement costs, transaction costs, insurance costs, and transaction and on-going tax. Or not being international. I would agree that it is hard to claim that these things are an overly exact science, but this index questions the premise that property investments are necessarily a huge profit centre.

However, we can also see why property was such a hot investment in the years before the sub-prime crisis (see Figure 9.2).

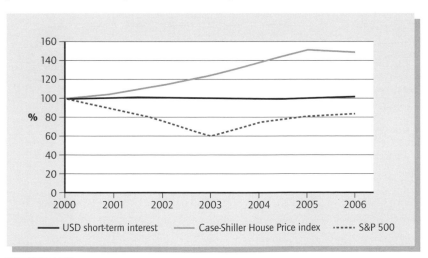

Figure 9.2 Case-Shiller House Price index versus short-term US government debt and S&P 500, all inflation adjusted

As property markets outperformed debt and equity markets, many saw this as a sign of things to come and jumped on the bandwagon, even as longer-term data did not suggest that residential property markets outperform in the long run. Besides, it's always easier to sell an investment in something that has recently done well, and property investments certainly did well until the bubble burst. Keep in mind that many countries have regulations or incentives that promote house purchase. As a good friend commented, 'Where else can you get a subsidised 90% loan-to-value investment with no taxes?' Of course, all those things should help house prices, but should already be reflected in the prices.

A home

A friend of mine and I were having a conversation a couple of years ago, soon after he had lost his job. He did not have much in the form of savings, about £20,000, but could probably support his family for a year without lowering their living standards. Almost as an aside, my friend said, 'Thank God we have the house.'

Five years earlier he and his wife had put all their savings into the equity of their house, obtained a loan-to-value mortgage of 80% and bought the cottage of their dreams in South London for £200,000. They loved the house and financially it had been a huge success. An estate agent had told them that they would have no problems selling the house for £250,000 – a tax-free gain of £50,000.

In my view, their situation is fairly typical of a London couple; the vast majority of their wealth is tied up in London property (see Figure 9.3).

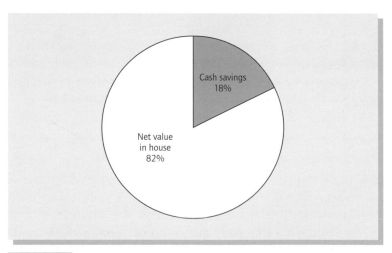

Figure 9.3 Net asset mix

Not only were my friends dependent on London property, but with their mortgage they were heavily geared. A decline in the London housing market could have a very significant impact on their net assets, the success of the house purchase not withstanding. Table 9.1 shows how this couple's net assets of £110,000 (house of £250,000 less £160,000 mortgage plus £20,000 other savings) would be affected by different movements in London property prices, assuming their house moved with the market.

Table 9.1   **London house price decline**

	Status quo	−10%	−20%	−30%	−40%
Total net assets (£)	110,000	85,000	60,000	35,000	10,000
Change		−23%	−45%	−68%	−91%

In essence, my friends were taking an incredibly concentrated bet on the London property market. If the housing market in general, and their home specifically, sufferered a decline of 20% they would see their assets decline by 45%; a 40% decline in the value of the house and my friends would almost be bankrupt.

I thought I was stating the obvious, my friend saw no sense in my argument. He pointed out that if they had taken the £40,000 that they put down for the house and put it in the bank instead, their life savings would be £60,000 today instead of £110,000. Where was the sense in that? I mentioned that if you ignored that a lot of people thought there was a lot of additional quality of life from owning where you live instead of renting, they had essentially taken a geared bet on London property and been lucky. Again my friend thought I was wrong. He felt that they knew the local market and had been able to find an extra-attractive house and that when they bought the house the local property market was about to take off. Instead of luck, they had been astute house buyers. At this point I kept my mouth shut.

I understand and appreciate the desire to own your house instead of renting, and also understand that we badly want to believe that we have made an astute purchase with what for many people is the largest investment of their lives. But buying a property may mean compromising the portfolio of our total assets, by increasing concentration risk and correlation risk in a leveraged way, and I would strongly suggest that any house owner takes a look at the fraction of total assets that local property constitutes.[1] Then question what would happen if your local property market dropped in value by various double-digit percentages. Would it matter? Is this likely to happen at the same time as you lose your job or other savings? Would you risk the scenario of being unable to make payments on a mortgage or forced to refinance the mortgage, thereby risking having to realise the price change and being unable to ride out the stormy market?

A major part of good portfolio management is about not putting all your eggs in one basket and subjecting yourself to the risk of bad things happening all at once in an unpredictable fashion. For many who were hurt in the recent property bubble, this was what happened. But I do understand why individual investors put great intangible value to owning their own house on top of the large monetary value many have realised over the past decades. My parents have lived in the same house for about 40 years. Their house is not an integral part of their portfolio or an investment – it is a home. If that is somehow sub-optimal from a portfolio management perspective, so be it.

The case for commercial property

Despite the questionable history of great returns in residential property and its presence in many portfolios through home ownership, general property investing has been a thriving investment for some over the years and an integral part of many diversified portfolios. While there is good evidence that the return profile for commercial property has been attractive in the past, to my knowledge there hasn't been a global diversified investable property index like there is in the stock markets with the MSCI World index and others. As an example, the FTSE EPRA/NAREIT Global index was not launched until 2009 and even while there is global data going further back, it is less clear how a globally diversified property investment product would have fared.

Proponents of property investment suggest that it is a separate asset class with limited correlation with equity and other markets. (Although only tracking residential property, the correlation between the Dow Jones

---

1 Although I would generally caution you against leverage, a mortgage on your property is often the cheapest form of leverage you can get, both because of tax advantages, but also because lenders are willing to lend you money at good rates against a fixed asset like your property. So if you need to borrow money and can do it through your property then that may be the cheapest way.

Industrial Average and the Case-Shiller index since 1900 is only 0.19.) Limited correlation with other asset classes is obviously a good thing and if this low correlation is replicated in future then commercial property investment could provide a good diversifier (although virtually all publicly traded property investments suffered in 2008 along with the rest of the market, suggesting low correlation is not universally the case). With low correlation you don't need that high a return expectation for a property investment to make sense and investing in a diversified global portfolio of property investments would also add geographic diversification.

But despite the promisingly low correlation and apparent good historical performance of commercial property generally, the FTSE NAREIT index mentioned above represents quoted underlying property investment companies with a market capitalisation that represents only 2–3% of the global equity market's total market capitalisation.[2] At the time of writing the largest constituent in the index has a market value of around $25 billion and the entire index of around 400 constituents spread around the world has a value of about $650 billion, or not much above the market value of a couple of leading individual companies. So while the global index provides the kind of good and well-diversified property exposure an investor should want, if you allocate far more to property than the sub-5% of the world market values, you run the risk of over-allocating to property, particularly considering the other ways you already have direct and indirect exposure to the sector.

Investors in equities are already directly and indirectly significantly exposed to the property sector on top of home ownership. A major constituent of equity markets everywhere is financial institutions, including banks. Those banks obviously serve many functions, but a key one is the provision or facilitation of capital for the property markets. The banks do this both in the form of residential property markets, but also by financing and investing in commercial property. Even in the cases where the banks only act as a facilitator and pass on the principal risks to other investors (as opposed to other cases where banks hold on to a property investment), they still have a huge interest in a positive property market.

---

2 Although the quoted property investment companies that are represented in the index trackers only represent a small proportion of the value of the world's total property that is also true of many other industries. Also, if this small quoted representation of property holding suggested that those quoted were extra attractive we would trust the market to have this reflected in the share price relative to other securities.

The bursting of the US sub-prime market bubble in 2007–08 and the subsequent default of many geared products connected to it was one of the primary drivers of the financial crisis. So even if the direct representation of property investment companies represents a fairly small portion of the overall stock market, we have indirect exposure to property through many other sectors of the stock markets. In addition to the banks, the listing of many large infrastructure and construction-related companies further adds to our indirect exposure to the property market because corporations in a wide variety of industries already are the largest holders of commercial property.[3]

Some might disagree that I'm leaving out property investments and I can appreciate why. For those investors who wish to add an investment in property, I would recommend you invest in low-fee and geographically-diversified property investment companies. A good option is publicly traded REITs (Real Estate Investment Trusts). REITs have a favourable tax treatment, particularly for US investors, and distribute most of the income from their diverse set of underlying property holdings (often mainly commercial, like offices and retail, but also warehouses, apartment buildings, hospitals, etc.).

If you do go ahead with adding property investments to your portfolio then consider the following:

- Invest broadly geographically and cheaply – there are some good global property ETFs (including one from iShares) that track the FTSE NAREIT Global index, or similar.
- Avoid concentrating in countries that you as an investor are already exposed to via your non-portfolio assets.
- Be clever about tax (REITs are tax-exempt from certain taxes); tax advantages could favour a larger allocation to property investments for some investors.
- When you consider adding property investments to the portfolio think hard about the exposure you already have to property, both indirectly via securities in your portfolio, but also potentially via your home.

3 According to Richard Ferri's excellent book *All About Asset Allocation* (McGraw-Hill Professional, 2010) about two-thirds of the total value of commercial property in the US is owned by corporations, many of which you are already invested in through the general equity market index.

Private equity, venture capital and hedge funds

I used to run a hedge fund in London and wrote a book about my experiences, *Money Mavericks: Confessions of a Hedge Fund Manager* (FT Publishing International, 2012), and still sit on the board of a couple of hedge funds. Also, earlier in my career, I worked at a private equity fund called Permira Advisors.

Private equity, venture capital and hedge funds (I will refer to them as alternative investments) do not belong in the rational portfolio.

All the alternative investment vehicles claim an edge in the market. They are essentially saying, 'Give your money to us and we will provide you with a superior return profile.' Time will tell if they are right or not, but by selecting them you are essentially saying that you yourself have an edge, not because you can make all the underlying investments yourself, but because you know someone who can, namely the manager of the alternative fund.

The perception of the alternative funds is often shaped by a couple of well-documented success stories. When John Paulson made billions for himself and his investors in 2008 from betting on a collapsing sub-prime housing market it was the kind of investment everyone wished that they had in their portfolio. Or when Sequoia Capital partners tell you that they have backed Apple, Cisco, Google, and other names you know too well the question almost turns into, 'How can you not invest money in alternative funds?'

In many ways, the logic behind picking an alternative investment is like that of picking an active manager. You do it because you think someone is able to perform well when investing your money. While you may acknowledge that you can't do so yourself, being able to pick an investment manager who can consistently outperform would be an incredibly valuable tool. But like stock picking it is a rare skill. Someone whose job it is to select alternative managers may say something like 'the East Coast biotech sector will massively outperform over the next decade', 'I think convertible arb will be resurrected', or 'John Doe fund manager is just brilliant'. Rightly or not, these are not the kinds of statements an investor without an edge can or should make. Particularly when you consider that the liquidity of your investment in alternative funds can be so poor that you may not get your money back for years, the need for an edge and superior returns is further increased.

Fees are very high

Besides the fact that investing in alternatives suggests a claim of having an 'indirect' edge on the part of the investor, the funds are also typically very expensive.

Many alternatives charge an annual management fee of 1.5–2% in addition to a 20% share of all profits above a certain hurdle rate, plus other expenses. While hedge funds in particular, at times with great justification, claim that the return profile they create is very different from one you can get through the markets, the aggregate fees mean that only the best-performing funds will be worth their fees. And therefore only those who have an ability to consistently select the best funds should invest in these alternatives. Most people simply do not have this ability.

To get an idea of the magnitude of fees consider Warren Buffett, one of the most successful investors over the past generation. If Buffett's fee structure had been that of a hedge fund instead of an insurance company the return to the investors would have looked very different (see Figure 9.4).

To illustrate the cumulative impact of fees, consider the example of a pensioner who invests money into a hedge fund through the normal route of a pension provider, via a fund of fund, with all the aggregate fees and expenses. Suppose further that the hedge fund made a return of 10% in a year, before any fees or expenses, and that it was a typical long/short

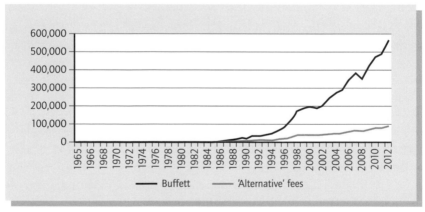

Figure 9.4 $100 invested with Buffett versus one with an 'alternative' fee structure

Based on data from Berkshire Hathaway, www. Berkshirehathaway.com fund with normal trading. What would be left for the pensioner once all the finance people had taken their bites? (See Table 9.2.)

This is, of course, before we have even asked how the hedge fund made its 10%. Was it because it simply had market exposure as it went up or was it all unique value added that could not be achieved elsewhere? If it was mainly because of markets going up, our pensioner has paid a shocking level of aggregate fees for exposure to the markets.

I'm not just picking on hedge funds: private equity and some structured products have as much to answer for. Despite similar fees they are unapologetically long the market often in a geared way: investors could do much better themselves through leveraged index trackers, and an investment in private equity is typically very illiquid. Be sure you get paid for the investment being illiquid, and that you don't pay to be long the market – you can do that much more cheaply with an index tracker.

This is not to say that alternatives never make sense but rather that the high fees mean that the bar is very high indeed.

Table 9.2   **What's left?**

'Gross' gross performance		10.00%
Hedge fund	Fee:	Net of:
HF trading expenses	1.50%	8.50%
Standard quoted gross performance		**8.50%**
HF fund expenses	0.20%	8.30%
HF management fee	1.50%	6.80%
HF incentive fee	20.00%	5.44%
Fund of funds		
FoF expenses	0.15%	5.29%
FoF management fee	0.75%	4.54%
FoF incentive fee	10.00%	4.09%
Pension fund		
PF external adviser	0.15%	3.94%
PF fees and expenses	0.75%	3.19%
Net return		**3.19%**

Alternative funds often argue that they provide investors with access to a different part of the economy (like a venture fund finding the next Facebook) or returns that are uncorrelated to the markets (like market neutral hedge funds). And they are sometimes right. Some alternative funds will undoubtedly do extremely well in future both in terms of providing investors with a unique exposure or just great returns, but the challenge is to select which one. Studies suggest that past performance is a poor guide to future returns so that doesn't help us. (That would almost have been too easy – just pick the past winners and away you go!)

In addition to staying away from alternatives because picking the right alternative manager suggests an edge, many investors already have a lot of the same exposure that alternatives give, for all its high fees. The correlation between the returns of alternatives and the stock markets is quite high as the alternative funds often invest in assets similar to those represented by the stock markets. (Venture funds would argue that they invest in companies too small for stock exchanges, but they are still exposed to the same economy and exits often involve sales to large companies or initial public offerings (IPOs).) It is not arbitrary that 2008 was the worst year in the history of the alternative industry. In the rational portfolio you have many of the same exposures you would have as an investor in alternatives, but at about one-twentieth of the fees.

In summary

Stay away from alternative funds for the following reasons:

- Picking the right manager of an alternative fund requires an edge, which we don't think we have.
- In the unlikely case that we could invest in all alternative funds and thereby get exposed to the whole sector, the combination of very high fees, poor liquidity of our investment, and the fact that we could have much of the same exposure but more cheaply through our stock market investment would render alternatives unattractive.

In reality, most investors couldn't get access to the alternative funds if they wanted to. Ignoring the access products or share classes that some funds have, this is often because either the minimum investment size is too large (often $1 million or higher) or there are other regulatory obstacles. There is, however, a good chance that you are already exposed to them. Public and private pension funds are among the biggest investors in alternative funds. If you are a present or future recipient of benefits you are therefore already exposed to their performance. You just hope that whoever chose the alternative funds to invest in on your behalf has the required edge that eludes most of us.

Commodities

Before the 2008–09 crash, certain commodities performed very well and often became an integral part of well-diversified investment portfolios. While gold and oil perhaps dominated the broader media picture there were also other success stories.

Until fairly recently it was very hard for most investors to buy commodities. Unless you were an institutional investor set up to take possession of the physical commodities or trade the futures contracts it was a cumbersome process to gain direct exposure to the commodities. This difficulty has greatly been reduced over the past decades. Today there are ETFs available on a wide range of commodities and gaining the exposure is therefore as simple as buying a share in the ETF of your choice. Some of the most popular commodity ETFs are the gold ones, but there is a wide range of other commodities also available in addition to some that track broad-based commodity indices.

The economics of commodities are different from that of equities or bonds. To physically hold commodities we may actually incur a cost instead of necessarily expecting our ownership of them to generate cash in the future. There are storage and insurance costs to holding commodities. Furthermore, commodities are not income generating: the cost of extracting the commodity may change and the usefulness of that commodity in the production of goods may change, but nothing suggests that this will be consistently positive.

Although the costs of commodity trading for most investors have come down greatly it remains an expensive proposition for most. Even if we hold a commodity such as gold through an ETF we are still indirectly subject to the same storage and insurance costs, in addition to management and trading costs. Also, unless it is our profession to trade specific commodities there is a great chance that we are at a significant information disadvantage. If you trade oil and do so while working at Shell or BP there is a reasonable chance that you have an information edge compared to someone in their pyjamas trading on their computer at home. Make sure you are not in the latter group.

Financial investors in commodities mainly invest through futures. The futures market for all sorts of things is many centuries old, but the first organised exchange was created in Japan in the 1700s. This was so that samurais who were paid in rice at a future date could lock in the value they received. We can buy or sell a future on cocoa, grain, oil or whatever for months hence and avoid the issue of storage, delivery, etc. The price of the future will depend on the expectation of the future price of the commodity and the interest rate we can earn on the money in the interim. The futures contracts are settled through an exchange that ensures payment on expiry so that we don't have to worry about the person or company we are buying our future from or selling it to.

But like the other asset classes we have discussed in this chapter, the main issue with trading commodities is the absence of an edge. Do you really have the knowledge or advantage in the market to profit from trading commodities? Chances are that you don't unless you work in commodities and trade them for a living. If you don't, don't trade commodities.

As with property or alternatives, you already have a lot of commodity exposure through your portfolio of listed stocks. In the world stock market index are many mining or oil-related companies with large underlying direct exposures to commodities, and adding commodities to the portfolio would lead you to double up on the exposure. For example, if you were to buy oil in addition to owning it via all the oil companies in your equity index you would be adding to an already large exposure to that commodity, but it's often hard to figure out exactly how much hedging commodity-related companies do themselves and what your indirect exposure to commodities from owning shares in a company therefore is.

Returns from commodities

Perhaps we could turn the question on its head and ask which commodities you would want to buy exactly and why you want to deselect others. If you buy cocoa beans, then why not wheat? If you buy copper, then why not iron scraps? Those that pick the individual commodities clearly claim an edge.

Investors in commodities claim that lack of correlation with the equity markets makes commodities attractive. One of the oldest commodity indices is the CRB Commodity index which tracks the performance of 22 commodities and first started tracking in 1957. Figure 9.5 shows the 12-month trailing correlation with the S&P 500 since inception.

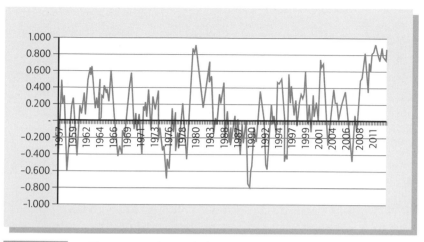

Figure 9.5   Trailing 12-month correlation between S&P 500 and CRB
Commodity index

As can be seen from the chart, commodities do indeed exhibit low correlation with the equity market, 2008 being a notable exception when they
plummeted with equities. (The index was down 36% in 2008, rendering
it a terrible hedge.)

But should we expect to make money from commodities?

Spanning only a couple of decades, the organised price history[4] of commodities is probably too short to be meaningful but Figure 9.6 shows a chart of
the CRB Total Return index[5] – this index was not created until the early
1980s – compared to an investment in US short-term bonds. This index
does not include the implementation cost which I have included at 0.5% a
year for the commodity index, more or less in line with current ETF costs.

It is not surprising that many advisers advocated investments in commodities until the crash of 2008. In the preceding decade, commodities had
performed strongly with a history of low correlation to the equity markets.

---

4 There is obviously a millennia-long price history of commodities, but to my
   knowledge not in an aggregated index that can be replicated in financial products
   like ETFs or mutual funds.
5 The total return index includes interest on the 'free' cash when investing in
   futures. The collateral on a futures contract is typically 5–10%, leaving 90–95%
   of capital free to be invested. The assumption is that this money is invested in
   treasury bills.

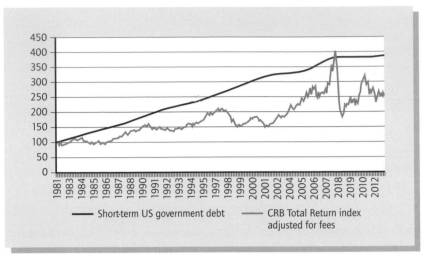

Figure 9.6   Commodity index versus short-term US government debt

But you can't get rich on low correlation; you need income and commodities are not income generating. Over the longer run, commodities trail the minimal risk rate of return and there is no reason to think that they will do so consistently in future. Because of that, and because you already have a lot of the same exposure through the existing portfolio, you should not include commodities in your rational portfolio.

Gold as a special case?

Gold has of course been a very public success story with the price per ounce well above $1,500, up from around $40 in the early 1970s when the US abandoned the gold standard. Gold does not have as much production use as some other metals and commodities, other than as jewellery and to some extent in electronics, but it has always been seen as a great preserver of value in times of distress.

If you want to avoid risk you should buy more of the minimal risk asset, and not buy gold. Gold is certainly not a low-risk asset – it is in fact very volatile in value. What attracts people to holding gold is the perception that it tends to move up in value when markets go down. It is therefore considered a hedge to the stock market or general economic/political turmoil.

I would caution you against viewing gold holdings as a hedge against stock market declines. If the stock market and the price of gold really moved

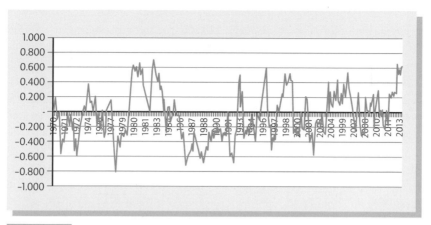

Figure 9.7 Trailing 12-month correlation between S&P 500 and gold price

in opposite directions (they do not – see Figure 9.7) and you had equal amounts invested in both, then in an economic decline you would make as much from the rise of gold as you would from the decline of the stock markets, and vice versa when markets were good. The only difference is that you would have paid expenses on your gold holdings as well as minor ones on your equity holdings. In that case you would have minimised your risk, but also your profits, and still be left with your expenses. Instead of having equity and gold exposures off-setting each other, you would have been better off just buying minimal risk bonds.

While the price of gold will continue to be volatile and perhaps even go up, as with the case of other commodities there is nothing intrinsic to suggest that gold as an investment will do better than the minimal risk rate, so I would suggest that you keep it out of your rational portfolio.

Private investments (or 'angel' investing)

In my personal life, the main way I differ from investing like the rational portfolio is through private investments. I'm incredibly lucky to have a group of talented friends and acquaintances who are doing very exciting things with their careers. Because of my background in hedge funds and finance, a large portion of this group is involved with finance, but certainly not all. Some are involved with various technology or related businesses. And quite frequently I'm approached to invest money as friends or acquaintances start something new or expand an existing business.

Private investments are perhaps an area of finance where we can slightly suspend the rational investment thinking. If you are approached by a friend to invest in his business you may have a lot of insight that other investors do not have. You know a lot about the principal and his history. You will also have heard him talk about the investment before he was trying to sell it to you so you have more of the real story. It could also well be that you are one of only a handful of people who was approached to invest money in the venture. As a result there is no real 'market' for the investment, but if there is then perhaps you are the investor with the most edge in that market. Since it's essentially the presence of an active market for securities that leads to a price that we don't think we can predict better, in the absence of that market there could be an opportunity for investing at favourable prices.

I was recently asked to put money into a New York-based private company that makes face recognition technology. A very snazzy presentation of how they will revolutionise social websites and everything else followed. The management team seemed very credible and knew the technology and the market very well. My main concern and reason I passed on the investment was that I felt that I was the one-thousandth person to be presented with the opportunity to invest. I also felt that most of the other 999 people who had passed on the investment were better positioned to gauge the viability of this company. This could be because they understood the technology or competition. Perhaps they could even write code and were able to look at the source code for the technology, which I can't. There was also the issue of why they needed money from a London-based non-technical person in order to make a New York-based technology firm thrive – didn't any of the locals want to do it? In short, I felt at a competitive disadvantage to others who had looked at but passed on the investment, and I did the same as a result. There was no edge.

There is unfortunately not a great amount of good and reliable data on private investments (outside the more institutional methods like venture capital, etc.). Many involved with private investments are notoriously bad at sharing performance data with the wider world. This is probably because many high-net-worth investors are reluctant to share information about their private portfolios, although exposure to the tax authorities may also play a role.

Poor information non-withstanding, according to a recent survey of studies on angel investing[6] the average annual return to angel investors was 27.3%,

6 'Historical Returns in Angel Markets' by David Lambert from Right Side Capital Management www.growthink.com/HistoricalReturnofAngelInvestingAssetClass.pdf.

which is obviously phenomenal. I would, however, suggest that there is an extremely heavy selection bias (only good results get reported, or people start reporting only after getting good results), and that if you had blindly invested in all angel deals the returns would have been substantially lower and perhaps fairly unimpressive. The report also states that 5–10% of the investments make most of the profits and the majority fail.

We all live in hope of being the first investor into the next Google or Facebook, but reality is probably far less glamorous. For most investors, making that investment has the probability of a lottery ticket even as many recount their near misses. But of course some people have become rich buying lottery tickets. I was president of the Harvard Club featured in the movie about Facebook (*The Social Network*) and knew people close to the founders. The endless 'could have/would have/should have' stories have inevitably followed.

Generally, and beyond the scope of this book, here are a few things to think about if you are considering potential private investments:

■ **Edge** Are you in the analytical or informational position where you are the right person to be making this investment? A private investment may be a bit like buying a lottery ticket – a bad idea if you have average odds, but potentially interesting if you can better your odds somehow. But someone who is without an edge or advantage who blindly invested in every private deal that came her way would see a queue of people trying to take her money and would soon run out.

■ **Portfolio** How does the investment fit in with your other assets? Would it tend to go wrong at the same time as everything else? Is it related to your job or area you live in? If you have several of them do they represent a substantial portion of your assets that may act similarly to each other?

■ **What do you invest?** A lot of private investments become very time consuming in addition to the money invested. Are you getting paid for the time and expertise? Of course you may think it's fun and could lead to future opportunities.

■ **Liquidity** Private investments tend to be very illiquid and there will often be no 'bid' for your stake. At least for short-term financial planning you should probably treat a private investment as 'dead' money.

■ **High failure rate** There may only be a 5–10% success rate in angel/private type deals. While the pay-out in case of success may be great you should be ready to lose the entire investment. Think about how this extremely high risk/return profile will affect your portfolio and investing life in general.

If you overcome some of the issues involved in making private investments there are some potential great advantages including:

- There are often tax advantages to private venture-type investing, particularly in development or clean tech sectors. Use them!
- You can use your expertise and skillset to add to your profits.
- Depending on the investment there are potentially large pay-outs that an investor investing in broad indices will not have in general (markets don't go up 100 times). In a book that is extremely anti-get-rich-quick, for the lucky/skilful few, private investments can offer the rare exception.
- If private investments are not dependent on general economic conditions, etc. they may be a good diversifier to the rest of your portfolio where the various assets will generally be correlated.
- If you make a private investment, despite being a rational and cautious investor, you will probably only do so after long study and serious consideration. This will probably serve you well. Good luck!

Collectibles

Occasionally there will be news about the sale of a painting for an eye-watering sum, triggering a discussion about collectibles as an investment. Collectibles can mean lots of things, but often include art, coins, vintage cars, antiques, coins and stamps – but also esoteric things like sports memorabilia, books or netsuke.[7]

The issue with collectibles as a financial investment is that it is hard to buy an index type of exposure to a broad range of them. You can't typically buy one-thousandth of a Renoir painting, only the leg of an antique chair or a sip of a fine wine. You are forced to pick individual items. If you are

---

7 *The Hare with Amber Eyes* by Edmund de Waal traces the history of a family netsuke collection through a century of tumult. Perhaps far-fetched, but a lesson from the book is how the netsuke maintain monetary and emotional value as the world collapses around them.

a great expert in a collectibles field then that may be a profitable venture, but if you are not, then chances are it is a losing proposition even if in some places there are tax benefits from owning art. You can, of course buy shares in fund-like structures, but even these only buy a small sub-set of the market.

While there are certain indices that suggest that art has been a great investment,[8] they suffer from a few shortcomings. For one, the studies often focus on segments of the art world that have been successful, suggesting selection bias, and are typically not easily replicable, so gaining exposure to them is not feasible. Also, many indices and the past performance of collectibles ignore the large transactional costs, insurance and storage costs. When you include all of these costs the return from collectibles is far less obvious, and you should not include them in the financial part of your portfolio.

There are, of course, non-economic reasons for buying collectibles. On top of the hope for a financial return, investors in a painting could derive great value from looking at it or reading a first edition book. Similarly, a stamp collector or someone driving in vintage car rallies may derive great pleasure or prestige from ownership. On a larger scale who had heard of Roman Abramovich or Mansour bin Zayed (owner of Chelsea and Manchester City football clubs respectively) before they bought their clubs? I don't think either expects to make money from ownership. Their objectives were perhaps prestige and having fun, both achieved in abundance if you ask me. And to that end they have spent the equivalent amount of their net worth to that of an average person buying a bicycle.

The non-economic benefit from owning collectibles obviously depends greatly on the individual and is very hard to quantify. Since most people gain some non-economic benefit from owning the asset, if you are purely a financial investor you will probably be disappointed. Perhaps a better way to think about collectibles is to be sure that you collect something you enjoy and that you are at least a reasonable expert. Combining the financial and non-economic gain from the investment may make it a worthwhile undertaking.

---

8 See for example www.artasanasset.com

three

Tailoring and implementing the rational portfolio

10

Financial plans and the risks we take

Any financial planner worth his or her salt will tell you that the amount of money that you have to spend in retirement will depend mainly on the amount of money you start with, how much you contribute to your savings, the rate of return on your assets and the taxes you pay.

But let's get concrete. As an example, suppose we wanted to find out how much we have to put aside each year to live comfortably in retirement. I will cover the opportunities and issues with pension plans and insurance-related savings products like annuities later, but for now assume you are saving up and have the luxury of ignoring tax.

Building your savings

Suppose you are 30 years old and have savings of £10,000 after finally paying off your student loan. Let's say you expect to work until you are 67, and plan to be able to put aside £10,000 a year in today's money (so real numbers) for your retirement. To be comfortable in retirement you think you'll need £20,000 a year in today's money (inflation will make the future number bigger but be equivalent to £20,000 of purchasing power today) on top of other pensions (e.g. the state pension) you have and you expect to live to 90.

Because you are a prudent person you have decided that the way forward is to put half your savings into the minimal risk asset and the other half into world equities. To ensure that the ratio between the minimal risk asset and equities does not get too out of kilter you plan to rebalance the portfolio every year to ensure that the split is 50/50 at the start of the year. The plan is then to move everything (i.e. 100% of your portfolio) to minimal risk assets when you are 67 and will start needing the money.

You may expect to make 0.5% on the minimal risk asset and 5% on the equities (0.5% + 4.5% equity risk premium) before minor fees. While the risk of the equity return has more frequent extreme outcomes than suggested by standard statistics – called fat tails – the annual standard deviation (SD) of that equity return is probably in the range of 20%. Taking into account these fat tails we increase our standard deviation assumption to 25% (a simplification).

To get an idea of the probabilities of having enough money in retirement here is a relatively simple excel model. The inputs are summarised as follows:

	Minimal risk	Equities
Expected net returns	0.50%	5.00% real returns
Standard deviation	0.00%	25.00%
Reallocation cost (trading)	0.25%	0.25%
Annual fees	0.15%	0.30%
Tax	None assumed	

In/outflows	Annual	No. years	Total
Starting amount:			10,000
Contributions:	12,000	38	456,000
Withdrawals:	−20,000	23	−460,000

You expect to live to age 90 and wish to withdraw £20,000 in today's money each year after you turn 67, so you will be withdrawing a total of £460,000 for your 23 years of retirement spending. Taking into account that you will make 0.5% on your investment in the minimal risk asset even in retirement you 'only' need approximately £434,000 in assets when you turn 67 to have enough money. This is of course excluding the fact that you probably want to have a buffer of additional money in case you live to be more than 90 (unlike an annuity, the buffer is not 'lost' when you die – it goes to your descendants)

So will you have enough? Well that depends on the volatility of the equity markets. The results are striking and highlight some important points.

I set up the model to re-run itself 1,000 times with the equity returns generated by a random function. Basically I told the computer to play this game 1,000 times where the return on average was 5% per year, but that this return should vary with a standard deviation of 25%. (Chapter 6 on risk discussed how this is roughly what risk has been in the past, and explained what that meant.) In roughly 68% of the cases the return on equities will be within a range of −20% to +30% (one standard deviation from the mean; average of 5% return and then add or subtract 25% depending whether it is a negative or positive 1 standard deviation move).

The 1,000 iterations of the model reveal greatly varying results. If equity markets are good between now and your retirement you will have far more money than you planned to spend. However, if equity markets between now and retirement are bad, the savings are far from enough to cover the future outgoings and you potentially have a serious problem. The results from the iterations are as follows:

	Age 90	Age 80	Age 67
Median	227,463	416,349	653,083
Average	342,081	527,031	758,940
Minimum	−281,350	−74,994	182,876
Maximum	3,569,477	3,643,613	3,741,168

The numbers above represent the outcomes of the 1,000 iterations and are based on the inputs above. The only thing that makes the outcomes vary so much is the impact of having the equity returns vary in risk by a standard deviation of 25% per year (more or less in line with what would equity markets have experienced).

The point I am trying to make is that the uncertainty of equity returns can lead to very large fluctuations in outcomes over a long time horizon and that you as an investor need to be aware of that and plan for it in your financial planning. Depending on how strong or weak equity markets are between now and retirement you might have less than half the money you need, or almost 10 times as much as you need. Those are pretty wild swings, brought about by decades of taking risk in the equity markets. I'm obviously not saying that you should rigidly stick to the strategy above, but the point remains that long-term financial planning can lead to a wide range of outcomes once you introduce risk into the portfolio.

Expected outcomes

If we are as lucky (or unlucky) as the average person we would expect to have the median amount of money, not the average. This has to do with the average versus compounded returns. Suppose two people over a two-year period had the following return profiles:

▶

	Year 1	Year 2	Average
Person A	5.00%	5.00%	5.00%
Person B	−20.00%	30.00%	5.00%

These people would have had the same average return. But when you compare the returns at the end of the two-year period the person with the least variation in her returns has the higher cumulative returns:

	Year 0	Year 1	Year 2
Person A	100.00	105.00	110.25
Person B	100.00	80.00	104.00

Simply put, this is the same scenario as in our example above. Because the returns vary greatly from year to year, the aggregate return at retirement will be lower with volatile returns than if we had been able to secure the average return every year.[1] While beyond the scope of this book, this realisation that as an investor you will over time fare worse than the compounding of your average returns is a critical and often neglected part of finance. You can't eat average returns – you eat compounding ones.[2]

1 On Youtube you can find a brief and instructive video called 'Geometric vs. Arithmetic Average Returns'.
2 There are a surprisingly large number of books and articles that seem to neglect this issue. A typical example will be an illustration that talks about $1,000 invested making an average of 5% a year so that after 30 years you will have made $4,320, ignoring the fact that high volatility in the yearly returns could significantly reduce the final value.

So, in returning to our model where we ran 1,000 iterations, the outcome we should expect if we are exactly in the middle is the median, not the average. If this was 1,000 outcomes, then we should expect the 500th, or median outcome.

Figure 10.1 shows the amount of money in our investment account at the age of 67, and the percentage of iterations that fall within various bands.

A couple of things are probably obvious about the graph:

■ Most cases cluster around the median return, but there are also a few very positive outcomes where we end up millionaires.

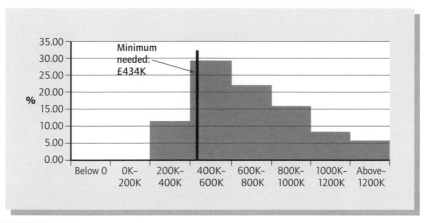

Figure 10.1 Amount in investment account at age 67 and percentage of iterations falling within various bands

- There are a high number of outcomes where we were unlucky and ended up with savings short of what we needed for retirement.

In my view, this second point is critical and goes to the heart of investment management and the risks we are willing to take with our financial lives.

As outlined above, we need to have accumulated approximately £434,000 by the time we are 67 in order to be able to withdraw £20,000 a year until we are 90. We also know that in the average (median) case we would have assets far in excess of that requirement. But now we also know that in a large number of cases our savings will fall short of that required:

Cases above £434K: 81.2%
Cases below £434K: 18.8%

So in nearly 19% of cases you will not have enough money for your retirement goals.

To most people a probability of approximately 20% that you will fail to meet your goals would cause great concern, particularly as you probably want some sort of additional reserve in case you live past 90. But what can you do about it?

As a rational investor, the worst thing you can do is to abandon your principles and pursue the promises of higher returns from various active managers or investment schemes. While you may get lucky, on average it would only make the situation worse.

In effect we have a few choices:

- We can contribute more annually.
- We can start with a higher amount.
- We can accept a lower annual amount in retirement.
- We can shift the mix between the minimal risk and equity to lower our risk, but at the expense of a lower expected asset base at the age of 67.

The super-cautious saver

If you are unwilling to take any risk that your savings fall short in retirement you could invest only in the minimal risk asset and your savings at age 67 would be £497,000, and far in excess of the £434,000 needed. By allocating some money to equities your expected savings would go up, and while that extra money would surely be nice to have it comes with a risk that there will not be enough. The greater proportion you allocated to equity, the more your median savings will be, but you will also increase the risk of falling short. The security of allocating entirely to the minimal risk asset comes at the expense of having significantly lower expected assets at 67 than if you had allocated some assets to equities – but that is a choice you have.[3]

If we had done the same exercise and found that our retirement savings fall short when investing only in the minimal risk asset we would have been faced with some tough choices. The way you respond to this shortfall relates to your personal attitudes towards risk:

- You could contribute more to your portfolio on an on-going basis if you are fortunate enough to be able to do so, or find a way to have a larger initial amount.
- If you are very risk averse you may not be willing to accept any risk with your retirement funds and simply accept a lower annual retirement pot.
- If you increase the equity allocation, the additional expected returns from equities will increase the chance that you have enough money for

---

3 If you wanted minimal risk you should buy inflation-adjusted government bonds with maturities similar to when you will start needing the money. In this case, that would involve some of the longest-dated bonds available, which typically carry a higher yield than the 0.5% used in this example.

retirement. But while you increase the chance of achieving the target savings and on average will have more money in retirement, you do so at the expense of potentially incurring a greater shortfall in the cases where future equity markets are bad.

Risk/return

We can use the example above to get a sense of the price we pay for the surety of having enough money at retirement.

In the 50% minimal risk/50% equity case we would expect to have approximately £653,000, while the minimal risk only portfolio would give us £497,000. A difference of over £150,000 to use in our retirement! And the cost of that expected additional amount? Accepting that there is roughly an 18% risk that you will not have enough money to take out £20,000 a year in retirement.

The decision whether those additional expected assets is worth the risk of a shortfall in retirement often depends on personal circumstances. What will be the impact on your life of falling short of assets in retirement? Will this be catastrophic or just a mild annoyance? Hard to tell. Similarly, what will be the impact on your life of having significant excess funds? Will it make you happier? Does it mean that you can afford a better life for your children than you had yourself? Or perhaps you can leave them with a nest-egg that you could not otherwise afford.

Below are the results of running the iterations with various fractions of the assets invested in the minimal risk asset:

Minimal risk portion	100%	90%	80%	70%	60%	50%
% shortfall cases	0.0%	0.5%	6.5%	9.1%	14.5%	18.8%
Median assets at age 67	497,000	536,000	576,000	604,000	633,000	653,000
Fifth percentile	497,000	468,000	420,000	392,000	352,000	317,000

The bottom line of the table illustrates the amount of assets we are left with in the fifth per cent worst outcome, or every twentieth case. It is no surprise that the fifth percentile number gets worse as we increase the equity portion. With the higher expected returns from equities come the higher risk and the 5% worse cases therefore get progressively worse as we increase the equity allocation.

An unfortunate soul caught out by the drop

It's 2007 and my friend had liquid savings of $500,000. She had decided that to live comfortably in retirement and to pay for the remaining years of her child's education, she needed $425,000. She was a couple of years from retirement so the potential to add to savings from her current job was limited. Because of what might be perceived as the attractive risk/return profile of the stock market she had half her money in an equity index fund abroad and the other half in government bonds. Given the low expected risk of the market at the time it seemed like a sensible and conservative allocation – also, while she *needed* $425,000 she could find a good use for any extra!

Now it's March 2009 and my friend is panicking. Her savings are down to $375,000 as she has lost about half on her equities, while the bonds are roughly flat. But not only has she lost 25% of her assets, her adviser tells her that now equities are super risky and that she could easily lose more.

Should she cut her losses and adjust her life choices to a lower quality of life, stay the course and consider this a large bump in the road? Or perhaps even double down and shift some assets from governments bonds into equities, in order to recoup the losses?

A lot of people found themselves in some version of this scenario at the peak of the panic.

Generalising the examples

Like any financial model this is the case of rubbish in, rubbish out. Models are only as good as the assumptions you put into them. The model above is based on some pretty generic assumptions about risk and return, and only incorporates the minimal risk asset and equities. You might disagree with those assumptions and be more aggressive about your return expectations or risk. You may want to run the model assuming 0% real return from your minimal risk asset in line with the current market, or introduce some risk to the return of the minimal risk asset.[4] Or you could move away from having a 50/50 allocation to minimal risk assets/equities in the portfolio, depending on your risk tolerances.

---

4 As you increase the risk of the minimal risk asset the importance of introducing correlation with your equity investment increases. This is a complication I have left out.

Instead of continuing to adapt a financial planning example that may not be entirely relevant to your financial planning needs, I would encourage you to do this kind of financial analysis yourself or to get someone to help you with it. You can do financial modelling in Excel, in Google Drive or use one of the many financial software packages available. In any case, make sure you spend enough time figuring out how everything fits together, and confirm that the model fits your specific needs.

It could be that you want to get an overview of what $100,000 invested in equities would get you in 10 years' time with the same assumptions on risks and returns (see Figure 10.2). Or it could be that you want to figure out the probability that the money you have put aside for your children's education will suffice. You might be an insurance company or pension fund that wants to find the probability of having enough funds to meet your future liabilities. The list is endless.

In any case, building a financial model that considers the range of potential outcomes will probably spark your thinking about the impact that the various outcomes will have. Take the model and amend it to roughly suit your situation. Then start playing with the inputs, assumptions and allocations:

■ Have you been too conservative/taken too much risk?

■ Could you bear bad equity markets in the decades ahead – what if they are riskier?

■ How much is your situation likely to change in future? How will that impact on your risk profile?

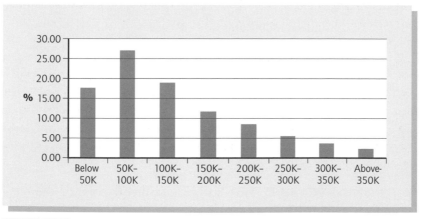

Figure 10.2 $100,000 invested in equity markets after a 10-year period

- Is it possible that your financial goals are incompatible with the risk you are comfortable taking?
- What is the lowest 5% of outcomes? Lowest 2%? Could you handle it? Would you be willing to accept that you could fall short in one out of 20 cases? One out of 50? Never?
- Do you have a 'drop dead' level of assets that you simply are not willing to fall below? How does that dictate your allocations?
- As 'touchy-feely' as it sounds, try to feel what would happen in various cases. What does your gut tell you? How would it affect how you sleep at night? Your career? Your marriage?
- What would happen to your other assets, job, etc. at the same time as any fall in the markets? Would they reinforce what is happening to you or offer respite?

Investing time in understanding the risks of your portfolio or financial goals is a worthwhile undertaking whether through a model like this or any other means. Even in the scenario when you don't change your thinking or portfolio as a result, the increased understanding will probably lower the emotional strain of adverse events. You have an idea of what might happen and what the consequences could be for you.

A few important points to remember when using a model like the one above:

- The model is very simple and built with some very basic assumptions, but be cautious about those that add lots of products with high returns and low correlations. This will enable people to come up with much better risk/return outcomes, but as rational investors we do not think it can be done (indeed rubbish in, rubbish out).
- The model does not incorporate corporate bonds and government bonds that could be a worthwhile addition to the simple rational portfolio. This is a simplification. Incorporating those two asset classes would involve estimating correlations between them and equities, which is a science in itself (and a constantly moving number). Besides, adding other government and corporate bonds is not a magic bullet for the portfolio; while those asset classes are good diversifying additions to the portfolio they are not without risk.
- The model is very sensitive to the inputs, particularly on risk, and does not account for some of the issues with using standard deviation to gauge risk that was discussed earlier (in Chapter 6). Changing the

inputs would make a massive difference to the range of outputs. If you do change the inputs, make sure you understand why – don't make 'nicer' assumptions just because you like the results better. The expected real return on equities will not be 10% a year just because you put it in a spreadsheet.

■ Keep in mind that all the returns are real returns. So the model is in today's money. Clearly the actual numbers decades from now will look very different because of inflation.

Keeping it real

If we have got to the point where we have built a financial model that reflects our situation and implemented our investment plan by purchasing the right products (see Chapter 14 on products and implementation) we are doing really well. Unfortunately that is not the end of it.

We have to keep an eye on our portfolio and financial model and adapt it to changing circumstances and, if nothing else, then the passage of time. Imagine a scenario where the market has moved up 50% in a year. As we look at our financial planning we would be remiss if we didn't somehow take our new and improved financial situation into account in our forward planning. It could be that with our higher asset base we are able to reach long-term financial goals with a far lower risk.

When we periodically look at our portfolio in the context of our overall financial health it may also be that our personal circumstances have changed, which in turn could affect our financial plans – we were promoted, fired, received an inheritance, got divorced, the uninsured car was stolen, our tax circumstances changed, etc. It all matters. How often we do this kind of review is a personal decision, but at minimum you should aim for yearly or whenever there has been great turbulence in the financial markets or your personal life. Since you should rebalance the portfolio periodically anyway that would be a good time to review its composition. I'll come back to rebalancing later.

Reacting to disaster

In the aftermath of the 2008–09 financial crisis many investors were understandably left aghast. Many had lost far more money in their portfolios than they thought possible, and often did so as their house and other assets also plummeted in value. The gut reaction for many investors was to sell their equity exposure at or near the bottom of the markets, only to miss out on the great rally that followed. 'A familiar story of retail investors abandoning their plans', some financial planners lamented.

I don't think things are that simple. During crashes like 2008 there is a natural tendency for everyone to have a view on the markets. The markets will dominate the headlines and be a topic of conversation at work, the gym, meals out, in homes and everywhere else. How can you not have a view?

The point is that we still don't have a view. While many people with the benefit of hindsight say they saw the rebound, 'just' because there is great market turbulence does not mean that an investor is better able to predict market movements. We don't consider ourselves smarter than the average dollar invested in the market, and that average dollar put the S&P 500 at an index value of under 700 in March 2009. The fact that four years later we see that same index trading around its all-time highs does not mean that we could predict in March 2009 that this would be the case.

When you look back at the 2008–09 crises or any crises preceding it, many people have a sense that there is a bottom somewhere, and great profits to be made for investors who find the bottom. And clearly that has often been the case. If you had stayed the course or invested more at exactly the right point in March 2009 (or July 1932) you would have made a lot of money. But you obviously did not know that then. For all you knew at the time, March 2009 was just a precursor to a really bad decline in the market, and you were scared to death. There is no guarantee that markets bounce back after a decline. Just ask investors who bought Russian equities in 1917 …

But that does not mean that there is nothing you can do. First of all, after bad declines in the market it is likely that the future riskiness of the market has gone up a lot in the general turmoil. While that does not give market direction at least you can prepare yourself for the increased risk. Those willing to bear the extra risk will probably see commensurate higher expected returns, but they have to be willing to accept that a lot of money could also be lost.

We know that losses like those in 2008–09 do happen with some frequency and it is at times like these that you hope to benefit from having had a conservative allocation policy, instead of selling your holdings in desperation.

In any case there are no easy fixes and we are faced with a few unpleasant alternatives:

- We can find a way to put more money aside in savings.
- We can accept a lower amount in retirement or the same amount for a shorter time period.
- We can reallocate between the minimal risk asset and equities if the large decreases have affected the risk we are willing to take with our portfolio.

Though it sounds like annoying hindsight, investment allocations are about ensuring that you don't find yourself in the position of making panic sales to start with. Have enough of a buffer so that you avoid selling equities at what might be the bottom of the markets. Over the long run, equity markets are likely to far exceed government bond returns, but they will also be far more volatile and periodically lose you a lot. Make sure your allocations allow for that.

A few ways to think about portfolio allocations

Here are some suggestions:

- **Drop dead allocation** If you need £100 for heart surgery, don't buy equities with your last £105. Have enough money in the minimal risk asset so that you certainly have enough in the short term, and only then start adding equities.
- **Pick a return point and see if you can handle the risk** You may expect 0.5% per year from the minimal risk asset and a premium to that of 4–5% from a broad equity index, both after inflation. You can pick the return point you are after, and then figure out the risk required to achieve your goals (see Figure 10.3).

  A word of caution: if you borrow money to achieve higher returns than those from equities keep in mind that those loans tend to get recalled exactly at the worst time and lock in your losses.

- **Pick a risk point and see what returns you can expect** How much risk you can handle is subject to your personality and individual circumstances. You can work out your worst 1%, 2%, 5%, 10%, etc.

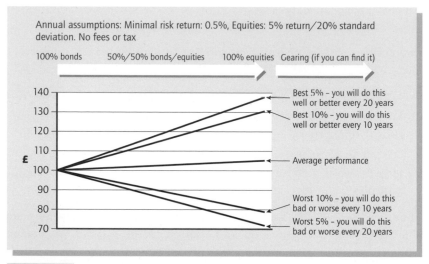

Annual assumptions: Minimal risk return: 0.5%, Equities: 5% return/20% standard deviation. No fees or tax

100% bonds   50%/50% bonds/equities   100% equities   Gearing (if you can find it)

Best 5% – you will do this well or better every 20 years

Best 10% – you will do this well or better every 10 years

Average performance

Worst 10% – you will do this bad or worse every 10 years

Worst 5% – you will do this bad or worse every 20 years

Figure 10.3 What can you expect at the end of the year from £100 invested on 1 January of the same year

scenarios to see what various portfolios look like, and get an idea of the risk you are willing to take. Put this in the context of the consequences of failing to reach your financial goal and guide your allocations that way.

■ **Think about the flexibility of your financial goals** As you consider your portfolio allocations it is worth keeping in mind what is implied by the end portfolio value you are trying to achieve. Does your goal suggest the minimum of financial survival or meeting a firm liability with its nasty potential consequences of failure? Or does your target really suggest more of a 'nice to have' lifestyle pot of assets? These considerations should play into the risk you take with the portfolio.

■ **Think about avoiding temptation** Set your portfolio up so you have some flexibility in case the markets move unexpectedly. Reallocations are costly and retail investors are notorious for selling their equity holdings at the worst time. Generally avoid trading in and out of things excessively – it's costly and will significantly reduce long-term returns.

■ **Use market experience** Think about how you react to losing money as the markets inevitably drop on occasion. If you can't sleep at night for worry about the future or sell after the decline then your equity allocation is probably too high. On the other hand, if you think 'that's nothing' and want to add more equities then you were probably too risk averse in your allocations. Sometimes it can be hard to know exactly how you will feel until the moment happens, and it can be hard to predict how other parts of your life would be affected by a drop in the markets.

▪ **Impact of non-financial assets and liabilities** As you think about the risk in your investment portfolio, consider how other assets and liabilities are affected by the same factors. Make sure that not too many bad things can happen to you at once, both from a value and liquidity perspective. Should the world equity markets experience a calamity, it is possible that the value of your house, job (an equity broker will be affected more than a civil servant, etc.), and other assets all decline at the same time. Those things are not as liquid as the rational portfolio. Be sure to avoid a distress sale of your only liquid asset (the rational portfolio) in bad markets by minimising illiquid assets that all drop in value at the same time. Meanwhile, your liabilities are often more fixed.

It is often a great idea to put your portfolio objectives and risk tolerances into words in a simple 'portfolio mission statement'. Unless you are so inclined, the statement does not have to be accompanied by a picture of a soaring eagle, but be something for you to look at occasionally, and particularly as your circumstances change. It helps to think of why you are saving up or allocating between equity and bonds and the maturity profile of those bonds. It could also be helpful for you to put into words how you would react and feel about bad things happening in your portfolio. If nothing else, this forces you to think about how you would react to various scenarios and potentially restructure your portfolio as a consequence of something not sitting right with you.

Stages of life

Your age will be a big factor in how you allocate your portfolio.

Early savers

It is generally the case that younger savers allocate a greater portion of their portfolio to riskier assets. They are in the early stages of saving and the cumulative benefits of even a small expected outperformance from a slightly riskier asset can add up to a large amount over the coming decades. Also, should markets be bad early on, savers have decades before they need the money and more time either for the investments to make up the shortfall, or for them to adapt their lifestyles or savings rate. My advice to you: take risk with your savings and put lots in the equity markets, be ready to lose a lot of it, but also keep enough in the bank so that you can afford a crisis. It's a good time to learn about the markets and how you deal with the risks. You should also familiarise yourself with all the tax benefits that might arise from pensions or other savings (such as ISAs in the UK). Getting into the habit of saving up and maintaining the discipline to stick with it is something that will serve you very well, particularly as you begin to see the cumulative gains from being a saver.

Mid-life savers

Once you enter the 30s and 40s you pass into the ranks of the mid-life savers. You might be at your prime in terms of earnings power and starting to get a good sense of how things will turn out careerwise. For many mid-life savers, tax considerations will play a major role in the execution of their portfolio, and many will want to allocate a greater fraction to the minimal risk asset, perhaps in longer-term bonds, than they did a decade or so earlier. Whilst these savers have accumulated some savings, the potential added return from allocating to equities is still important in reaching their financial goals in retirement. And should the equity markets be bad in future there are still some working years to address the losses from those investments, either by saving up more and reducing current spending, expecting to work longer or reducing expected retirement spending. At this point in your life savings cycle you might start to get a sense of what your expenses in retirement will look like, and perhaps how many income-earning years you have left before retiring.

In terms of practically shifting your investments from equities into lower-risk assets as you age I would encourage you to do this as you either put money into your savings or take money out anyhow, as that reduces trading costs and potentially taxes.

Retirees

At the other end of the spectrum is someone already in retirement. Particularly those without a great amount of savings to see them through their remaining years typically have a far lower risk tolerance as there are fewer options to make up a shortfall if markets turn against them. At the risk of over-simplifying, if you don't share the upside of having more savings (with limited years left to enjoy them), but would experience the painful downside, then don't take risk and stay with minimal risk bonds. Of course estate planning and passing on assets to the next generation will play a major role here in terms of the exact structuring of your portfolio. Also think about what non-investment income you can expect in the form of company pensions, social security, etc. and compare that to your expected outgoings. The difference between the two will need to come from investment income, or liquidating part of your portfolio. While many rules of thumb don't apply universally, if you stick to only spending 4% of your portfolio a year, you will probably be fine (you can increase that percentage as you grow older).

For those in retirement I would encourage you to get ready for the day when you can no longer handle your savings yourself, or even plan for eventually passing them on. Keep things simple; have only a couple of accounts and not too many investments, and make clear to whoever is going to take over the management of your assets how you want them managed and why.

For those retirees with savings in excess of what they need, the risk profile of the portfolio may be different. These retirees are no longer only investing for their own needs, but also for the longer-term needs of their descendants or whoever the assets will be going to. Since the time horizon for those descendants can be much longer term, the portfolio could well include some equities and a generally riskier profile than if it was just for the retirees.

It really does depend on your circumstances

Like most things in investing, allocations are highly subject to individual circumstances and risk tolerance. Figure 10.4 shows how an investor's allocations may change over his or her life, ignoring the complication of risky government and corporate bonds in the rational portfolio.

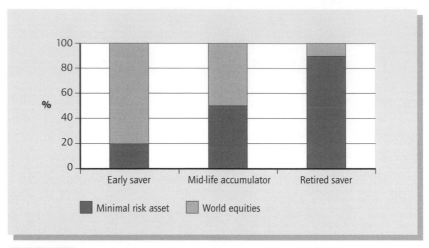

Figure 10.4 **Stages of life: moving from equities as you age**

Risk surveys

As discussed above, getting a handle on your risk tolerances is not only critical in investment management, but also a very individual thing. In my view, far too often investors rely on their gut feelings in deciding on the risk levels in their portfolios, or are guilty of what some call 'recency' where we over-emphasise recent events in planning for the future.

Risk surveys are increasingly common in the financial industry and are sometimes mandatory for companies taking on new clients. You find them at most banks, insurance companies, asset management firms or your local regulator. As suggested, they are meant to give you an idea about your risk tolerances, often via stress tests, but in my view risk surveys often leave a lot to be desired.

Risk surveys that I have completed are too simplistic to give a really detailed view of your risk profile, often because they don't ask enough questions about your specific situation. Sometimes I find that the surveys are a prelude to someone trying to sell me a specific 'tailor-made' product (read: expensive), instead of objectively trying to help me understand my risk tolerance. In addition, risk surveys often fail to properly incorporate all my other assets and liabilities, including seemingly odd ones like education, inheritance, future tuition for children, or other critical things like what stage of life I'm at regarding career or retirement. The surveys therefore often fail to get a full picture of my financial life and in my view suffer in quality as a result.

With the caveats listed above, I would still encourage you to undergo a few risk surveys and to be on the lookout for new and improved surveys. Particularly if you are someone who is not used to thinking about your risk profile in the financial markets it probably makes sense to try a few surveys either through your financial institution, your domestic regulator or one of the many you can find on the internet. Who knows, they may tell you something you hadn't thought about, or perhaps you will have added comfort from confirming what your gut feeling tells you – see Figure 10.5.

The understanding and integrated tailoring of risk profiles will be a future growth area in financial services. While a risk survey is only as good as the information you put into it, if there was a seamless way to integrate all major aspects of our life to provide a fuller risk picture then those results could be very helpful to individual investors. One day I imagine that risk surveys will be informed by an incredibly detailed profile of you based on your portfolio, annuities, insurance, credit card bill, LinkedIn/Facebook profile, where you holiday, your tax filings, how you drive your car, online games, if you tend to book flights last minute, the state of your marriage, and how you play golf, etc. While all that sounds distastefully intrusive I wouldn't be surprised if some IT companies already know most of it.

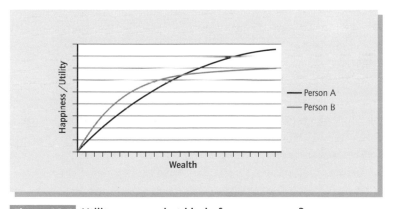

Figure 10.5 Utility curves: what kind of person are you?

A few rules of thumb

In researching this book I came across several publications on the topic of investment and savings which had rules of thumb that were pushed as gospel truths. While I think rules of thumb fail to incorporate individual circumstance and attitudes here are a few to consider:

- Your age in bonds (60 year old = 60% in bonds).

- Don't withdraw more than 4% of your portfolio a year in retirement.
- If you react badly to losing money in your portfolio, reduce the equity exposure by 10%. Keep doing that until you are OK with portfolio falls.
- Equity exposure = amount of years until retirement in percentage terms. So with 10 years to retirement your equity exposure should be 10%.
- Equity exposure = 120 – your age.
- Put aside 10% of income for retirement.
- The value of your house should be less than three times your annual income. (It was staggering to see how often and by how much this rule was broken particularly pre-crash.)
- Base your retirement needs on 100% of pre-retirement expenses plus 10%.
- Have at least 7–10 times your annual income in life insurance.
- Have at least 6–8 months of living expenses in cash in the bank.

Clearly these are exactly that, rules of thumb. Obviously these rules don't apply to everyone, or indeed most people (and some are even slightly contradictory). Instead, in this chapter I've tried to give you a sense of how to think about your individual risk and some ways to understand the probabilities of encountering tough conditions when saving.

Adding government and corporate bonds

In earlier chapters, I suggested that there could be merit in adding risky government and corporate bonds to the portfolio, but we have not incorporated them in the examples above. This is not out of neglect, but to keep the discussion above simple and practical. If we attempt to add risky government and corporate bonds to the excel model outlined earlier we would significantly add to its complexity and you would need to have a view on complex things like asset correlations. Taking an average correlation between risky government bonds, corporate bonds and equities would be too much of a simplification. During times of great distress, correlations between asset classes tend to go up (just like they do between various equity markets), and as we run the multiple scenarios we would need different correlations for different states of the equity markets, resulting in something like this:[5]

---

5 This is still a significant simplification. The correlations in the various return scenarios would be an average expected correlation. Since each crisis is unique there is no guarantee that the actual correlations would be like those in the table.

Equity return	Sub-AA government bond correlation	Corporate bond correlation
15%+	0.35	0.40
5% to 15%	0.28	0.32
−5% to 5%	0.22	0.28
−15% to −5%	0.34	0.38
Below −15%	0.55	0.67

What this adjustment incorporates is that the addition of risky government and corporate bonds adds less diversification when you need it the most, namely when equity markets are poor. Since the bonds I suggest adding here are sub-AA rated return generators, in a crisis they may not be seen as a 'flight to safety' and go up in value. Your minimal risk asset will probably be seen as a safe haven and increase in price.

At the risk of oversimplification, other government and corporate bonds will add less risk to the portfolio than equities, but will not be risk free. Depending on the exact mix of sub-AA government bonds you add, you could perhaps see the other government and corporate bonds as adding half the risk of equities, although realise that this more a guesstimate than a precise calculation.

Adding great complexity to the simple model misses the point that all this is far from an exact science. The point of the excel model is to show that even the best-laid plans are subject to market risk, and to point out how we can incorporate this element of chance in thinking about our portfolio allocations and planning. By making the model excessively complex we run the risk of giving a false sense of precision.

Tax

Benjamin Franklin famously said that death and taxes are the two certainties in life. The residents of Monaco may disagree, but for most people tax planning is an integral part of investment management.

A book on investments ignoring tax would be incomplete. With state finances around the world in tatters, taxes are going to be a bigger, not smaller issue. New taxes will be introduced, either to close former loopholes or simply to raise revenues. And with the sentiment in the general population being one of anger towards banks and the wider financial community, taxes will probably go up for this sector and the products it offers. What this means in individual jurisdictions will vary a great deal, but as an investor it's well worth understanding tax.

Let's remind ourselves that the point of the rational portfolio is that we have a more optimised, liquid, cheap and risk-adjusted portfolio. Those are undoubtedly good things. But if we construct that portfolio in a tax-inefficient manner, all our good intentions can quickly disappear.

In general the taxes I will refer to are:

- income tax, including taxes on dividends and coupons;
- capital gains tax (CGT): this covers a broad range and depending on jurisdiction will be greatly affected by the holding period and type of asset;
- transaction taxes, such as stamp duty in the UK;
- other taxes such as inheritance tax, corporation tax, taxes on gifts, etc.

Owing to its simple construction with a strong bias towards minimum turnover and very long-term holding periods, the rational portfolio is very tax-efficient for most people. Below are some of the most obvious tax benefits most people would realise from holding a rational portfolio:

Low turnover = less capital gains and transaction tax A passive investment product will have fewer trades than an active fund. This will typically lead to lower capital gains (including short-term ones often taxed at higher rates), but also fewer payments of transaction taxes such as stamp duty. In addition to tax, there are other obvious advantages such as trading costs associated with the low turnover.

Fewer fund changes = defer tax on gains into the future Related to the low turnover of securities in the fund, investors in index trackers also change funds far less frequently than investors in active funds. They are not chasing the next 'hot manager'. On top of the advantages of not constantly triggering 'one-off' or front-loaded charges in some active funds and avoiding higher fees, this has the tax advantage of deferring the tax on the gains.

Diversity of products = getting the right product to help reduce tax As the underlying securities in the rational portfolio consist of an extremely broad and easy-to-construct array of securities, product providers can easily create construct products that cater to specific investor needs. For example, some investors would prefer to have dividends reinvested in the fund rather than paid out. So instead of having an index tracker valued at $100 and receiving a $2 dividend, the index tracker would be valued at $102. For some investors there are large tax advantages with this kind of structuring. It is such dividend versus capital gains advantages that are among the features making some exchange traded funds (ETFs) tax efficient.

Jurisdiction = pick the right one for your investment product Should you be buying an ETF or index fund through a Dublin or Frankfurt listing of the same underlying exposure? Understand the tax implications of your choices as they can be very different for different investors. Since setting up an ETF in a new jurisdiction is not that costly, not that many investors need to demand it before a provider will meet the market demand. This issue of jurisdiction is one that is perhaps of overriding importance for some investors and not a big deal to others.[1]

Tax wrappers = because of a simple portfolio, tax wrappers and planning should be cheap Since the underlying product of the rational portfolio is relatively straightforward, potential tax saving wrappers should be

---

1 Some investors see the opportunity to invest in multiple jurisdictions as an opportunity not only to minimise current tax, but also as a way to be less liable to a sudden increase in taxes in one jurisdiction.

more transparent and cheaper. You are not paying for a complicated investment product, even if the specific tax structure is complex. If you find yourself investing in a film project to get a tax saving that may be fine, but it's probably not an investment you would have made without the wrapper and there is therefore an implicit additional cost of the tax structure.The rational portfolio is so simple and transparent that at least the investing part of your tax wrapper should be simple. This simplicity should give you greater transparency regarding any other charges you face in implementing the tax savings.

My mother bought some insurance-related savings products to reduce tax in the late 1980s. These products invested money in a portfolio of stocks, and had the advantage of saving her about 40% in tax on the money invested. It all looked good at the time, but my mother recently realised that there is absolutely no way to move the tax structure/wrapper away from the large Nordic bank it is with currently. Not that the tax wrapper legally requires it, but because the contract with the bank says so, and they won't let my mother move her business elsewhere. I think she has been overcharged at about 2.5% a year for over 20 years for a wrapper which consists of very normal equity investments. For decades the bank in question has essentially used the structure to tie in my mother as a very high fee-paying client. If instead she had received only the legal and tax advice and implemented the underlying investment as a separate matter there would have been massive savings relative to the expensive current structure. If my mother had used the rational portfolio as the baseline investment, instead of having the tax structure and investment product bought combined, it would be far more transparent what she is being charged for – in both advice and set-up fees – and she would realise that those costs are a small fraction of what she is being charged now.

Tax adviser or accountant

Tax planning is an area of investing where I highly recommend getting expert advice, if you have enough assets so that the cost of getting advice will be covered by the savings you can hope to achieve from the advice. I am a non-domiciled UK resident, being a Danish national. Over the years I have tried to keep track of applicable tax rules for myself, my family and the businesses I was involved with. After initially fancying myself a bit of an expert on the topic I soon gave up. The rules were changing too quickly and I had a day job to keep. I found myself in the situation where knowing things were 'sort of OK' was a bad solution, and that I was either not entirely sure that what I was doing was 100% correct, or I was not being particularly clever about it.

Keep in mind that at the end of the day the rational portfolio consists of a few relatively simple products. While the logic and theory of why it makes sense may be complex, the end result is not: it is simple. Taxes, however, are not simple.

On top of everything, taxes change continuously and it is your responsibility to ensure on-going compliance. By the time you read this, the optimised tax thinking at the time of writing may out of date, or even illegal.

Finding the right tax adviser may seem daunting. Below are a few things to ponder as you look at various candidates.

- Do they understand your situation and have experience of it?
- Are they transparent about how they make money from you – you don't want them to make commissions from any investment products they sell you. This additional indirect fee still happens to an unbelievable degree although rules are increasingly in place to prevent it, such as the UK retail distribution review that led to greater transparency in the charges you face from an adviser.
- Are the charges in line with the competition? What are the charges compared to the kind of tax savings you could hope to make? Do you get a sense that they charge less because they think they can sell you other products like special tax structures? If so that is a concern as they may not be entirely objective.
- Are they up to date on latest tax changes and how those affect you?
- Will they be with you for a while and understand your whole picture, potentially including family and inheritance tax issues?
- Do they have correct authorisations and membership of the right bodies? If not, why not?
- Is there good chemistry between you? Do they pass the gut test?
- Will they save you time and money?
- Can you talk to their existing clients for references?

A friend was making good money in a growing IT business. She paid her taxes and was more concerned with being a successful business woman than a tax planner. In the early days of the business she had been more preoccupied with making sales than optimising her company's tax structure, which she regretted now things were going well as it was hard to change the tax structure. She recently succumbed to the relentless persistence of some people that wanted to help her minimise taxes. A whole new and complex world showed itself. She knew that it would be a labyrinth of complexity and on-going fees once she entered. But she was also getting to a level of assets and income where the fees were worth it. So she went ahead and hired a tax firm. It made sense now, but it hadn't earlier.

Ask your adviser

In addition to the tax advantages specific to the rational portfolio outlined above here are a few more potential ways to save money on taxes. Like anything in the area of tax, clear these with a tax adviser, just to ensure that changes in rules have not rendered any of them ineffective or illegal.

Different accounts Many investors will have different accounts that in aggregate add up to their investment portfolio. One may be a fully taxed normal deposit account whereas another is tax-free (e.g. a UK ISA). Generally, different accounts may have different tax characteristics; by putting the high-income generating investments (typically fixed income) in the tax-free accounts you may lower your overall tax burden. Being informed about which investments fit best into various accounts can save you taxes. In the UK, for example, if you pay tax it almost always make sense to have an ISA account and benefit from its tax advantages.

Tax efficient proxies In some countries certain government bonds are tax advantageous. For example, in the US certain municipal bonds are exempt from certain taxes. If you are able to take advantage of such tax relief these bonds may be a more tax-efficient way to gain the virtual equivalent of the minimal risk asset. In other words, in this case you may not be holding US government bonds in the way you would be if there were no tax issues, but the municipal bonds are fairly similar and the tax advantage renders this compromise well worthwhile.

Enterprise Investment Scheme (EIS) or equivalent In the UK there are certain tax advantages or government subsidies in making start-up and certain types of clean-tech investments. Depending on your tax rate these are well worth knowing about. Your tax adviser should know all about them (these are outside the scope of this book).

Gifts Instead of realising a capital gain it may be advantageous to gift securities to your spouse and have him or her make the sale (thus utilising your spouse's CGT allowance). Likewise, think about gifting relatives instead of them incurring inheritance tax. (You can't do this just before death so check the rules!)

Realise losses When realising the capital gain on your portfolio you may be able to sell another security at a loss (to offset the gain) and reinvest the proceeds from the sales in a very similar investment. The rules on how similar the investment can be depends on the country, but be sure to stay compliant. You may, for example, sell an investment in the S&P 500 and reinvest the proceeds in the Wilshire 5000 index to get a different product with substantially the same exposure.

Create trading lots Keep track of your investment lots. If you buy 100 shares at £10 and later another 100 at £15 your average price is £12.50. If you later sell 100 shares at £20 you want your tax to be due on the second lot (i.e. a £5 gain) instead of your average gain of £7.50 per share. You can do this by designating each lot you buy separately and making clear that you are selling the lot bought at £15 per share.

Tax schemes If you enter into a tax-saving scheme of some sort, make sure in your planning that you calculate a realistic probability of it being found non-compliant and the fine this implies. Too often I have seen people involved with the tax authorities who find the whole thing incredibly draining both from a financial, emotional and time perspective, far beyond any potential tax savings are worth. Being the protagonist in a Kafka novel is never worth it.

It's hard to generalise about something as specific as tax. The potential to minimise tax is often very specific to the individual person or institution, but always important. In addition to the points above, you need to keep as much flexibility in your tax planning as possible and avoid locking yourself in. Not only might your individual tax circumstances unexpectedly change, but the tax regimes that you operate under may also change. This 'option' on future changes is another reason not to pay your taxes sooner than you have to. It may be difficult to estimate the probability of such events, and some people have no options or flexibility in their tax planning, but for others the advantages could be great.

Rational portfolio adjustment

Throughout this book we have discussed the rational portfolio. While one of its many advantages is its simplicity, taxes can hinder this simple portfolio.

As an unrealistic example, imagine you are a US-based investor who would be taxed at 0% on dividends or capital gains if you invested only in US securities, and 50% tax in the case of foreign investments. Let's say that there was no way to get around this geographic tax (e.g. by buying US-listed securities that invest abroad). What should you do? It would make sense to create a US-only portfolio, rather than incurring the tax. You could have your minimal risk asset in the short-term US government bonds and your equity exposure in the US equity markets. In this instance you would have compromised on geographic diversification, but since the alternative would be to pay 50% of your profit it would be worth it.

If you consider the equity risk premium to be 4–5% a year in addition to a minimal risk rate of 0.5% and annual inflation of 2% (because we pay tax on nominal amounts, inflation causes us to pay extra tax, you would expect your annual equity return to be around 7% (0.5 + 4.5 + 2.0) and the tax you pay on that is zero in the US and 3.5% abroad after the 50% tax. In simple terms, you would then be deciding if the diversification benefits from investing in the world equity markets as opposed to only the US one would be worth 3.5% tax a year.

A similar argument can be made for expensive tax wrappers. If the only legitimate way to gain the cheap, broadly diversified portfolio was through a complex wrapper, again you would have to consider the all-in costs of a rational portfolio. Did the annual charges from the wrapper in addition to an adverse ruling from the tax authorities really merit the benefits from the rational portfolio? If not, then perhaps we would be better off with an alternative portfolio that did not incur those costs. However, if someone tells you that you can't have a rational portfolio because of your specific tax or other situation, but suggests what looks like an expensive alternative, then ask: 'Can I buy quoted securities through this structure?' If yes, then ask: 'Is an ETF not just another quoted security even if it represents an underlying exposure to a broader equity or bond portfolio?' Well, yes it is!

There is a reason that so many product providers offer tax-sheltered or optimised products; many investors are in the same boat. Some of the products charge far too much, particularly in on-going fees, but similarly many would work well for the rational portfolio while being tax optimised. Since many products change frequently, make sure you are up to date on developments in this area.

Those that claim that you should not consider your investments in the context of your tax situation in my view are just plain wrong. Each tax situation is specific but the point applies broadly. There are certainly situations where taxes may mean that it makes sense to have a tax-optimised imperfect portfolio rather than a tax-inefficient perfect portfolio. But hopefully you will be able to have both. Most people can.

12

Liquidity

Perhaps one of the most underappreciated advantages of the rational portfolio is its excellent liquidity. The rational portfolio will outperform most actively managed portfolios in the long run, while being tax efficient and tailored to our individual risk profile. But it is also advantageous from a liquidity perspective.

Liquidity is one of those things you mainly hear about in a negative context because things went wrong and there wasn't enough of it. The rational portfolio is also affected by liquidity issues in the market; times of decreasing liquidity are typically synonymous with declining markets. And the rational portfolio with some risky equity exposure will probably lose money in declining markets, like most other portfolios with risky assets. But compared to most portfolios the rational portfolio is less at risk from a liquidity perspective as the index-tracking investments are very liquid.

The importance of having liquidity in your portfolio depends on your circumstances. One friend commented to me that liquidity is his number one requirement when considering new investments, while some endowments and foundations have predicted their capital needs decades into the future and are more relaxed about being able to sell their investments for cash within days or hours. Most investors are perhaps between the two extremes regarding liquidity requirements. Some investments that are meant to be held for the very long term, perhaps for retirement, but there is also a desire to have available liquidity for unexpected needs.

Selling your investment

Liquidity is really a question of how quickly you can transact your investment portfolio. If you hold 10,000 shares in Microsoft that may be a lot of money to you (about $300,000 at the time of writing) and a significant share of your investment portfolio. But if you needed to sell the stock, you could do so in minutes without moving the share price. Around 50 million Microsoft shares trade every day so your entire holding represents a tiny portion of a day's volume.

If on the other hand you owned $300,000 worth of shares in a company that trade only $100,000 worth of stock every day, then you would have a problem if you needed the money quickly. Let's say the share price is $20 and there are 5,000 shares traded every day, then you own about three days' volume of the stock. But as a rule of thumb you can trade about 10% of the average volume of a stock without affecting the price too much, so in normal markets you would own 30 days' volume of shares, not three.

Suppose you were looking at your illiquid investments in the middle of a crisis like the one in 2008–09. You knew that the stock was illiquid, but in your mind there was no need to sell quickly. You had other stocks and generally felt good about the portfolio.

Now the world has changed and you need liquidity. You look at this stock and to your horror see that it is no longer a $20 stock, but a $15 one (see Figure 12.1). But not only has the $300,000 investment become a $225,000 one, but the liquidity in the market has dried up, and the bid/offer spread has widened massively.[1] To make matters worse the bid/offer spread looks erratic and selling now will really affect the share price. These are panic markets and everyone worries that there is something about the company that they don't know. They are jumpy at any suggestion of bad news, including the prospect of other investors needing liquidity – why are they selling? Who knows how low a stock like this one can fall?

You are now panicking. The value of the company and your ability to raise cash from selling the stock is evaporating simultaneously. If you didn't before, you now certainly realise why you should have a broadly diversified portfolio and not just be holding potentially illiquid investments. But not only that, this is probably all happening at the same time as everything else is going wrong in your life.

A similar version of this could be faced by the manager of a fund that invests in small- and medium-sized companies facing redemptions from

---

1 The bid/offer spread is the difference between what you can buy the stock at and what you can sell it for.

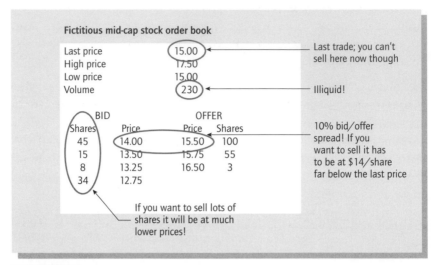

Fictitious mid-cap stock order book

				Last trade; you can't sell here now though
Last price	15.00 ←			
High price	17.50			
Low price	15.00			
Volume	230 ←			Illiquid!

BID		OFFER		
Shares	Price	Price	Shares	
45	14.00	15.50	100	10% bid/offer spread! If you want to sell it has to be at $14/share far below the last price
15	13.50	15.75	55	
8	13.25	16.50	3	
34	12.75			

If you want to sell lots of shares it will be at much lower prices!

Figure 12.1 You don't want to have to sell 1,000 shares by the end of the day!

many investors. While she has more stocks that she can choose to liquidate from, she also has more potential investors that want to sell when things are bad (and if she sold only the most liquid stock, the remaining portfolio would be even less liquid). So even if you are one of the investors in the fund who doesn't have to liquidate in the crisis, the performance of your investment will still be hurt as other investors in the fund scramble for the door.

Compare that to the Microsoft investors. They have also taken a hit as the stock is down of about the same magnitude as the smaller company, but although liquidity has also declined, they can still realise the value of their holdings quickly. And when panic hits the market, cash is truly king!

Minimal risk liquidity

The minimal risk asset consists of high-credit-quality government bonds. There are literally trillions of dollars of these government bonds outstanding and many billions in each currency and maturity, and the trading of them is extremely liquid. But also, consider for a moment what actually happens during a crisis. People sell their risky assets like equity investments, sometimes in a complete panic, and realise cash from their investments. The cash from the sale will be deposited into an account with their bank or custodian once the trade has settled. Now what? Particularly after the last few crises many people are, quite rightly, not content to leave a lot of cash sitting in an account; they want to move the money into something secure. And there are no investable assets more secure than the minimal risk asset.

As a result of the flight to safety that happens during any crisis the value of the minimal risk asset typically goes up in value with the longer-term bonds experiencing the greatest gains.[2] People worry less about the low return on offer and more about not losing more money. Minimal risk assets become like a bullet-proof insurance policy and they often go up in value.

The equity portfolio and 'risky' bonds are highly liquid

The world equity portfolio is among the most liquid of investments you can find. Let's remind ourselves that a large fraction of the world equity portfolio consists in part of the largest traded companies in the largest economies of the world. As a result the portfolio consist of companies like Apple, Exxon, Vodafone, PetroChina, General Electric, Nestlé, Google, IBM, Royal Dutch Shell, Petrobras, etc. While you also have some exposure to smaller companies in the broadest equity indices, the proportion of those stocks in the portfolio is far below what it would be in a portfolio of exclusively small- or medium-sized companies.

Unless you have an investment portfolio the size of a sovereign wealth fund there should not be much of a liquidity concern with the world equity portfolio. Even if the values of your holding are dropping, you would be able to liquidate your portfolio in far less than a day without causing price movements.

Likewise the liquidity of a rational portfolio that includes sub-AA rated government bonds and corporate bonds is very good. As with the case of the broad equity indices, these are broad and diversified exposures. The underlying securities in these exposures are mainly individually liquid and considering that each security only represents a small fraction of the overall portfolio, the aggregate risky government and corporate bond

---

2 In the panic, investors demand lower interest rates for the security of these bonds. For short-term bonds the price rally will be limited as the bonds will already be trading at close to par, but longer-term bonds could rally more substantially.

exposure is very liquid as a result. But not only that. For many index-tracking products, 'authorised participants' (think of them as brokers or market makers) are actually able to 'disaggregate' the tracker into its constituent parts, ensuring liquidity. So if the authorised participants held an exchange traded fund (ETF) of the FTSE 100, instead of holding the tracker, they have the choice of getting the underlying 100 stocks instead, ensuring that other market participants have similar liquidity. You therefore indirectly have the choice of the liquidity of the index tracking FTSE 100 ETF or the liquidity of the underlying 100 stocks.

The exposure of the rational portfolio is indirectly an exposure to literally thousands of underlying securities all over the world. While the rational portfolio will suffer in falling markets, along with the rest of the world, the exposure to liquidity issues is far more limited.

Since liquidity only ever seems important when you don't have it we forget about it in our daily lives. Most people don't live their lives like a portfolio manager with live prices feeding into an excel spreadsheet, and live updates on volume statistics. We look at our portfolio on occasion and perhaps pay more attention when we add to it or sell something, or when there are major price movements. Otherwise we leave it and get on with our lives.

By having our equity exposure in a large and broad index, like the world equity index, we avoid taking a liquidity risk that is incredibly real, but typically only rears its head when we really don't want it to. If you hold in your portfolio a number of smaller companies, property, private equity investments, private investments, etc. then make sure you understand what your liquidity position would be in the case of a crisis with its typically resulting liquidity squeeze.

Getting paid – illiquid investments should generate better returns

Investors need to be paid for the lack of liquidity. Imagine the scenario where you have two investments that are very similar. Both have the same risk/return profile, tax profile, and diversifying effect on our portfolio. I now tell you that you can unwind one of them today, but that you have to hold the other one for five years or potentially longer, as you do in most private equity or many property investments. Hopefully, it's obvious that you would rather have the option of cashing out of your investment, even if you don't use that option. The illiquid five-year investment needs something else to make it as attractive as the liquid investment (see Figure 12.2).

In some illiquid investments there is virtually no price to get out at (traders would say there is 'no bid' to buy the investment). Because of this, illiquid investments have to offer a return premium which compensates you for the fact that your money is tied up. The size of the premium demanded by investors varies a great deal. For me personally, the world is just too uncertain a place and the potential future opportunities for my money too great for me to want to sign up for something which ties up capital for five years unless there are massive expected returns. But people differ. If you know that you don't need the money for 20 years or have only a small fraction of your assets invested in illiquid assets, then perhaps there is less of an issue with tying capital up for longer periods of time.

The example above points to one of the main issues I have with private equity, property, private investments or long-term investments. But structured products or hedge funds are not immune to liquidity issues either. During the 2008–09 crisis many hedge funds suspended redemptions as the underlying investments the fund had made were out of sync with the liquidity terms of the investors. As a result of the hedge funds' failure to honour their liquidity terms, many investors were left in a bind.

While comparing products with easy daily liquidity, like products for the rational portfolio, to alternatives with five-year lock-ups may seem

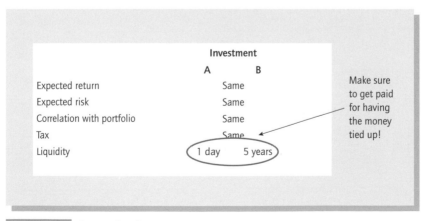

Figure 12.2 Comparing investments

unfair, finance literature is often guilty of simplifying the issue. Certain works will say things like 'buy a UK small-cap index or emerging markets mid-cap fund' sometimes without discussing the liquidity constraints and issues with those products.

Liquidity rethought

Just as tax is a topic which is difficult to generalise, individual liquidity concerns vary a great deal. But while this is the case, investors must look closely at the overall liquidity of their investment portfolio and consider how drastic changes in their ability to realise the value of their investments would affect them. There is a great tendency for liquidity to be something we consider only when we are forced to do so, and that is rarely at an opportune moment.

Furthermore, the potential risk of being caught short of liquidity in some investments increases the attractiveness of very liquid and broad portfolios like the rational portfolio, without compromising the return expectation. I imagine that some people underestimate the importance of these issues and hope that they are never forced to face them. But in the unfortunate case that you need to raise capital quickly, the ownership of the most liquid instruments on offer will lessen the distress caused by having to sell.

13

Expenses

In this chapter we are going to look at the cost of your portfolio. There are too few people from the world of finance that are interested in emphasising the importance of low fees to investors. They are, after all, the ones making money from those same fees. I have nothing to sell you, other than the book you have already bought.

Fees are always important in finance, but even more so for the rational investor. Since we don't think we'll be able to outperform the market, we are not asking anyone to be particularly clever about investing. We just want someone to replicate the market. As a result, we can expect to pay very little for it. It's worth repeating a lesson from earlier (see Figure 13.1).

Inertia is a powerful force. It either makes us leave our investments where they are or makes us buy the well-known active funds, like so many others. Most investors are aware of the extra costs, but often don't seem to react – please don't let that be you. It seems paradoxical to me that many investors spend endless hours comparing the prices of laptops or holidays

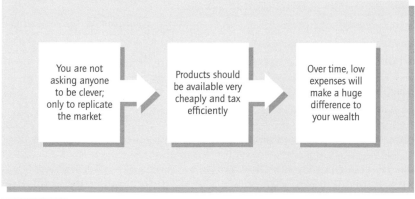

Figure 13.1 The simple solution again

when hours spent researching better and cheaper financial products could far outweigh savings made elsewhere.

An expensive, active choice

Let's compare the costs of investing in a passive, index-tracking product to that of a typical active fund tracking the same index:

	Active fund		Index tracker		
Up-front fee	2.00% *Do not pay this!*		0.00%		
Annual:					
Management fee	1.00%		0.20%		
Other expenses	0.20%		0.15%		Audit, legal, custody, directors, etc.
Trading costs					
Bid/offer	0.35%		0.25%		Rebalance at times of liquidity
Commission	0.15%		0.10%		Trackers don't pay for research, etc.
Price impact	0.25%		0.25%		
Transaction tax	0.25%		0.00%		ETFs can typically avoid stamp duty, etc.
Total per trade	1.00%		0.60%		
Turnover	1.25×		0.10×		
Total trading costs	1.25%	1.25%	0.06%	0.06%	
Additional taxes*		0.00%		0.00%	
Annual cost		2.45%		0.41%	

*From turnover of portfolio and shifting active funds occasionally.

While thankfully many investors can avoid the increasingly rare up-front fees, in simple terms you can save about 2% a year by investing in an index-tracking fund compared to an active fund (some funds have exit fees too, but those are increasingly rare).

If the annual saving does not seem like a lot to you, consider the power of compounding returns.

Let's assume that you are a frugal investor who diligently put aside 10% of £50,000 income from the age of 25 to 67 that you put into equities.

(Assume income will go up with inflation but to simplify this is an average over the time span – most 25-year-olds don't make £50,000.) How much of a difference should you expect from the allocation to an index-tracking product as opposed to an active fund?

Let's further assume the following nominal cumulative returns before fees (ignoring taxes for now):

Minimal risk rate	0.50%
Equity risk premium	4.50%
Annual inflation	2.00%
	7.00%

It is worth reiterating the key point that we should not expect the active manager to outperform the index before fees. Obviously some managers will do so, but in aggregate the active managers perform in line with the index before fees. It is because of their significant trading, management and other fees that the outperformance is so stark compared to index-tracking products.

So where does this leave you? As you get ready to retire at age 67 the difference in the savings pot is staggering. You are left better off by £643,000 simply by investing with an index fund as opposed to an active manager (see Figure 13.2).

This is calculated by simply taking the annual savings each year (so £50,000 × 10% = £5,000 in the first year, etc.) and either investing it in

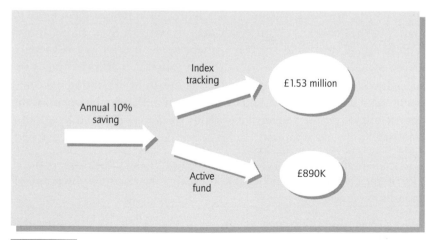

Figure 13.2   Result of investing with an index fund as opposed to an active fund

the index tracker or the active manager with a return of 7% a year before fees.

Adjusting the £643,000 for inflation, the saving is still around £280,000 in today's money. If you had managed to avoid paying the up-front charges your active fund investment would have been greater by about £23,000 at age 67, hitting home the advantage of avoiding this initial charge, if possible. If you had avoided the up-front charge and there had only been a 1.5% annual difference in costs, the difference in savings at retirement would still amount to £494,000. If you think you have a great edge in the market and think you could easily make up this 1.5% or 2% annual cost difference, then good luck to you. If not, then the sooner you shift out of the expensive investment products and into cheap index-tracking products the better off you will be.

Think about that. By not giving money to an active manager who probably was not able to outperform anyhow you saved £280,000 in today's money over your investing life. Just imagine the difference in quality of life that kind of money would make in retirement or for your relatives after you are gone. Suppose now that you are an institution administrating assets for a large number of customers – the cumulative savings from shifting assets into the index-tracking products can quickly become truly astounding.

Conversely, consider the 85–90% of investors who invest in active managers as opposed to index-tracking funds either directly or via their pension funds. Over the long run only a very small percentage of those investors will be lucky enough to invest with active managers that will give better returns after fees. The rest have simply paid a staggering amount of money to the financial industry over their investment lives. To put things in perspective, next time you see a finance person driving a Porsche or jetting off to a holiday home in Spain just consider that these additional and unnecessary fees for just one saver over his or her investing life could buy at least seven Porsches. And paradoxically this is money paid to the finance industry from a saver who would typically not be able to afford a Porsche.

If you know all of the above and are still happily paying the fees then at least stop complaining about people in finance making too much money and driving fancy cars.

You are obviously not forced to choose only between an active manager or an index tracker. As many do, you could manage your own portfolio with individual security selection. The decision whether or not to do this goes back to the question of having an edge in the first place. If you don't have an edge you know that this 'do-it-yourself' approach is a loser's game for you as you will not be able to pick a superior portfolio to that of the market, and will end up buying the market index trackers as this is far less hassle and more cost efficient.

Patience

The problem with the focus on fees is that we don't receive instant gratification. There is no stock that doubles next month. To really notice the additional profit we gain from being clever about expenses takes years or even decades. The key to reaping the most savings is to have the patience to wait for the compounding impact of the lower expenses to take effect. I compare it to making money while you sleep; lower fees make a little bit of money all the time.

Consider Figure 13.3 that illustrates the aggregate savings of the saver mentioned above. In the early years you can barely tell the difference between the active and index tracking investments. In the later years the benefits are apparent, but obviously only exist for the investor who maintained the discipline of lower fees.

Saving 2% or more a year in fees may sound like a lot, but are we going to notice that amid the noise of the investment markets? The index tracker

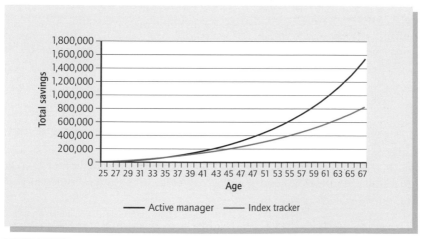

Figure 13.3 The importance of sticking with it: your aggregate savings

performs slightly better than the average active fund – outperformance coming from the lower fees. Meanwhile the active fund performance will be all over the map, with the best performers screaming the loudest about how their special angle or edge ensured the greatest performance. We might be tempted to believe the manager and abandon our boring and average index-tracking strategy, but please don't unless you can clearly explain to yourself why you have an edge. Chances are you don't and you will be wealthier in the long run from acknowledging this.

Believing in an edge can be expensive

Once the CFO of a mid-sized European insurance company proudly showed me around his internal investment group. We came to a large open-plan floor and he showed me analysts that were actively trading securities in individual stock markets, with the team being divided geographically. There were perhaps 25 of them in total, with a trader who would pass on the orders to brokers around the world. When I asked the CFO, 'Do you think these guys have an edge in the markets', he looked at me like I had just asked him a nonsense question, like how long to cook a chicken.

The CFO made some comment to me that instead of caring only about edge, by actively trading stocks the analysts were able to create the kind of risk profile that suited their overall investment objective. I thought that they would be better off combining equity indices with a broad bond portfolio in proportions that suited their risk profile. And then there was the issue of costs. Even excluding the Bloomberg terminals, office space, real-time price feeds, bid/offer spreads, commissions, risk of fraud, research costs and so on, in total these guys cost the company millions every year in salary, bonuses and expenses. Was that worth it? I thought not – I didn't think they had an edge. In fact in the financial models I built for this insurance company I built in an expectation that they would underperform the equity indices by 1.5% a year in their equity exposure (but I doubt they made the same assumption internally). They should not have spent the large resources actively trading in the market, but realise that they were without an edge and have an index-tracking portfolio as a result. Over time this would serve them and their shareholders better.

In another case I visited a commodity firm with large and fluctuating euro/dollar exchange exposures. There was a small team of traders in charge of hedging the company's currency exposure. Fair enough. But instead of thinking about what kind of exposure the company wanted and implementing it these guys had effectively set up a small trading operation where they were actively trading multiple currencies, depending on their views of the market. This made no sense to me. The euro/dollar foreign exchange market is one of the most liquid markets in the world, and anyone with a real edge in this market has a fantastic opportunity to realise great riches from it. It just seemed to me that the three or four traders at this commodity firm did not possess this edge and would be better off not playing those markets.

In both the company examples above it seems that the shareholders would be better off without the implicit assumption of an edge. Unfortunately in far too many cases, trading decisions are made on the basis of how things have always been done or perhaps as a result of someone who was given some leeway to trade, only to have things mushroom from there.[1] Instead these companies and many like them would have been far better off if they had started with a basic question: 'Do we have an edge, and if so why, where, and how can we best exploit it?'

Where are we heading?

In my view, expenses in connection with investing will be a major point of debate over the next decade, as awareness and dissemination of information increases further in the investment management industry.

Particularly in the 1970s and 1980s the mutual fund industry grew explosively. The benefits of diversification espoused by academic portfolio theory also became wider known, even if not necessarily in technical terms. When I was attending classes on financial theory in the early 1990s, mutual fund investing was discussed in great detail as a great tool for the private investor.

As the mutual fund industry grew so did the index-tracking industry. The index-tracking firms were not generally as widely known as the mutual funds, probably in large part because their low fees did not leave a lot of room for general marketing expense. They were led by Vanguard and the legendary John Bogle.

The growth in the index trackers was a natural extension of the disaggregation that the finance industry had moved slowly towards for decades. Disaggregation ▶

---

1 In my view there are many cases where it is in the employees' but not the company's interest to have these kinds of trading operations. The employee may get a bonus or share of the profit if there are gains, but will not share in the losses.

is perhaps too big a term and I'm sure that nobody had a grand plan, but the basic idea was that you paid for what you got. If you only wanted market exposure as defined by the creation of some index, you only paid for that, with the simplicity of the product continuously pushing down its costs. Unless you wanted to, you didn't have to pay for a supposed star mutual fund manager at the same time or the friendly advice from your local broker. And doing it all yourself was not only time consuming, but the cost and information disadvantages compared to professional investors meant that it was increasingly a bad choice. Those things are certainly still available, but so is the bare-bone version of only buying the index.

Index-tracking investments consist of approximately only 15% of stock-market investing so there is a lot of room to grow. This continued growth will benefit investors at the expense of the financial industry as the aggregate fees will decrease.[2]

I hope a future development in the world of index tracking will be a focus on lowering the costs of this essentially commodity product. There is today far too great a disparity between the charges imposed by index-tracking providers (like index funds, ETFs, etc.) and some are simply too expensive. Vanguard is at the forefront of an extreme focus on costs and that firm's massive size suggests investors are receptive to the improvements. Competitors including iShares have responded to the challenge and lowered fees, leading to an encouraging industry trend. A rational portfolio should be driving a Volvo, not a Porsche. Taking cost reductions further, investors could be offered the chance of investing in a white-label index[3] instead of a more well-established index like S&P or MSCI, and thus save the licence fees. In one of those moves that cause great ripples in the world of index investing, but hardly noticed elsewhere, Vanguard recently changed some of their products to track a FTSE index instead of an MSCI one to save money on licence fees. This kind of cost focus among the product providers ultimately benefits customers.

2   There is clearly an upper limit on indexing. If there was only index investing there would not be an efficient market with prices reflecting the future prospect of individual securities. However, I think index tracking could more than triple and still be very far from this point.
3   A white-label product is one that is produced by one company, which is then rebranded by others.

14

Products and implementation

To implement the rational portfolio:

- We need to find the best products that give us exposure to geographically broadly diversified equity markets, minimal risk government bonds and other government and corporate bonds.
- We want to do this in a way that is tax optimal.
- We need to combine the securities in a way that reflects our risk preference.

The past decades have seen an explosion in the number of products available to the index-seeking investor, and this development continues unabated. As new products come to market there is a risk that the information outlined here grows stale quickly and I would strongly encourage the reader to survey the market for new and better products before making investments. With the large growth of index funds and exchange traded funds (ETF) investing over the past decades, the abundance of different product offerings leave even professional investors confused; it's no wonder that many investors say 'forget it' and revert to doing what they have always done.

The two main ways to gain index-type exposure is through ETFs and index funds (this term covers a few different structures). The main difference between the two is that an ETF is traded like any stock while index funds are more akin to mutual funds or unit trusts in their structures.

If you can find a product provided by Vanguard, iShares, State Street or one of their major competitors that meets your needs from an exposure and tax perspective, this is probably a very good way to gain your exposure. These are clearly among the cheapest and largest providers of index exposure in the world; sort of the Ikea/ Ryanair/Walmart of finance – no frills, but you are very likely to get the best price

▶

in town. Until recently Vanguard's presence outside the US was limited, but that is rapidly changing. iShares recently lowered the prices of a number of its products as it was losing market share to Vanguard because of higher prices. The iShares CEO quite tellingly said that its overall margins (i.e. your costs) would still be good as there were lots of ETFs other than the major flagship ones where there was lower pricing pressure. (In comparison Vanguard is a mutual so owned by the investors and thus perhaps less inclined to charge higher fees.) You should not buy these specialised and expensive products even if they are called 'index XYZ' and sold as an ETF. Investors who buy an ETF that tracks EU insurance companies, Canadian mining companies, etc. essentially claim an edge by their selective exposure to the market, just like those buying Microsoft shares do.

Index-tracking products outside the US have historically been more expensive than in the US, but thankfully that is changing and in the future I would expect to see close to cost parity. Investors will be left better off as a result.

Total expense ratio tells you the cost of owning the product

When comparing different suitable products look at the total expense ratio (TER). The TER tells you the annual cost of owning the products including fees, custody, administration, etc. Additional costs not included in the TER mainly consist of trading costs (bid/offer, commissions, market impact, etc.) although these are small for index-tracking products because of the portfolio's low churn.

TER (per year)	Comment
< 0.3%	Very good and increasingly the norm in the large and liquid products.
0.3%–0.6%	Still OK if the product you are after is not straightforward.
> 0.6%	Be sure you need to pay this much. Don't forget trading costs come on top!

So if iShares has a TER of 0.3% for a product when Vanguard has a very similar one for 0.2% then that difference should be the deciding factor (disregarding tax and liquidity differences).

Investors can save quite a bit of money by looking at different products and selecting the index-replicating product with the lowest cost. I recently went to speak at a conference on ETF and index investing. At the conference all the product providers had large stands with gadgets and toys to lure investors. That was all fine. But what was also clear to me is how much some of the people that work for these providers get paid. Much like some of their peers in the investment banking divisions of the big banks, someone who works at a big ETF provider is no stranger to generous pay packages. When you add a culture of being paid like a banker to the large marketing budgets, licence fees to the index provider, administration and corporate profit margin, it's no wonder that many of the ETFs or index products are not as cheap as they could be. Like any other for-profit business you can't blame the providers for trying to create the most profitable product portfolio they can, but you may find equally good products at a cheaper price. And it is certainly worth our while looking for them. So while you have got 90% of the way there by picking an index-tracking product like an ETF for your rational portfolio you could do even better by picking the best and cheapest of those products.

It used to be that investment books suggested that people refrained from investing abroad (abroad to the US in most cases) because the costs were deemed prohibitive. Thankfully this is no longer a real issue as the easy movement of capital and investing in various domestic markets has increased significantly over the past decades. There are clearly some countries where trading is expensive or transaction taxes are an issue, but far fewer than in the past. However, also keep in mind that if you buy the broad world equity markets, around 70% of your money will be invested in the US, Canada, Western Europe, Japan and Australia, which all have cheap access. So if you found yourself paying 0.25% TER for access to these countries and 0.5% for an all-world product you would effectively be paying 1% TER for access to the rest of the world, which is too expensive.

While the TER is an important component in selecting an index-tracking product it is not the whole story. Some ETFs that track less liquid bench-marks could incur significant trading costs and impair returns as a result, just like you incur costs to trade the ETF (commission, etc.). Likewise you may incur costs like exit and up-front fees (you should avoid these except if they are very small and only relate to the costs the fund incurs in trading your additional money in the fund), or costs from advice or platform charges.

The best ETFs: liquid, tax efficient and low cost

The main difference between an index fund and an ETF is that the ETF is a traded product. You buy and sell the ETF like you would any stock. In the case of ETFs tracking world equities, the ETF will try to replicate the performance of that index by buying the individual stocks represented in the index. As a holder of the ETF you should then end up with the performance of that index, subject to a few things that we will return to later.

Advantages to owning ETFs

These are as follows:

- They are easily traded like any stock (you should avoid trading your portfolio, but it's nice to have the option). Even during the most volatile and distressing days of 2008 and 2009 there was liquidity in the markets for the biggest ETFs and the bid/offer spreads did not widen materially.
- They almost always trade very close to the value of the underlying holdings.
- ETFs are relatively easy to create; there is a huge array of product offering and far in excess of that of index funds, even if many of them are irrelevant to the rational portfolio.
- In the UK ETFs don't pay stamp duty.
- The right ETF is a very low-cost vehicle.
- Fee-chasing advisers and banks sometimes neglect to push them to you (there aren't enough fees for them to get a cut), suggesting that they are definitely worth looking at!

ETFs have grown massively in prominence over the past couple of decades. In the mid-1990s they were still a fairly limited asset class, but in the early part of the following decade they exploded in number and size. There are today almost $2 trillion invested in ETFs, mainly in equity-related products, but increasingly in fixed-income funds. The assets are spread among literally thousands of different ETFs and you can use them to buy exposures to anything from the various standard indices, to volatility indices, gold bars, oil, sectors and more. This array of offerings is a good thing for the wider investor. It used to be practically very difficult for most investors to buy direct exposure to something like gold or oil without buying a gold mining or oil company stock. Now they can. However, this does not mean that these products are suitable for you: stick to the simple rational portfolio.

iShares is the largest ETF provider, although as the sector has grown a large number of competitors have entered the space. Table 14.1 shows the

Table 14.1 Number of products and market share by provider

	Number	Assets	
	ETF/ETP	(US$ bn)	Share
iShares	622	809	39%
State Street	177	362	17%
Vanguard	88	278	13%
PowerShares	193	80	4%
db X-trackers/Deutsche Bank	310	52	3%
Luxor	210	40	2%
ETF Securities	331	28	1%
Others	2,875	433	21%
	4,806	2,083	

Based on data from Blackrock Industry Review, Q1 2013.

leading providers (Vanguard was a late entrant to ETFs but has since made up for lost time with impressive growth rates).

You need to peruse the websites of the market leaders outlined above for products that suit your needs (tax, regulatory, domicile, liquidity, cost, etc.).

Below are examples of products I would consider suitable for the generic rational investor (assuming you have no restrictions, which is obviously unrealistic), although other providers also have competitive and good alternatives. The ETFs listed here are probably good options at the time of writing, but there are many more products available so look around. As you do your own research on which ETFs best suit your needs, here is a list of things to consider:

- Does the ETF track the right index for your portfolio?
- Is the TER very low (< 0.3% a year)?
- Is the ETF and underlying index liquid? Are there many assets in the ETF and it is frequently traded (look at the bid/offer spread and how much is traded daily compared to other ETFs)?
- Is the ETF tax efficient for you?
- Is the ETF in the right currency and jurisdiction for you?

Exposure	Product	TER	Comment
World equity	Vanguard Total World Stock ETF (VT)	0.22%	Relatively new product
	HSBC MSCI World ETF (HMWO)	0.35%	Developed markets only
Minimal risk asset	iShares 1–3yr Treasury Bond Fund (SHY)	0.15%	Vanguard's product is a similar price and still too new to have significant assets. Shorter-term products exist, but are less attractive due to larger transaction costs
	Vanguard UK Gov Bond ETF (VGOV)	0.12%	UK equivalent
	DB Trackers IBOXX Germany 1–3yr ETF	0.15%	Germany (for euro exposure) equivalent
Government bonds	DB Trackers Global Sovereign Index ETF	0.25%	Too few of these products exist and have fairly low assets under management, but a one-stop shop to buy a broad, global, government bond exposure
	iShares S&P/Citi Global Gov Bond ETF (IGLO)	0.20%	Ex-US government bonds
	State Street Barclays Emerging Market Local government bonds	0.55%	This ETF holds Turkey, Russia, Brazil, etc.
Corporate bonds	iShares Global Corporate Bond (CORP)	0.20%	Very recent product, but with global exposure. Look out for more of these or combine the products of a few countries yourself.

- Does the ETF have a history of performing very differently from the index it is tracking (tracking error)? Why?
- Can you execute the ETF easily and cheaply?

Just like new product launches occur frequently in the index space, the fees of the various products can change continuously. Particularly the bond ETFs leave a lot to be desired and this is an area where a cheap and broad active fund with the perfect profile may make sense (if it exists), but this is a growth area for the ETF sector so hopefully there will soon be suitable index-tracking products available.

Traditionally, there have not been as many world equity or bond (government or corporate) ETFs available, but this is a fast-growing area of the indexing space (the best known index – the MSCI World – was not even created until 1970, much less followed by an array of product alternatives). Index exposure was more tied to the national markets where the products were offered, such as the DAX in Germany or the S&P 500 in the US. (The world's largest ETF tracks the S&P500 with around $100 billion in assets under management.)

Physical or synthetic ETF?

ETFs are roughly divided into two kinds: synthetic and physical. Simply put, physical ETFs are those where the owner of the ETF owns all or a majority sample of the underlying securities through the ETF. So if you have an ETF on the S&P 500 then you are actually the owner of your representative number of shares in each of those 500 stocks. When an index-tracking ETF does not own all the constituents of the index in exactly the same proportions as the index all the time, this introduces a tracking error. This tracking error is entirely normal and unless a provider consistently underperforms an index as a result of it (suggesting other issues) it's not something you should expect to make or lose a lot of money from at least among the major ETFs.

Synthetic ETFs are a little different. Here the provider, such as Deutsche Bank (their brand is DB Trackers) will aim to replicate the performance of the index, but you as an investor do not own the underlying securities. This creates a credit exposure to the provider (here Deutsche Bank) in case it goes bust. The synthetic ETF providers argue that they are better able to replicate the performance of the index they seek to produce by using certain derivative products. Furthermore they argue that there is a great deal of collateral backing the ETF. So if you have $100 in a synthetic ETF there may be $120 of collateral of other securities backing that ETF. The providers also argue that this renders the risk of the synthetic ETF minimal and well worth taking to get more accurate tracking of an index, and perhaps slightly better returns from the financial manoeuvring the synthetic provider can undertake.

> I was recently helping an African development institution select some ETFs for their investment portfolio. As I tried to explain the difference between physical and synthetic ETFs one of the directors cut me off.
>
> 'So you are saying that in one of the cases we own what we think we own, and in the other we may own a bunch of other stuff if Deutsche Bank goes bust. Try to explain to my minister that we invested in a synthetic or in any way a derivative product with taxpayers' money. He would eat me alive.'
>
> So we went with physical ETFs.

I see why many people choose physical ETFs. The synthetic somehow doesn't feel right to a lot of people, and explaining it in simple terms often doesn't make them feel much better. Personally I have no problem with the synthetic products and accept the minor extra risk that come with them. That said, from my perspective the decision between physical and synthetic ETFs is less important than selecting the right ETF on the basis of tax considerations, liquidity or cost.

Index-tracking funds

The index funds work like a regular mutual fund or unit trust, even the terminology and exact fund structure vary slightly between jurisdictions (in the UK, for example, they are often called unit trusts or OEICs – open-ended investment companies). In the case of the index funds, the simplest way to think about these is that you give them £1,000 to invest and they then take that £1,000 and buy the underlying securities that make up the index exposure. If you want to redeem or sell your index investment that same index fund will then sell shares in proportion to your index investment and give you back the proceeds from those sales.

The index fund sector is more local. Unlike the ETFs that you can buy from any location in the world, like you would a stock, index-tracking funds are typically local financial institutions and the major player in the US is thus not the same as that in Germany, the UK or elsewhere. What this means in reality is that in some countries the choice of index funds is still far more limited than it is in major financial centres, to the detriment of the local investor.

In the US, the index space is dominated by Vanguard, but Fidelity, Blackrock, PIMCO (for bonds) and American Funds all have assets in excess of $100 billion (not all index tracking), and Dimensional Fund Advisors and State Street are potentially also worth a look. In the UK the leading players are Legal & General, Blackrock, State Street, HSBC and increasingly Vanguard.

If you are outside these two jurisdictions search the internet and look at the offerings from four or five asset managers or banks in your country, using the ETF checklist above as a rough guide. Keep in mind that if you call these companies and ask if they have some cheap index-tracking funds they may try to sell you a more expensive alternative, like an active fund or a structured product. Please don't give up so easily.

The problem as I see it with the index trackers is that there is not as broad a range of products. Even a strong leader in its sector, like Legal & General in the UK, does not have a broadly diversified world portfolio. It has an index fund of the top 100 blue-chip companies, but this is quite different from any kind of world equity index. Also, that product comes at an annual charge of 1% plus extra expenses of 0.15%. John Bogle, the founder of Vanguard, would be aghast at those kinds of fees. So if you wanted to gain access to a world equity portfolio through Legal & General you would be forced to put a portfolio of index funds together yourself, instead of having a one-stop product like a world equity product.

Generally speaking, some index products can be incredibly expensive and best avoided. The Virgin FTSE All-Share Tracker fund charges 1% a year in fees while the Vanguard FTSE All-Share index charges 0.15% in on-going fees.[1] Why people would pay six times as much for the same product unless their circumstances did not let them invest in the cheap one is beyond me. Add to this that some index-tracking funds have up-front fees

---

1 At the time of writing, in the UK the only way to buy the Vanguard funds below £100,000 is through Alliance Trust. Vanguard has been making noises about introducing easier and more direct options.

and the cost differential for what is essentially the same product becomes eye watering.

So with index funds like ETFs on top of the checks you need to make to ensure that you get a product that is suitable for your specific needs, make sure you get proper diversification and that you are not being overcharged by the product provider.

A few issues with index replication through ETFs or index funds

As I'm suggesting that we should be investing through broad-based and cheap investment products I want to flag a few things that some people could see as issues with these products. In no particular order, they are as follows.

Different indices on the same market will perform differently?

Index providers have different rules on things like free float (the fraction of shares that freely trade as opposed to being owned by controlling shareholders or management), liquidity, re-balancing, etc. and as a result will perform differently even if they follow the same market. So one index provider might lower Facebook's weighting by 50% because of its low fee float while another reduces it by 66%. Who is right or wrong is open to debate, but the index returns will be different as a result of the different weightings. While this is correct and leads to slight differences in performance there is no reason to expect one index to consistently outperform another. The index providers are trying to do the same thing: provide a good representation of that market and while their interpretations differ slightly you can expect different indices on the same markets to act very similarly. Most of the securities in the index are the same and in roughly the same proportions.

(Related to first one) Index tracking funds and ETFs have a tracking error

Correct. Practically speaking, product providers can't match the index 100% all the time. Sometimes the rebalancing is done slightly differently or perhaps providers have slightly different proportions of the less-liquid constituents. Indices typically rebalance quarterly. Imagine that because of a reweighting you have to include Facebook in your index-tracking product with a 5% weighting as of the 1st of next month. Theoretically you would buy all those shares at the closing price on the day prior to the 1st, but that is not practically possible. Instead you have to decide how you scale into the stock. Perhaps some traders buy the stock five days before and after the 1st while others do it all 10 days before the 1st. As a result, their performances will be different and one will track the index less closely than the other. If an index tracker/ETF consistently underperforms other products on the same index it may point to problems in its implementation (or hidden fees) and it may be worthwhile looking for alternative products.

Not all countries are in the world equity and bond indices

Correct. One day they probably will be, but not for now. Some countries don't have functioning capital markets (try buying shares in North Korea). That said, the world equity indices represent countries that in aggregate constitute more than 95% of the world gross domestic product (GDP), in my view making it representative enough.

Most indices don't represent all stocks or bonds in a country

Correct. Having all traded stocks or bonds represented in an index would make it extraordinarily tough and expensive to implement or increase tracking error as index trackers would often not include them in trading for practical reasons of liquidity and cost of trading. (Similarly, as discussed earlier, the stock or bond markets represent varying proportions of the domestic economies in different countries.) Besides, if we have an index that represents 95% of the total value of all stocks in a market then the last 5% outside the index would have to massively outperform before the omission is material.

Licence fees will eat into my returns

Index providers charge the product providers an annual licence fee. The size of the fee is mostly confidential, but 0.02–0.03% a year is probably a decent guess. This is what iShares pay to MSCI to call it the World MSCI index instead of just the World index. While I would personally be happy to save the 0.02–0.03% a year for a white-label index brand the product providers obviously think the association with the MSCI, S&P, FTSE, Stoxx, Russell, Dow, etc. is worth it. I would not be surprised if firms like Vanguard not only pay far lower fees, but also eventually consider its own brand strong enough so that it follows its own index creations or very cheap independent ones.

Your performance will only be average

Yes. Hopefully. The point is that we can't outperform the market and as a result should buy broad market exposure in the cheapest and most tax-efficient way. Of course this means that we won't only own the next Apple going up 500%, but nor will we have all our savings in the next Enron or Lehman.

Comparison sites

There is every chance that by the time you read this there will have been new product launches or changes in the fees of some of the products mentioned above. With that in mind, you need to do some of your own research on the best available products before investing. Here are a few comparison websites you may consider (there are many others):

- Morningstar.com
- Trustnet.com
- Indexuniverse.com (or .eu)
- Funds.ft.com
- Bloomberg.com
- Reuters.com
- Investmentfunds.org.uk (UK biased)
- Barrons.com

I would caution you against taking the information on the websites as fully correct and complete. Before making any investments ensure you go to the product provider's website and look at the fund facts in detail. Only there can you be sure that the information is up to date and correct.

If you have a financial adviser it would be a reasonable expectation that he or she has an educated view on how to best to get similar information.

On the site you should be looking for the fund screeners. The categories are not always straightforward and sometimes the sites don't allow you to screen for 'index tracking'. A good way to get around that is to search for the funds/ETFs with lowest total expense ratios (TERs); perhaps even look for terms like 'index' in the names of the funds. Likewise you will find lots of different styles like 'mid-cap value' or 'high yielding', etc. but not the simple 'global' portfolios we are after. Also, in some cases certain products will simply be absent from the product offering section of some super-markets so be sure to check a few. Have patience and keep trying – it's worth your while. Failing that you can always revert to browsing through the ETF or index fund providers listed earlier. While many other product providers try to compete with them there is a reason that those listed are among the market leaders.

Some index fund providers charge a small trading fee to get into the fund, just like they do if you redeem from the fund. This charge just reflects the cost to the fund of investing your money in the underlying securities. If there were no charges and you were a long-term holder of the fund (like you hopefully will be) you would instead indirectly be paying the trading fees as other investors come in and out of the fund. While entry/exit fees are explicit in index funds, in ETFs those charges are implicit in the bid/offer spread, or in some cases if the ETFs trade at a premium or discount to the net asset value. (So there is a discount if the ETF trades at £99, but the aggregate value of the holdings is £100, etc.)

For all its growth, index-tracking products still only represent around 10–15% of investments in equities (less in other products), and will not be pushed hard by the comparison sites. Keep in mind that index-tracking products like index funds or ETFs charge low fees and as a result far greater profits are to be had for the finance industry from flogging other products on the platform.

Execution

If you are at the point where you know what index fund or ETF you want to invest in, all that remains is to execute the investment and start reaping the benefits of index tracking.

Since buying an ETF is like buying a normal stock, you can use a normal online discount broker for this. The commission rates should be very small even if you buy via some of the more established banks, although in both cases be sure to avoid 'hidden' extras. You are a 'bare-bones' customer. The products we have discussed are all liquid so your order should not have a market impact, unless you have investment assets as large as those of the Emir of Qatar. For less-liquid ETFs study the daily volume and normal bid/offer spreads before making an order. If your order seems like it could move the market of that ETF you may want to reconsider if that is the best choice of investment product for you.

Buying an index fund is often best done via one of the fund supermarkets. Make sure that you get 'execution only' and withstand the offers of expensive services. Because there are so few fees in the cheapest index tracking funds some of the supermarkets charge a maintenance fee if you buy the tracker through them. (The supermarkets often get a cut of some funds' fees so no wonder that they push ....) While the fees at a couple of pounds a month may look small, make sure that your investment is of a size that this will not eat into your returns in a significant way. (£2 a month on a £10,000 investment is still 0.24% per year, so you are probably better off owning an ETF.)

A few suggested (UK-specific) supermarkets are as follows:

■ bestinvest.com

■ hl.co.uk

■ cofunds.co.uk

■ fidelity.co.uk

■ alliancetrust.co.uk

■ iii.co.uk (Interactive Investor)

In many countries, including the UK, you can buy government bonds directly from the treasury at little or no cost. While there is a small cost saving to doing so this means you are responsible for ensuring that the maturity profile of your bonds is in line with your target on average time to maturity as it naturally changes with time. For most people it is worth paying the cheap product providers' small costs so that everything is taken care of for you.

Trading is expensive and pulling the trigger can be nerve wracking

Trading is expensive and one of the main reasons many investors under-perform, but by changing allocations when you are trading securities you will be able to save money on transaction costs. Some product providers offer combined products with fixed weightings between bonds and equities. While they have the same issues outlined here they also have the huge advantage of large natural flows from customers and have lower costs as a result. If you find a product that suits your profile this added advantage is worth noting.

When rebalancing your portfolio also consider your ticket size. If you are trading a $10,000 position and split that into four ETFs or securities, even cheap commission charges will add up. If you pay $15 per trade you will have incurred a 0.6% ($60/$10,000) brokerage fee. Do consider if you really need all four securities this time around. Keep in mind that, for example, the equity portion of the rational portfolio can easily consist of only one security, which is an advantage when it comes to keeping down commission costs.

If you are just getting started on saving money up and building your portfolio from scratch it may be a bit daunting to pull the trigger and invest the money all at once. You would hate to buy into the market only to see markets drop 10% in the weeks after making the decision. All that hard-earned money up in smoke just because you were unlucky and picked the wrong week to invest.

While it may be harder emotionally you should put the money to use sooner rather than later, once you have made your plan, decided allocations and figured out the best products for you. We think markets will increase slowly over the long term, but also know they can go anywhere in the short term. Of course if you invest everything at the same time you increase the risk that you randomly picked a bad moment, but while you wait to implement your portfolio you are expecting at least the equity portion of it to go up at an annual rate of 4–5% equity risk premium. So unless you know something about the short-term direction of the markets and can pick a better moment to invest, there is no time like the present.

If this 'all at once' allocation seems too risky you may consider splitting the allocations into chunks where you add a little at a time over a certain period, although don't forget that you will pay more in commission that way. (Investors typically pay a fixed amount each time they trade.) If you are fine with the higher commissions and hassle of doing multiple trades you may consider strategies like dollar-cost averaging (where you buy more as markets are dropping) or value averaging (similar but subject to investing a fixed amount over a period of time).[2] Personally I don't subscribe to these methods as I think you are essentially saying the market follows a mean reversion pattern (and thus you claim an edge), but if it gives you greater comfort in getting started it may be a good idea.

Rebalancing your portfolio

Any investment book worth its salt will tell you that you need to think carefully about formulating a plan and sticking to it. Swapping in and out of securities will significantly reduce long-term returns, mainly because of the transaction costs and taxes you incur.

While market movements or changes in your personal circumstances may alter your risk/return perspectives, generally you want to set yourself up so that you have a fair bit of flexibility in your portfolio before those factors force you to trade securities. Suppose, for example, that your risk profile

---

2 See *The Intelligent Asset Allocator: How to Build Your Portfolio to Maximize Returns and Minimize Risk* by William Bernstein (American Media International LLC, 2004).

is such that you want a 60/40 bond/equity mix in your portfolio, but that strong equity markets made this ratio 55/45. Should you sell 5% of equity and buy bonds to get back to the 60/40 split?

How far you are willing for your portfolio mix to diverge from your ideal allocation is an individual choice and partly depends on how fixed your split was to start with. Obviously you want to avoid trading too narrow ranges: if you reallocated every time the allocations got more than 1 percentage point away from your ideal allocation (so 61/39 or 59/41) you would end up trading very frequently which would be expensive and probably not necessary. One rule of thumb you might consider is to reallocate once a year if the allocations are more than 10% out of sync, or during the year if more than 15–20% out.

Keep in mind that just like you originally planned your allocations and came up with a 60/40 split, that split is not written in stone. Your circumstances may change, prompting a rethink, or development in the markets may change your desired allocations. If, for example, you started with £100,000 and a 60/40 bond/equity split, and equities rallied 50%, without rebalancing the split would have become 50/50 (£60,000 in bonds and £60,000 in equities). You might find that you don't need more than £60,000 in bonds to be comfortable and you therefore could keep all the additional money in the higher risk/return equities (and not rebalance in that case). Note how rebalancing typically involves selling the better-performing asset and buying the underperformer, something which sits uncomfortably with many investors.

So a few thoughts on rebalancing your portfolio:

- After you determine your initial mix of the portfolio, have an idea of what kind of bands you are happy to operate within before rebalancing. If you are more than 10% out of sync, that is probably a good time to rebalance.

- Whenever you have money coming into or out of your portfolio use that as an opportunity to rebalance a little bit. So, if your ideal mix is 60/40 bonds/equities and you are currently at 62/38 and have money coming in, use that money to buy equities, not a 60/40 mix. In the long run this will save you money in rebalancing the portfolio as you save additional trading costs.

- Periodically, and at least yearly, review the portfolio and make sure you are still happy with the mix. Have things changed in your life so that 60/40 no longer is the best ratio? This could include the passage of time; as you get closer to retirement you should have fewer assets in equities and more in bonds.

Summary

Portfolio implementation is obviously incredibly important, but the choices you have are much better than they were only a couple of decades ago. Cheap and liquid index exposure is now commonplace and something most major financial firms offer.

The right product for you is really an individual choice dependent partly on your tax and currency situation. But the key facts are the same. Buy as broad an index tracker as you can and as cheaply as you can. If you do that, you are doing pretty well.

four

Other things to think about

Pension and insurance

For many individuals their investing lives are dominated less by issues relating to their rational portfolio, but rather by the options and choices with regard to pensions, life annuities and related products. Wearing the rational portfolio hat, here are some thoughts on these topics.

Defined contribution pension plans

Defined contribution plans have increasingly become the main option for employees at private companies. Instead of offering defined benefit plans or final salary schemes where the companies underwrite the risk that there is a shortfall in the size of the pension assets, companies now let pension plan participants take the investment risk.

Does it make sense to participate in a pension plan? In short, yes, but it depends ...

Pension plans are generally a very tax-efficient way to save money for retirement. Depending on rules and jurisdiction, contributions are tax deductible and potentially subsidised or matched by the company you work for. In reality this could mean that for every £100 of regular post-tax income you could put into a rational portfolio, you could effectively put £200 into a pension plan. The potential drawbacks of a pension plan for the rational investor are often not significant enough to negate such a great, effective subsidy of an investment and participating in a pension plan therefore makes sense. In other cases, the investor has no choice in the matter and is forced to participate, which for all its faults at least eliminates indecision.

As discussed earlier, rational investing is all about realising that you can't beat the market and putting together a portfolio that reflects that while considering your individual risk and tax circumstances. Pension plans are an example of where the tax (or related) benefits of those schemes may make them preferable to investing in the rational portfolio without them. That said there are a few issues to consider before blindly signing up to a pension plan:

- Will you have flexibility to choose the investment portfolio in the pension plan to match the investments you would make in the rational portfolio? If not, does the pension plan contain many expensive investment products or active funds that will negate the savings?

- What are the fees and expenses generally? Some pension funds charge an annual fee of 1% or more which, depending on your time in the scheme, may mean you would be better off without the benefits and investing in a rational portfolio yourself. In my view, one of the great financial scandals of the next generation will be the aggregate charges investors generally face when making pension investments that are sometimes virtually mandated. According to a recent study, an estimated half (50%!) of investment gains will disappear into the abyss of fees and charges for the average pension plan member.[1] I find that absurd and shamelessly beyond reason.

- Does the risk profile of the pension fund match your personal risk preference? Do you have any choice in this?

- Can the pension plan easily be transferred to another provider or country if you change jobs or simply find the first one too un-economical? Do you even have a say in this?

- Do you have flexibility to access the capital in your pension if you need to? Even if you do have access to your capital are the penalties prohibitive?

- Does your pension plan have lots of hidden charges, even if they only apply in various cases? One friend's pension plan discounted his holdings by 50% in case he died before his spouse.

Consider the example where you have the choice of either taking the advantage of your employer matching your contributions and the tax advantages for an investment of £100 into a pension plan, or foregoing all those advantages and only investing £75 into the rational portfolio with everything else the same. Let's say that you invest 50/50 into minimal risk

---

1 www.telegraph.co.uk/finance/personalfinance/pensions/9407283/Fees-that-can-halve-the-value-of-your-pension.html

assets and equities with an average return of 3% and that the difference between the two portfolios is an annual charge from the pension fund structure of 1.5% (ignoring the benefits of flexibility from managing your own money in the rational portfolio).

Over time the benefits of the pension plan may be negated by higher charges (see Figure 15.1). If you can invest as cheaply through a pension plan as you could via a rational portfolio you should obviously take advantage of the tax and other benefits of the pension plan, but there are also cases where things are less clear cut.

I was working at a firm that was setting up an employee pension scheme. The tax benefits from the scheme were such that we would effectively save around 20% in taxes for the amount put in, but we had to keep the money in that scheme for about 25 years. I estimated that there would be an extra 1% charge by having my money invested with the scheme compared to buying a simple index fund. There was also the benefit of accruing returns on my tax savings which further benefited going with the scheme although I could probably get some of them in any case. I compared the small net savings, estimated after comparing the lower tax and higher charges to doing it myself, against a pretty hefty illiquidity discount in tying my money into a scheme for 25 years, and ended up not going with the scheme as a result; much to my boss's dismay.

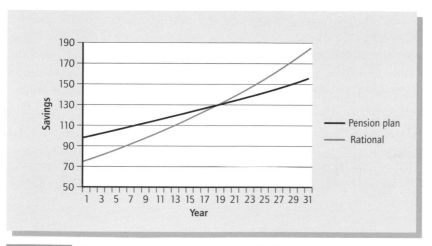

Figure 15.1 Comparing pension plans to a tax-inefficient rational portfolio

The point is not that you should not save for retirement. Of course you should, and in fact many schemes, like the UK workplace pension scheme that recently came into effect, are compulsory. But you should be conscious of the impact of potentially large fees and expenses that come on top of the lack of flexibility often associated with pension plans, and consider if you can find cheaper ways of achieving the benefits from pension fund investing, or as a last resort save up for retirement outside a pension scheme.

The rules regarding pension investing and the tax consequences vary greatly between jurisdictions and over time.[2] Considering that rational investing, to a great extent, is about saving pennies it is well worth your while to educate yourself about the best way to be efficient about achieving the benefits from pension schemes.

If you are uncertain about your pension plan options this is an area where the expense of an adviser is probably well worth it. Given the choice, I would encourage you to pick a no frills and very cheap pension plan where you are free to select your own mix of securities. This would allow you to keep all the tax and other potential benefits of the pension plan whilst investing in a rational portfolio and would be a clear win/win situation.

Defined benefits schemes

Defined benefit schemes are increasingly rare, especially in the private sector. If you have a defined benefit scheme I would encourage you to consider who the guarantor of the future stream of cash flows is. Depending on the scheme you may be receiving benefits 30–40 years from now, and who knows what companies will be in business that far in the future. Is your scheme backed up by guarantees from your government (many such schemes are required to buy insurance that is backed by the government) or, if not, what happens to your pension if the company fails with an underfunded scheme?

The issue of failing pension schemes will be bigger in a poor economic environment, which may be exactly when you particularly don't want your pension scheme to fail (there is probably never a good time though).

2 For UK specific thoughts on financial planning and pensions I recommend Jonquil Lowe's *Be Your Own Financial Adviser* (Pearson Education, 2010).

More companies fail during recessions and as this is also typically when investment markets have performed poorly, the risk of a company default combined with an underfunded pension scheme has gone up significantly.

In future, I think there will be huge issues with underfunded pension schemes, both public and private. In the relatively benign environment of good markets and higher interest rates that prevailed prior to 2008 some schemes used too optimistic assumptions on future returns and had too few reserves as a result. The pension funds use a discount rate to predict how much money they need to fund their future obligations. If they need to pay someone £1,000 in 20 years' time the amount needed now will be around £550 with a discount rate of 3%, but only about £375 with a discount rate of 5% – and it's easier to ask someone for £375 than for £550. This may seem like a spreadsheet abstraction until the day someone tells you that you will receive less from your pension than what you were promised because someone used the wrong discount rate and was too optimistic about the future.

Unless the coming decades see benign markets and interest rates to help rectify the issue of underfunded pension schemes I predict there will be many failing schemes. Governments will then have to step in to protect the retirement payments of many pensioners, at a time when they are already facing other pressure from high debt and an ageing population. If you are in a defined benefit scheme and expect to receive payments in several years hence then make sure you know where you stand if this calamity happens.

Annuities and insurance

Annuities are an important and sometimes dominant part of the investment portfolio for millions of savers. While in some cases there is a requirement for pension scheme participants to put a part of their pension savings into an annuity many other investors find great comfort from having a secured cash flow until they die (some annuities continue payments for dependants).

I certainly don't have a problem with annuities. There is great intangible value to be had in knowing that you are going to be OK in your old age, regardless of how old you become. Particularly if you have an annuity that is adjusted for inflation (some adjust for changes in the retail price index), you have a very good picture of your spending power in retirement, without worrying about the oscillations of the markets or dying with a lot of money that you will have no use for (you'll be dead ...).

But there are a few things you need to think about when purchasing an annuity:

■ **Who guarantees your payment in the future and what is their credit quality?** Keep in mind that you will be expecting payments many years into the future. If you buy an annuity at age 50, with some luck you'll be looking for a payment up to half a century into the future, and at that time your quality of life may greatly depend on actually receiving that payment. In most cases annuity providers are insured by a government-backed scheme, but you want to make absolutely sure that this is the case. You certainly don't want to be in a situation where a Lehman-style bankruptcy means that you are left with nothing in retirement when your earnings potential has greatly diminished. (Keep in mind that annuity providers are likely to be struggling exactly when markets are tough and you probably need the money the most.)

■ **The price of the annuity may be very high – be sure you need it!** You are essentially lending money to the insurance company for a very long time. You can try to figure out at what rate in the following way for a standard (non-inflation adjusted) annuity:

1 Figure out your life expectancy. There are many life expectancy calculators on the internet.[3] It will be more accurate if you can incorporate where you live, etc. This will give you a good idea of how long the insurance company expects you to pay your annuity for (make sure you tell them all the bad health stuff – as morbid as it sounds, in this case you want them to think you are going to die soon). I was surprised by how long I can expect to live, which according to a friend in insurance is a common reaction.

2 Search around for the best annuity and be sure that the payments are in fact guaranteed by someone other than the annuity provider's general corporate credit. Assuming you are buying an annuity for £100, what will your yearly payments be?

3 Figure out the internal rate of return (IRR) on your payment. Your IRR is the rate at which the insurance company effectively borrows from you. So year zero: −£100, year 1: +3.75, year 2: +3.75, etc. You can do this in Excel.

---

3 I used a couple including one from University of Pennsylvania: wharton.upenn. edu/mortality/perl/CalcForm

Keep in mind that unlike a bond you don't get the principal back at the end (there are annuities that do this, but the interim payments are just lower to reflect this).

4 Figure out the average time to future payments (the duration – also use Excel). Depending on your circumstances it will perhaps be 15–20 years. If you start receiving the annuity payments now this will be half the years you are expected to have left to live.

5 Compare your IRR to a government bond of a maturity similar to the duration and in same currency (your average time to payment in 4 above).

6 Apply some sort of discount to the annuity IRR to reflect the inflexible nature of the product and perhaps stiff penalties if you try to get out of the annuity.

7 Consider any tax advantages of the annuity; these are at times significant.

As an example, when I did the above exercise as a potential annuitant, the IRR I received on my investment was slightly lower than the equivalent UK government bond. So essentially I would be lending money to the annuity provider decades into the future at a lower rate than I would the UK government, ignoring the flexibility I would have in trading the UK government bonds if my circumstances changed. In other words, the insurance I received from the annuity provider against running out of money in very old age was very costly.

It is not surprising that the IRR for your annuity is not great. Annuity products are expensive to manage, and not necessarily great business for the insurance companies as they deal with the administration of cash transfers to thousands of annuitants, in addition to marketing, overheads, re-insurance that the annuity provider will be able to pay you, and the profit and capital requirements of the annuity provider. Just think that it costs money every time someone calls up to complain that they have not received their £300 and multiply that by a million customers – even if you are not the costly customer you share in paying for those costs by being on the same annuity platform.

My conclusion on annuities is that if you don't have a lot of savings and worry about having enough into old age, annuities are well worth the poor return they promise on your investment. If you don't have a lot there is great value in knowing exactly what you have and that it will be enough. An annuity can give you that.

If you have more assets and are highly likely to leave an estate for your descendants then perhaps reconsider annuities. After adjusting for potential tax or other benefits the return on the assets you put into an annuity is quite poor and you could make more money investing on your own. You will of course not have the guarantee of additional payments if you live beyond your life expectancy, but considering your other assets you will be fine even without that additional money. Also annuity providers make large sums from the hefty penalties from changing or cancelling annuities and if there is any chance that you may be doing that then take it into consideration when evaluating an annuity (a lot can change in decades ahead so even if you consider that unlikely now, that may change in future). This could include if you wanted out because you no longer considered the future annuity payments secure. Just imagine how you would feel if your old-age living cost was promised by a Greek insurance company that was backed by the Greek government. You would hopefully have run for the hills a long time ago.

As shown by the IRR on the annuity, the return profile is extremely low risk/return and that may not suit your risk profile – if you can afford greater risk in pursuit of greater returns in your portfolio an annuity may lock you in to lower return expectations for decades ahead.

Buying insurance

In very rough terms the world of insurance is divided into life and non-life insurance. Non-life insurance is for things like your car, house, travel, business and other *non-life* things. We all know how it works. You pay £500 to insure your car against a number of things, including for example theft. Let's say it's a £10,000 car. In simple terms, the probability of making a claim against the full value of the car in any one year has to be 5%. Without necessarily doing it in those terms, most buyers of insurance probably consider that about right and therefore worth it.

The reason I would not buy the £500 insurance on my £10,000 car (other than the third party insurance which is required by law) has to do with my knowledge of the insurance company's combined ratio. The combined ratio is the sum of the claims and expense ratio. The claims ratio is exactly that – what the company pays out in claims to people whose cars were stolen or damaged. And the expense ratio is all the other costs of the insurance company; marketing, administration, overhead, etc. Insurance companies can have combined ratios over 100%; if claims don't come due for a while the insurers earn an interest on the premiums they collected until the claim falls due. But since car insurance is typically a one-year policy the combined ratio for this policy should be below 100% to be profitable.

For car insurance, the risks are somewhat predictable and the insurance company is likely to have a good idea of the number of claims and expenses it will face (insurers can reinsure risks they don't wish to hold fully themselves). Using very rough numbers the insurance company might have a combined ratio of 95% for these policies made up of a 70% claims ratio and 25% expense ratio (my friends in insurance will bemoan this simplification). So, essentially, if you are an average risk customer, every time you pay £100 in premium on your car insurance you get £70 back in claims and it costs £25 for the insurance company to make it all happen, and they take a £5 profit. In other words, you are paying £30 for the peace of mind of having the insurance. You obviously don't get £70 back. Most of the time you get nothing back as you didn't make a claim on the insurance company, and then when misfortune strikes you get your £10,000 back; but on *average* you get £70 back.

So the reason I don't buy insurance is that I don't want to pay the 30% in cases where I can afford the loss (25% expenses plus 5% profit to the insurance company). Obviously it would really stink to have my car stolen or damaged to the tune of the full £10,000, but I see this as a risk I can afford to bear and don't need to pay to protect against. Importantly, I don't think that I save the full £500 in annual car insurance. I think that I save the 30% difference between what I paid and the average claims. In my view the insurance company knows as much about my risk as buyer of insurance as I do, and if they set the average pay-out for me at 70% of a £500 policy then that is probably about right. So using this case of car insurance to extrapolate how I think about insurance in general, on average over all the insurance policies I don't buy I would expect to have a loss of £350 (70% of £500) on my car in any one year, and have saved £150 by not buying insurance (30% of £500).

Not buying insurance against things we can afford to replace or have happen does not mean that those things don't happen. It just means that instead of having the small bleed of constantly paying small premiums for lots of small things we will once in a while be paying out larger replacements amounts for things we did not insure against. Personally, I also think the whole hassle of keeping track of insurance policies is a pain I would rather avoid and I also seem to constantly hear stories about insurance companies that either fought claims or made claiming on a policy a huge headache.

Without being scientific about it, including all insurance forms that I don't buy (including life insurance) I think I save about £500 per year in expense ratio

▶

and insurance company profit. Assuming that I took this money every year for the next 30 years and invested it in the broader equity markets and was able to return 5% on that money, my savings from not buying insurance over the period would amount to around £35,000 in present money. This is money I have instead of it being in the insurance company's pockets in 30 years. Importantly this saving does not assume that I don't have accidents or have my car stolen. In fact it assumes that I'm at risk of those things exactly with the same probability that the insurance companies assume.

There is probably going to be a massive 'always seek expert advice' or 'don't try this at home' disclaimer from my publisher in the front of this book, and here it really applies. *You should not save on insurance premium payments in instances where you can't afford the loss*; and everyone is different in terms of what they can afford to lose. Almost nobody could afford to lose their house in a fire so they should insure against this possibility (you probably couldn't get a mortgage if you didn't). Most people in countries without national health services couldn't afford episodes of bad health so should get health insurance. Many can't afford to have bad things happen to their car or have their homes broken into, so they should insure against that. But most people can afford to lose their mobile phone, having to cancel a flight or holiday, or an increase in the price of their electricity bill, and they should not insure against those things. And even if there are things you need to buy insurance for you should always get a high deductible, which in turn will lower the cost of the insurance policy. Over time, having no insurance or a good discount when you do will save you quite a bit of money, and that should make you sleep better at night. And perhaps you will look after that mobile phone just a little bit better because it's not insured, which in turn will lower the risk that you inadvertently lose it.

Similarly there are many instances when life insurance makes sense. As with the case of annuities, many life products have an investment component to them, but obviously also a life component. If you are in a situation where your death or disability will cause unbearable financial stress on your descendants then the premium you pay on these policies makes sense. As with the example of car insurance, you should do so when you or your descendants can't afford the loss. Whether they can or not is obviously a highly individual thing, but bear in mind that as with all insurance products there is a tangible financial cost to the intangible peace of mind many people cherish by being insured. Make sure it is worth it.

chapter

16

Apocalypse investing

Not long before the financial crash of 2008 a book called *The Black Swan – The Impact of the Highly Improbable* (Penguin, 2008) written by Nassim Nicholas Taleb was published. The book caused quite a stir in the financial community. The title of the book refers to the common assumption that swans are white. Swans had always been white and it had almost become part of the definition of being a swan, that it is a beautiful, graceful, *white* bird. The swan-watching community (if there is such a thing) was aghast and confused when a black swan appeared out of nowhere. All that it took for granted was thrown to the wind if such a fundamental assumption as the swan's colour could be shattered in an instant.

Taleb goes on to make a mockery of common parameters of risk used in finance. He describes how if you assume that the annual standard deviation of the S&P 500 was 15%, a drop of 45% would represent a 3 standard deviation move and without skew or fat tails (i.e. big moves are more likely than suggested by a normal distribution, as discussed earlier) this should happen approximately 0.14% of the time, or about every 700 years, when in reality it seems to happen every couple of decades. I'm grossly simplifying, but I think Taleb would forgive me in the interests of getting a complex point across in a paragraph.

Where am I going with this? I think a book on how to invest your assets would not be complete without commenting on how to think or react in what most of us consider highly unlikely and undesirable scenarios. We discussed the short-term government bonds of the most creditworthy governments in the world, and how there are probably no securities that are lower risk than those. But what if we, for a moment, allowed the possibility of a complete collapse of society with governments going bust and law, order and property rights negated?

It's hard for most of us to imagine what this kind of complete breakdown looks like without knowing much more about the reasons it happened.

It struck me as odd, in the recent movie *Contagion* about a deadly virus that even with 40 million people dead in the US, and in a state of complete panic, the main characters still seemed to walk around in clean clothes and drive their cars. Would there really have been functioning general stores or petrol stations with the world in such a state? Would your credit card be working? Electricity and water? Could you get your money from the bank and if you could would that money actually be worth anything?

I am going against the logic of Taleb's book in even discussing how society's breakdown could happen or its consequences. Taleb discusses the 'known' unknowns and the 'unknown' unknowns, and in my mind basically concludes that we don't know squat, other than the fact that unlikely events are more likely to happen than we think. (Paradoxically he discusses buying government bonds and put options to protect against this, which both assume somewhat functioning financial markets to profit from the disasters.) However, even discussing ways that the highly unlikely may happen and its consequences, in Taleb's mind I may be missing the whole point that the unknown is exactly that and trying to forecast it is a doomed undertaking.

Still, how we protect ourselves and our loved ones from an investing perspective if society breaks does depend slightly on how it happened. Was it due to a massive natural disaster that we survived? Was it war? Was it an epidemic that wiped out half the world's population over a couple of months of science-fiction-type mayhem?

Gold as security

The ownership of gold in such a meltdown may make a lot of sense. Over the past centuries gold has served as a great bartering tool, whether held as gold bars or in the form of jewellery. Thinking of gold as a good hedge for markets that are so desperate that your investment in assets such as AAA-government bonds is worthless suggests a state of almost complete collapse. We all remember the horrible stories from World War II when people bartered gold or jewellery for things like food or shelter, or the possibility of escape. People who have studied history and worry that it may indeed repeat itself may find that owning gold has some insurance value to them.

One point of caution on owning gold: suppose you own it by owning a gold-mining company or an exchange traded fund (ETF) that tracks gold.

The value of those assets will track the value of gold closely as the world heads towards turmoil. But would they be of value to you in the case of complete breakdown? Perhaps not. Depending on the disaster there may not be a functioning stock exchange where you can sell your gold correlated securities, and the bank where you held the securities in custody might be long gone.

Perhaps as a cautious investor you have some gold bars at a very conservative bank in a vault that could withstand 10 atomic bombs or whatever disease the evil spirits have thrown our way. But again the gold here may not be of use to us when we need it. Would the bank actually be open for us to go and collect the gold? In that desperate state of the world would we trust that the employees of that bank had not broken into the vaults and stolen the valuables if that meant feeding their children? Even in the case where you were able to go to the bank and pick up your valuables, you may not want to. In a completely broken-down society imagine what it would be like to walk out of a bank with a bunch of gold. You would undoubtedly glance nervously over your shoulder as you exited and police protection on leaving may be non-extent.

If not gold, then what?

Obviously the scenarios I describe above are extremely unlikely. Major disasters of the magnitude described have only happened a couple of times over the past century, and even in those cases it was not everywhere in the world simultaneously. Of course those caught up in the horrors of war or mayhem find it scant comfort that things are better elsewhere, as they are forced to deal with what is in front of them. If you can't realise the value of securities or even pick up valuables in a safety box at a bank the breakdown of society as we know it today would be so complete that we individually would probably be worried about other things such as shelter, security, food and water. Probably the last thing on our minds would be how to best invest our assets. In fact people with the paper version of this book would probably burn it for warmth while mocking the apparently orderly and stable society most investment books take for granted.

In certain circumstances, ancient jewellery has historically been a great preserver of value in times of great distress. It is easy to store, hide and transport. That said, as with gold I would caution you against storing lots of expensive jewellery at home: the risk of theft could quickly eliminate any benefit from holding it. (My wife thinks jewellery as a store of value is an excellent idea, encouraging me to get some.)

In certain cases property may be a good asset in times of great distress even if it is illiquid for immediate use. Ignoring the possible benefit of it as arable land, if the crisis passes there may well come the day where the rule of law prevails and you can reclaim your assets. While shares in companies may be worthless with companies long gone, property will probably maintain some value.

Finally, there is some protection through the holding of the broadly diversified portfolio. Although the scenarios discussed above are clear calamity scenarios there is some chance that part of the portfolio will survive and maintain some value as a result. Even in an highly inter-connected world the rational portfolio is highly geographically diversified and holding securities in companies in diverse locations such as Australia, Brazil, Canada, Europe, the US, China and Japan may be of some value if calamity strikes your London home base. For all the securities in a rational portfolio to be worthless a calamity would have to strike simultaneoulsy all over the world.[1]

How could 2008 and 2009 have happened?

My point with the crazy stories above is that your best investments in times of great distress depend on how you define great distress. If you define great distress as what happened in 2008, the AAA-rated government bond is indeed a great preserver of value. In fact, things could have gone a whole lot worse than what happened in 2008 and that would still be the case. But although my suggestions of societal breakdown may seem alarmist and like scenes from a bad science fiction novel, if we are talking about extreme 'black swan' events then conventional thinking would be out the window.

---

1 Many companies in the world equity portfolio have large net cash holdings (Apple has over $100 billion in cash at the time of writing) unlike governments which are typically large net debtors. In a really nasty world scenario those cash holdings could prove invaluable and ensure survival longer than many governments. To ensure that you actually own those underlying stocks you would need an ETF to be physical instead of synthetic, where you take credit risk with the issuer.

I remember talking to a few friends at collapsing financial firms in October 2008 and again in March 2009 as they were navigating their way through the mayhem. One phrase I remember hearing a couple of times, mainly as a joke, was 'If this gets any worse, it is guns and ammo time.' While I chuckled at the time, it was interesting and scary how fast the world moves into panic mode, even without an obvious trigger like war, epidemics or natural disasters. This was a panic caused by the falling house of cards that most of us had helped build through the creation, purchase, regulation, complicity, or ignorance of a crazy, headless, expansion of credit. (I recommend *How I Caused the Credit Crunch* by Tetsuya Ishikawa (2009, Icon Books). Tets, who was very involved with crisis events while at Goldman and Morgan, has written a funny book about the financial crises.)

As bad as things were at the worst point of the 2008–09 crisis they could clearly have been much worse. There were still functioning financial markets, no governments had defaulted (they had in fact been able to oversee large and necessary bailouts), there was no hyperinflation or threats of war, and there was no widespread civil unrest.

Suppose now that instead of the world recovering from the darkest days of the 2008–09 crisis things had taken a bad turn for the worse. We would probably have had a complete collapse of the financial system. Virtually no banks would be in business, or at least not be operating like we take for granted they do today. Your insurance policy would probably be worthless with the underwriter bust. Many governments around the world would be unable to meet their short-term debt maturities and be in default. There would be nobody with liquidity to buy their debt.

With no functioning financial institutions, trade and commerce would completely dry up. Why would you deliver goods to store when there was no real way you could get paid? Similarly, petrol stations might not be working and public transport would be a mess. A friend told me that the UK has about three months of food reserves and six weeks of fuel assuming normal consumption patterns. Tax revenues would plummet further as there would be far lower incomes to pay tax on and commerce had come to a halt (so no sales tax or VAT). The absence of tax income and inability to refinance their short-term bonds would cause the government to severely cut back on spending, including benefits, pensions, education and medical care. Sensing what was in store the government might increase spending on police and the military. With the inability to fund itself the government might start issuing IOUs (promissory notes), but these could lose credibility quickly as it became apparent that the prospect of repayment was poor.

The main losers of large-scale government cutbacks would probably be extremely agitated and civil unrest would break out. We have seen cases of civil unrest (like the London riots) or larger protests at government spending cuts in relatively normal states of the world and since the picture I'm painting is much worse, even more widespread unrest could dominate. Where that could lead is anyone's guess, but probably nowhere good. The whole infrastructure of society would come under great stress.

The scenario I describe above probably won't happen in my lifetime, the lifetime of my children or even the grandchildren I hope to have one day. More than anything my point with this chapter is to demonstrate that we must have a flexible mind when we consider all the possible outcomes in our investing lives. The question is: how should we think about investments in a state of complete societal breakdown, not seen in my lifetime, at least in the Western world? These include potential scenarios where property rights have broken down, there is no police or food on the shelves of the stores, and your money is worthless anyhow.

As I see it the rational portfolio remains superior in virtually all states of the world, except in the scenario where the world is left without property rights and all investment assets across the world are worthless. In a highly unscientific ranking of different levels of societal breakdown here are some thoughts on what you might want to own[2]:

- Depending on the level of breakdown we could still be safe with AAA-government bonds (they would not still be AAA) potentially from countries other than our own.
- In slightly worse scenarios we would probably want to own fixed assets such as a house or property, and there would still be value somewhere in the broadly diversified rational portfolio as the whole world probably did not go bust all at once.

---

2 The emergence of virtual currencies/commodities like Bitcoin may provide financial shelter in the future and a potential alternative to gold. These currencies are still in the nascent stages, but if they end up as a recognised asset that can be stored securely I would not be surprised to see its value go up at times of turmoil and stress in the financial markets.

■ In an even worse scenario than this where property rights are out the window we would probably want to own high-value, yet easy to hide and transfer, goods like gold or jewellery.

■ And in complete mayhem we want to own shelter, security, food and water. And indeed guns and ammo.

Avoiding fraud

While different from the broader kind of calamity discussed above, for some people Bernie Madoff and other fraudsters like him have become their personal equivalent.

Whole books have been written about how to avoid investing with the next Madoff, and rightly so. Madoff is the epitome of the worst the world of finance has to offer. He was stealing from people whose confidence he had gained, and left many people bankrupt while he was living the high life.

A couple of former investors of mine were hurt by the Madoff debacle. Knowing these investors I can attest that they were not naïve simpletons, but sophisticated and diligent managers. That they could still get caught investing in what turned out to be frauds has served as a reminder to me that few people are entirely safe from the prospect of becoming the next victim.

While every measure and precaution should be taken to avoid something like Madoff's scheme happening again, there are undoubtedly people concocting elaborate schemes right now. It is something different every time and the explosion of international finance with increasingly sophisticated instruments only adds to the possibilities of tricking investors.

I don't have a guaranteed way of avoiding fraud, but I do think that the kind of index-type investing recommended in this book minimises the probability of fraud. We are not paying an intermediary to be clever on our behalf. We think that is futile and expensive, and we trust the market to find the best value for securities. Most frauds over time have been committed by someone who was entrusted with other people's money to generate great returns. We are not entrusting anyone with our money and telling them to go perform miracles. We don't think it can be done.

It is of course possible that either the product providers like iShare and Vanguard, or the execution brokers or custodians, are massive fraudsters. Ultimately anything is possible, but in my view extraordinarily unlikely partly because of the simple structures of these companies. These are not the kinds of firms where one star manager will make all the decisions. Many people would have to be in on the fraud and the chance of detection would therefore be much greater than the kind of scam Madoff ran. If you wanted to protect against this extremely unlikely possibility I would suggest that you diversify across different product providers, products, brokers and custodians.

A wish list aimed at the financial sector

Frustratingly, some simple tools that could help the investor make the best investment decisions are not readily available from the index trackers, banks or financial advisers that have the greatest interaction with individual clients. Sometimes these institutions can sell higher-margin products to their clients and are not interested in selling the cheapest, simplest solution, and in other cases the lack of economies of scale of advisers or the thin margins of product providers prevent the provision of a few simple tools I feel investors would be better off having.

The portfolio described in this book is actually pretty simple. By creating a portfolio that combines a minimal risk asset with a world equity portfolio and potentially other bonds, an investor is already doing very well. Adjusting this portfolio for the optimal risk levels and doing so in a tax optimised way will in my view leave the investor better off than the vast majority of investors.

So what tools or information do we really need to do this? The short answer is that we can do it pretty well with what is available today, but a couple of things could make the search for the most suitable rational portfolio even easier.

Enhanced independent comparison sites

First of all we need a simple place to find out which products are available to us and what the costs of those products are. In Chapter 14 we discussed how there are now a very large number of index-related products available to the end investor. That is a good thing. But with the large increase in choice also comes confusion over what is the best product for any one investor. We should have a simple comparison site that compares the all-in costs and liquidity of the various products, seen in the context of the customer's currency of assets, eventual currency of liability and tax situation. In particular, investors outside the major currencies are at times confused as their local choices of investment products seem more limited, even if they are not.

In short, it's not that simple to compare the all-in costs of owning an index tracker and applying an educated view of your risk tolerances. A large, independent and credible website that did this would be incredibly valuable to the investing community. Of course it would have to have huge scale as its charges would have to be minimal and paid by the investor to maintain its independence. A site that is paid for mainly by product providers is unlikely to advise you that their products are too expensive.[1]

Risk expertise

Perhaps as a supplement or component of the enhanced comparison site, a website on investments would be inadequate without some detailed tools to help the investor think about risk. In the few surveys I have seen over the years, investor risk is almost taken as understood or subject to a few simplistic questions. I remember having to answer, 'Do you like risk? Please tick yes or no', and thinking how incredibly inadequate a help this was in figuring out my risk profile.

What an investor should have is a thorough understanding of the risks in the market. This should involve very generic things such as 'how likely are you to lose 25% of your investment?' with thorough explanations of how this likelihood can change. There should be more in-depth sections with more technical or mathematical calculations for those who want it, along with discussions of the Black Swan theory of Taleb's books (see Chapter 16). I don't think there is enough of this kind of information available for investors today.

---

1 I'm sure some people will say, 'Oh, that exists. Just go to XYZ website.' Perhaps so, but I maintain that when someone as involved in the financial world for the past decades as I have been is not familiar with the offerings there is room for improvement. That said, I would love to hear about the sites, perhaps for a later edition of this book.

This risk section could be tailored by incorporating information given by the investor. The more information you as the investor are willing to share, the more detailed analysis you would get back. This could include pension age, other assets, potential liabilities, tax, etc. presented in a fairly generic way, but with the possibility of getting very sophisticated and more detailed. Subject to proper data protection and guarantees of confidentiality, this risk assessment could include data such as your job, education, residence, mortgage, marital status, family wealth, tax returns, Linkedin and Facebook profiles, etc. that are already available subject to a few clicks and permissions. While intrusive sounding, I wouldn't be surprised to see the advisory world move in that direction with the happy complicity of customers. Done correctly the customer could be better informed and invested.

Governments and regulatory authorities could also do more here than their current barren and infrequently used websites. They could be the vital provider of sophisticated web-based tools that could help investors understand risk better, and perhaps serve as a valuable double check on what the investor has found in the private sector. Through its social safety net, the government is the ultimate source of help for investors that have lost it all, perhaps because they didn't properly understand the risks they were taking or products they were sold.

Tax advice

Just as there should be a web-based service that would advise us on which products would be the cheapest way to buy an index-type exposure, there should be a good website for simple tax advice. The private banks are always paranoid about this. Whatever investment idea they pitch me, they are always incredibly keen to point out that they don't give tax advice and that I should get my own counsel. I find this frustrating. The few times I have gone ahead and talked to tax lawyers on a specific idea the whole thing often ends up expensive and at times even less clear. So I stay away.

I miss a website that would give very simple advice about taxes for investors in the context of index-tracking products like those of the rational portfolio. It could be something as simple as: 'I am a Danish citizen living in the UK with taxable income of X and expected capital gains of Y. What would be the best way for me to buy index exposure? What other tools are currently available to save me taxes? What may change in the future that could affect my circumstances?'

I'm perhaps making things too simple, but I think a lot of people are left with tax sub-optimal investments because they were unaware of some fairly basic facts. Also, as tax regimes constantly change, the time spent finding out what is indeed tax optimal would be done better centrally by an investment-related service like the one discussed above.

In cases where the simple tax advice on investments was inadequate the site could then refer to a network of tax experts in the area who had been vetted and approved by the site's hosts.

Customisation

We have discussed how we should really be looking at our investing lives in almost a holistic way (see Chapter 8). When considering our risk and portfolio we also need to incorporate non-investment assets and liabilities. Since many non-investment assets are often geographically quite concentrated near where we live or work it sometimes make sense for us to have fewer of our investment assets based there.

It's partly because of this kind of thinking that there are today several exchange traded fund (ETF) products that offer exposures like 'The World ex-US' or similar. And those are good things to consider. But why stop there. Since a world ETF is really just an aggregation of the exposures of the individual underlying countries, there is no reason why you should not be able to customise your exposure quite cheaply. You might for example like to own the world equity markets, except Southern Europe. You should then be able to de-select the countries you didn't want and end up with your own tailor-made adjusted world equity exposure. With this kind of customised exposure you would be better able to tailor the investment portfolio to that of your overall assets. Other than painstakingly creating this kind of exposure by buying ETFs for each of the underlying countries that you want (so every country in the world, bar a few Southern European ones in the example above), this kind of service is unavailable today. The customisation could also allow you to pick tax-optimised products by geography, if there was an advantage to this, and thus ensure that the overall portfolio is tax optimal.

Related to the customisation where you exclude countries or regions, the exclusion of industries could be interesting to some. As an investor you may already have great exposure to the IT sector and therefore don't want this to be a part of your world portfolio. But you still want the rest of the world ex-IT. As above, there is no reason why this kind of customised exposure could not be created cheaply and tax efficiently. The underlying products are there – you are still buying the same underlying stocks in other countries and in the same proportions to one another: you are just excluding certain sectors.

How it used to be and how it might become!

My maternal grandfather mainly lived in Southern Spain for the last 25 years of his life, until he passed away in the 1990s. With some time on his hands and a bit of money to invest, my grandfather enjoyed following the stock markets. He would keenly read the *Herald Tribune* and other publications that came with some regularity. Unfortunately, like everyone else in the area my grandparents lived in, there was no phone in the house. Even into the 1980s we would send a telegram to my grandparent's local post office that would then dispatch someone to their house with the message.

My grandfather would trade shares frequently, often after conferring with the adviser at his bank. They would plan certain times that my grandfather would call this adviser and they would go through what had happened in the portfolio since the last conversation, and decide which stocks should be traded. The commission was around 1% in addition to the trading and foreign exchange costs, which was probably a decent rate at the time.

I remember visiting my grandfather during the 1987 stock market crash. He would plan his day around a few radio programmes that partly covered finance and study the few articles in the *Herald Tribune*. He would also try to reach his adviser to get perspectives on the crash, but was frustrated as he had been unable to get through (they had a phone by then).

Today, the story of my grandfather's investment management seems crazy. He was miles from having an edge and was in all likelihood incurring incredible costs, not only in commissions, but trading, custody, currency, and probably even phone bills. My guess would be that every year my grandfather would spend about 4–5% of his portfolio on all of this, before considering the validity of his stock picks. Even Warren Buffett would have a problem making up this shortfall.

The world has clearly moved on massively in the past decades since my grandfather's investing. I find it fascinating that just over a decade after seeing his reaction to the 1987 stock market crash I was working at a New York based hedge fund, using the internet for my information and getting real-time news and stock quotes. Ten years after that virtually anyone around the world who looked seriously at investments would have access to the internet, webinars, Twitter, message boards, blogs, instant news alerts, etc. and be able to trade easily across borders.

Ten years from now my grandfather's story will seem crazier still. By then I imagine there will be even fewer barriers to international capital flows and even more investors will consider 'the markets' not as their home equity market but the global ones. As a result world markets will be even more efficient and accessible for investors. Hopefully index-tracking products will meet this demand and respond with better-suited products and increasingly low prices that are easy to compare. There will be far more detailed and informed risk assessments of the individual investors, and good tax advice will be more seamless and incorporated in product reviews. This will all be done online and each investor will probably have a 'Facebook' page equivalent of his or her investing life that is unique and secure, and incorporates all aspects, including portfolio customisation, or notices of any relevant information. How this comes about I don't know, but investors will hopefully be far better off as a result and I for one would sign up.

Do you need a financial adviser?

I'm cautious about this book sounding as if we could do away with the entire finance industry and do everything by ourselves. There is no doubt that in my perfect world the aggregate fees paid to the finance industry should only be a small fraction of the fees paid today. There are far too many people getting paid far too much for adding too little value. But this does not mean that we should not use financial advice at all. There are a few of places where we need it: tax advice, advice on pensions, help with finding the best products when thinking about our specific circumstances regarding our rational portfolios. With very few exceptions, the financial advisers I have met have been honest, hard-working people with their clients' interests at heart, and I fully understand the advantage of having someone like that in your corner. It's nice to have someone to talk to when you are unsure of something or things have not gone to plan, in addition to the specific expertise mentioned above.

Getting a financial adviser may help you answer some of the questions posed above. Finding the right adviser is certainly not easy and obviously involves costs. Many advisers charge a fee of 1% of assets every year, which at least alleviates the concern that they are somehow making more out of you than the fixed fee and try to profit by selling you products you don't need. Of course, if we are generally discussing investing methods that in aggregate should cost around 0.2–0.3% a year, the adviser fee seems disproportionally large, but depending on the size of your portfolio may not imply a high hourly rate. Also if you are not after the kind of standardised advice you might find online there is probably a limit to how cheap you want to go. Bad advice will cost you a lot more than the fees. As a client of an adviser what you are asking for is a lot simpler than many clients who want a tailor-made portfolio built from scratch. You are not asking the adviser to find you the best portfolio to put together. You now know all that: you are a rational investor.

18

Conclusion

This has been a book about demystifying investing and making it simple. Simple because once you embrace that you do not have an edge to beat the markets, the best way to invest money becomes a lot more obvious. At this stage I hope you agree.

You are potentially now at a critical junction. Now is when you have to take the next step, move ahead and do what the book suggests. It is a critical junction because inertia leads many of us to put the book away and promptly forget about it, or perhaps store a few memorable points or anecdotes at the back of our minds. It's a bit like when I read about sensible diets. I tend to think, 'That makes sense. Must go do that. Starting tomorrow.' And then have myself another coffee and piece of chocolate, and promptly forget about it all.

Please don't be like me. Do something – you will be far better off in the long run. Here is a simple checklist of things you can do now.

A checklist of things to do now

- Consider if you have an edge. For most people, in most sectors, it is highly unlikely that you do. If you stop here and embrace this conclusion, that alone will probably lead to better investment decisions in future. But please do plough ahead and implement the rational portfolio.

- Consider the building blocks of the rational portfolio: the minimal risk asset, world equities and potentially other government and corporate bonds, and why they make sense. Those building blocks will be the same for all rational portfolio investors and combining them in the right proportion for you gets you a very long way towards your best possible portfolio.

- Consider your circumstances and risk profile. What stage of life are you at and what is your time horizon? Are you generally a risk taker or risk averse? Depending on your risk profile you should invest in different combinations of ▶

the building blocks. If you have zero tolerance for risk, put all your assets in the minimal risk asset; if you want a lot of risk, you can buy all equities.

■ Think about your non-investment assets and liabilities in the context of your portfolio as it stands today. Are you running the risk of everything going badly for you at the same time by being unduly concentrated in your assets? Think about how having a broadly diversified rational portfolio will help remedy this problem.

■ Think about tax. You probably are already, but do so in the context of how it can reduce your investing costs. Perhaps this means an ISA in the UK, or a tax-efficient pension product, but there may well be other opportunities to be smart about taxes. It probably makes sense to get some professional help here.

■ Whatever you do, implement your portfolio cheaply and don't trade a lot. This alone will serve you well in the long run. You will be getting a little bit richer while you sleep than you otherwise would be.

Our simple rational portfolio enjoys massive advantages over traditional approaches to investing:

■ We're much closer to a theoretically optimal allocation so have a better risk/return to start with.

■ We're much, much cheaper. The compounding drag of fees makes it very hard for an active approach to beat us in the long run.

Please act on the advice in this book. You will be investing without speculation and that should make you sleep better at night.

Index

Also by Lars Kroijer

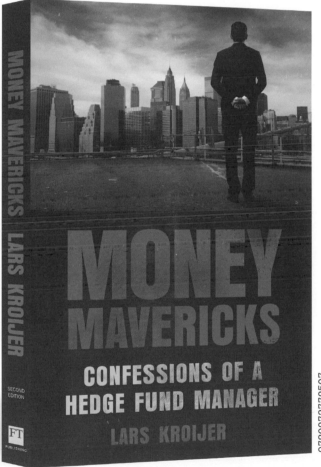